Public Policy under Blair

ONE WEEK LOAN

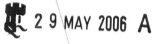

Public Policy under Blair

Edited by

Stephen P. Savage
and
Rob Atkinson

First published 2001 by
PALGRAVE
Houndmills, Basingstoke, Hampshire RG21 6XS and
175 Fifth Avenue, New York, N. Y. 10010
Companies and representatives throughout the world

PALGRAVE is the new global academic imprint of St. Martin's
Press LLC Scholarly and Reference Division and Palgrave
Publishers Ltd (formerly Macmillan Press Ltd).

ISBN 0–333–76410–2 hardback
ISBN 0–333–76411–0 paperback

This book is printed on paper suitable for recycling and
made from fully managed and sustained forest sources.

A catalogue record for this book is available
from the British Library.

Library of Congress Cataloging-in-Publication Data
Public policy under Blair/edited by Stephen P. Savage and Rob Atkinson.
      p. cm.
   Includes bibliographical references and index.
   ISBN 0–333–76410–2
   1. Political planning–Great Britain. 2. Great Britain–Social policy. 3. Great
Britain–Economic policy–1997- I. Savage, Stephen P. II. Atkinson, Rob.

JN318 .P286 2000
320'.6'0941–dc21   00–048312

10   9   8   7   6   5   4   3   2
10   09 08 07 06 05 04 03 02 01

Copy-edited and typeset by Povey-Edmondson
Tavistock and Rochdale, England

Printed in China

To Jonathan P. Savage
and
Olive and Ken

Contents

Preface

This aim of this book is to provide a broad-ranging assessment of policies and the policy process in Britain under New Labour. While it is an entirely new book, it follows in the tradition of two predecessor volumes, *Public Policy Under Thatcher* (1990) and *Public Policy in Britain* (1994), which looked respectively at the extent to which the policies and ideology associated with Margaret Thatcher constituted a radical break from a supposed post-war consensus and at the extent of policy continuity and change under her successor as Tory leader and Prime Minister, John Major.

This book takes a similarly 'comparative' approach to public policy under Blair. The comparisons it seeks to draw are of two kinds. On the one hand we have attempted to compare public policy under New Labour with public policy as it has been formed over eighteen years of Conservative government. To what extent does New Labour entail a continuation rather than a rejection of Conservative principles? On the other hand, at least where possible, we have drawn comparisons between New Labour and 'old' Labour. Has there been a 'Blair revolution' which has swept away the traditions of the Labour Party and replaced them by the new politics of the 'Third Way'? In many respects this sort of question is parallel with that posed in the first of our studies of public policy: to what extent has Tony Blair emulated Thatcher and transformed or overturned the political and ideological traditions he inherited? Through an analysis of each of the major areas of public policy, these are the sorts of issues which this collection seeks to address.

As with *Public Policy in Britain*, the book is presented in two parts. Part I examines the 'policy context' through the study of a range of generic factors which have influenced the policy agenda, including the ideology of 'Blairism', changes in structures of governance and the 'Europeanisation' of public policy. Part II then addresses each of the substantive areas of public policy, both in terms of the comparative analysis outlined above and by way of an account of the major developments which have taken place in each of those areas of policy under both the Conservatives and Labour. To this extent each of these chapters can be treated both as 'stand alone' studies of specific areas of public policy and as parts of a wider, cross-sector examination of public policy under New Labour.

The editors would like to thank all of the contributors to this volume for their patience and perseverance as this collection has taken shape. Some policy areas in particular have experienced phenomenal change over relatively short periods of time and, in order to reflect those changes in this text, the authors in question have had to return all too often to their chapters and make the necessary amendments. We would also like to thank our publisher Steven Kennedy for his 'firm but fair' approach to ensuring that the books under his wing actually see the light of day. Finally, the editors would like to offer a special thanks to Kellie Diggins, Administrator at the Institute of Criminal Justice Studies, University of Portsmouth, who, once again, has played a special role in production of this text.

STEPHEN P. SAVAGE
ROB ATKINSON

Notes on the Contributors

Rob Atkinson is Urban Research Director in the Cities Research Centre, Faculty of the Built Environment, University of the West of England, Bristol. His major areas of research are in the field of urban policy, urban regeneration and urban social exclusion. He has published widely on these subjects and is the co-author of *Urban Policy in Britain* (1994, a new edition of which is in preparation) and co-editor of *Public Policy in Britain* (1994).

Arthur Aughey is Senior Lecturer in Politics at the University of Ulster at Jordanstown. He has written extensively on Northern Irish politics, in particular on Ulster Unionism, and has also contributed to studies of British Conservatism. Amongst his publications are: *Conservatives and Conservatism* (with Philip Norton) (1981); *Under Siege: Ulster Unionism and the Anglo-Irish Agreement* (1989); and *Northern Ireland Politics* (edited with Duncan Morrow) (1996). He is currently writing a book on the politics of constitutional change in the United Kingdom.

John Bradbeer is Principal Lecturer in Geography at the University of Portsmouth where he teaches environmental management and policy. His main research interests are in environment–society relations and in learning and teaching in higher education. He has published in both areas, contributing to books and writing papers.

Fergus Carr is Head of the School of Social and Historical Studies at the University of Portsmouth and Principal Lecturer in International Relations. He is co-author of *NATO in the New Europe* (1996), editor of *Europe: The Cold Divide* (1998), and co-editor (with Andrew Massey) of *Public Policy in the New Europe: Eurogovernance in Theory and Practice* (1999).

Stephen Cope is a Principal Lecturer in Public Policy in the School of Social and Historical Studies, University of Portsmouth. His primary areas of research are the governance of Britain and policy analysis, on which he has written widely.

Paul Durden studied for his masters degree in social policy and administration at the London School of Economics and, after a brief spell back in further education, was appointed Lecturer in Social Policy at Portsmouth Polytechnic (now Portsmouth University). At Portsmouth he has contributed to the BA Honours degree in Social Policy and Administration, teaching courses on the history of social policy, education policy, housing in the UK, comparative housing policy, and social policy in the United States. Currently his main academic interest is comparative pensions policy.

Dan Finn is recognised as a leading expert of employment programmes, the benefit system and Welfare to Work strategies. He has contributed to many of the political and academic debates about unemployment and benefit dependency, and has been published widely. At Portsmouth he has developed a national and local programme of work on unemployment, social exclusion and Welfare to Work strategies. He is a member of the Advisory Group for the UK New Deal Task Force and is also a Special Advisor for the House of Commons Education and Employment Select Committee.

Michael Hill is Visiting Professor of Social Policy at Goldsmiths College, University of London and joint editor (with Helen Jones) of the *Journal of Social Policy*. He is Emeritus Professor of Social Policy at the University of Newcastle upon Tyne, having left that university in 1997 on taking early retirement. He is author of *Understanding Social Policy* (sixth edition 2000), *Social Policy: A Comparative Analysis* (1996), *The Policy Process in the Modern State*, and other books.

David Holloway is Principal Lecturer in the School of Education and Continuing Studies at the University of Portsmouth. His research and teaching interests focus on post-16 education and he is currently undertaking research on the regulation of public services with Ian Kendall and other colleagues at Portsmouth.

Norman Johnson is Professor of Social Policy in the School of Social and Historical Studies at the University of Portsmouth. His main research interests are in the voluntary sector, civil society and mixed economies of welfare, where he has published widely. Recent work includes a study of contracting in the personal social services and the impact of the New

Deal on voluntary organisations. His most recent book is *Mixed Economies of Welfare: A Comparative Perspective* (1999).

Ian Kendall is Professor of Social Policy in the School of Social and Historical Studies at the University of Portsmouth. He has written on many aspects of social policy. He is the author of *Health and the National Health Service* (1998) with John Carrier, and several recent articles on the voluntary sector with Martin Blackmore, Yvonne Bradshaw and Norman Johnson. Current work includes research on the regulation of public services with David Holloway and other colleagues at Portsmouth.

Andrew Massey is Professor of Government and Director of Postgraduate Studies in the Faculty of Humanities and Social Science, University of Portsmouth. He is the author of many articles and books on public policy and public administration.

Mike Nash is Principal Lecturer in Criminal Justice at the University of Portsmouth. His research interests include criminal justice policy with a specific focus on the probation service. He has published widely in the field and has specialised in the role of the probation service in its work with serious and dangerous offenders. His first book, *Police, Probation and Protecting the Public*, was published in 1999.

Nancy North is Principal Lecturer in Health Policy at the University of Portsmouth. Her research and writing interests have focused on commissioning in the NHS, consumerism and accountability and inter-professional collaboration. She co-edited *Perspectives in Health Care* with Yvonne Bradshaw and has recently co-authored, with Graham Moon, *Policy and Place: General Practice in Britain*.

Stephen P. Savage is Professor of Criminology and Director of the Institute of Criminal Justice Studies, University of Portsmouth. He has published widely on policing and criminal justice policy. His most recent publications include the co-authorship (with Charman and Cope) of *ACPO: The Changing Role of the Association of Chief Police Officers* (2000) and co-editorship (with Leishman and Loveday) of *Core Issues in Policing* (2000). He is also co-editor of the *International Journal of the Sociology of Law*.

Rob Thomas is Principal Lecturer in Business Environment and Course Director of the MBA at the University of Portsmouth. He has written and broadcast extensively on local business and was Hampshire Business Journalist of the Year in 1992. His primary research interests are UK and European economic and business policy and the role of professional bodies and associations.

Part I

The Policy Context

1

Introduction:
New Labour and 'Blairism'

ROB ATKINSON AND STEPHEN P. SAVAGE

Introduction

The objective of this introductory chapter is not to prejudge the content of the individual policy chapters which follow, but to provide an overview of the ideas and contexts that appear to inform the thinking behind the policies pursued by the Labour government. In this sense we will attempt to search for any coherence that may, or may not, underlie this thinking and therefore provides a coherent basis for a 'New Labour' worldview – or the Third Way as it is often referred to. At the same time it will be necessary to identify how 'New Labour' differs from 'Old Labour' and the continuities and differences between New Labour and its Conservative predecessor, Thatcherism. There is, however, still a great deal of uncertainty and difference of opinion surrounding these issues and readers should not expect to find a single coherent view of what constitutes New Labour's thought, or a consensus over the relative merits of New Labour and its policies.

For many people who followed the results emerging from the 1997 general election it appeared that what was taking place before their eyes was a landslide of truly epic proportions resembling the results of the 1945 and 1983 elections. For many people this appeared to represent a veritable sea change in the nature of British politics that would usher in a new political landscape. At first sight this is a very plausible interpretation; Labour had 419 MPs, its largest number ever, the largest working majority (179) of any post-war government and had been the beneficiary of a 10.3 per cent swing across the country as a whole. Yet as Curtice (1997, p. 2) notes, 'at 44 per cent, Labour's share of the vote was lower than that secured at any election between 1945 and 1966 ... Indeed, just three in ten of those registered to vote cast a ballot for a Labour candidate.' Both Labour and the Liberal Democrats benefited from a considerable amount of tactical voting, which, according to Curtice (1997) gave the former an additional 48 seats and the latter 18 more seats than they would have won on a uniform national swing. Clearly a decision was taken by voters in a sizeable number of seats to vote tactically in order to defeat the Conservatives; conversely it appears the Conservatives lost seats due to the geographically even spread of their vote. This points to a key element in the Conservatives' defeat – a general feeling of disillusionment, caused in part by the events surrounding their decision to withdraw from the Exchange Rate Mechanism in 1992 (arguably *the* turning point in Conservative fortunes), the constant accusations of 'sleaze' and general mismanagement which dogged the Major government and a general feeling of the need for a change after 18 years of Conservative government. Prime Minister John Major could justifiably have claimed personal responsibility for the Conservatives' electoral victory in 1992 on the basis of his 'unThatcher-like' style, but his modest and conciliatory style seemed less suited to holding together the factions and splits which emerged within the Conservative Party almost immediately after the 1992 general election.

Whatever the weaknesses of the Conservatives, Labour still had to perform to win the election and in order to do this the party needed to convince the electorate that it was fit to govern and no longer the party of the early and mid 1980s riven by internal factional disputes and 'extremism' – in other words to win the trust of the electorate. For many (e.g. Mandelson and Liddle, 1996; Gould, 1998), one of the major achievements of Tony Blair was to carry forward the reforms of the party begun by his predecessors, Neil Kinnock and John Smith, and thoroughly modernise the party in order to give the party leader both control over the party and autonomy from entrenched 'Old Labour' interests (e.g. the Trade Unions). Part of this process involved the abandonment of former 'sacred cows' such as Clause IV and the assertion of New Labour's independence from both public sector and trade union interests. Moreover it involved a willingness to accept a reduced role for government, a central role for markets, a dramatic reduction in trade union influence and greater individual choice. For many it was this 'electric shock treatment' (Gould, 1998, ch. 6) that created the platform which allowed New Labour to reoccupy the centre ground of British politics and appeal to those sections of the electorate (e.g. skilled manual workers) lost to the Conservatives since 1979 and to go beyond Labour's traditional heartlands and appeal to the voters of 'Middle England' – in other words, to create a winning electoral coalition which reunited Labour with 'ordinary suburban people' (Gould, 1998, p. xii). A key part of this strategy was for New Labour to do what no other Labour government had done before – to win a second term of office with a sizeable working majority; in other words, to develop a long-term strategy for power. The outcome of the 1997 election appeared to vindicate these changes and to provide the platform for what Tony Blair has described as the 'forces of progress' to dominate the politics of the twenty-first century and for Labour to become the natural party of government. However, as we have already noted, the results of the 1997 election are somewhat more ambiguous than they appear at first sight, and while it seems highly unlikely that the Conservatives could mount a credible challenge at the next election, not least due to their internal difficulties, it should not be assumed that Labour will repeat its landslide victory. This is particularly the case as there are signs emerging that key sectors of Labour's traditional support may not actually turn out to vote and that sections of 'Middle England' are becoming disillusioned with the new government over key issues such as health and education (see Dunleavy, 2000).

How then does New Labour's time in government stand up to scrutiny? While the individual policy chapters will review these issues in depth it is worth noting that the government could point to major achievements such as economic stability and growth, low inflation, the creation of an independent Bank of England in charge of monetary policy, devolution, the establishment of a National Minimum Wage (NMW), incorporation of the European Convention on Human Rights into British law, partial reform of the House of Lords, increased spending on health and a long-term strategy for eradicating child poverty. Indeed the Conservatives seem to have accepted that many of these key changes (e.g. NWM, devolution, an Independent Bank of England) are irreversible, signalling perhaps that Blair has already moved some way towards his ambition of creating a new centre-left political consensus. Critics on the other hand would point to Blair's 'presidential' style of government, his dominance of Whitehall and an apparent desire to control all aspects of politics and policy (Hennessy, 1999). Outside the centre it could also be argued that, despite an apparent growth in decentralisation, central government has increased its control over sub-national government through increased control over public expenditure and an ever-growing army of inspectors (e.g. in education and health). Others would also argue that the government has failed to attack entrenched poverty, refused to tackle the deep inequalities created by the market and has generally moved the welfare state towards a 'workfare' state.

Interpretations of 'Blairism'

Clearly many questions remain regarding the nature of New Labour in government. For instance, does New Labour represent a new political constellation with a distinct set of ideas that it can call its own – or, for want of a better term, 'Blairism'? Are we faced with a version of 'Thatcherism with a human face', a British version of Christian Democracy, a 'modernised' New Liberalism or perhaps some combination of all three which synthesises, but goes beyond, them to create a post-Thatcherite politics, or the 'Third Way' as it is frequently termed (see Thompson, 1996; Hay, 1997; Kenny and Smith, 1997; Giddens, 1998; Marquand, 1998; Marr, 1998; Driver and Martell, 1999)? It is these political and ideological issues that we will focus on in the remainder of this chapter. In *Public Policy in Britain* we argued that:

> Thatcherism may be seen as the contradictory articulation of neo-liberalism and neo-conservatism presented in a populist manner, constrained by the exigencies of a competitive party system, a liberal democracy and pre-existing institutions, organisations and political forces. (Atkinson and Savage, 1994, p. 9)

Margaret Thatcher was the pivot around which this political constellation orbited; in a very real sense she was the person who wielded these contradictory tendencies into a political programme and held them together in an unstable coalition. Thatcher's appeal was one that transcended her party and she frequently appeared to appeal directly to the electorate. This, allied with accusations of increasing prime-ministerial control of Whitehall, led to frequent accusations of presidentialism. Moreover, Thatcher was often at odds with sections of the Conservative Party and ultimately she was unable to carry the party with her and resigned. However, as we noted, there was also a pragmatic side to Thatcher that reflected her political instincts regarding the political and electoral viability of particular policies. In many ways Tony Blair resembles Thatcher in that he too has been central to the transformation of his party, its political success and political image, and has also been accused of having a presidential style. Furthermore, he has expressed admiration for Thatcher and accepted key elements of the reforms carried out by Conservative governments (see Blair,1996, esp. ch. 9). But one should not necessarily assume that even those changes deemed irreversible are accepted *in toto*. For instance while Blair and his political associates have welcomed the greatly increased role for markets, they argue, in contrast to the Thatcherites, that markets should be seen not as an end in themselves but as a means to an end (i.e. greater economic growth and more choice).

Given this situation it should come as no surprise to see that Blair and New Labour, both in and out of government, have been accused of wholeheartedly embracing the political consensus established by Thatcherism. Thus Hay (1997) has argued:

> Britain has become a one-vision polity. Indeed, that Britain is no longer a one-party state may be seen as a direct consequence of New Labour's acceptance of the neo-liberal political and economic paradigm that is the sole vision animating contemporary British politics. (Hay, 1997, p. 372) (see also Thompson, 1996)

As a result, Hay claims that New Labour was (and is) unable to offer the electorate an alternative political vision; it is simply claiming that it is more competent at managing the affairs of Britain than its Conservative predecessor. Such claims find support in New Labour's commitment, during the run-up to the 1997 election, not to increase direct taxes and to adhere to Conservative public expenditure projections for the first two years in government. Many would also argue that New Labour's abandonment of Keynesian demand management techniques, the stress on supply-side actions (particularly with regard to the flexibility of labour markets), the emphasis on duties/responsibilities, attempts to reform the welfare state and an unwillingness to tackle poverty and inequalities through redistributive policies provides further evidence of a capitulation to Thatcherite orthodoxy.

Whilst there is a general recognition amongst academics that New Labour has accepted key elements of the Conservative legacy, the counter-argument is that this is too simple a picture (Kenny and Smith, 1997; Marquand, 1998; Driver and Martell, 1999). For example even commentators who have at times been critical of New Labour in government claim that it has actually begun to tackle issues of poverty and inequality (Toynbee, 1999). The claim here is that New Labour has done so largely by stealth in order not to alienate its new voters. For many New Labour supporters it should actually be publicising its achievements in policy areas that benefit Labour's traditional electoral constituency rather than covering them up. However, there is a general feeling that New Labour appears to have accepted crucial elements of Conservative orthodoxy in two key areas – macroeconomic policy and morality. We shall examine each of these in turn.

Macroeconomic Policy

Kenny and Smith (1997) argue that on economic policy New Labour has not simply accepted Conservative neo-liberal orthodoxy; its position reflects the changed conditions and constraints imposed by globalisation on the actions of national governments. Is this the case? For instance, in an attempt to justify the 'Third Way' Blair exemplifies some of the ambiguities of New Labour which many critics point to. He argued:

> The Third Way in essence seeks to combine economic dynamism with social justice. Indeed, it does more, it avows that the one depends crucially on the other. If a country generates no wealth, it cannot afford social justice. (Blair, 1999a) (see also Blair, 1996, esp. ch. 11)

In turn, Blair accepts that for markets to work efficiently they require a degree of social justice (primarily defined in terms of equality of opportunity). However, in a manner which for many is consistent with Thatcherite orthodoxy, there is a reluctance to intervene in the distributional outcomes of markets; the primary area of intervention is to be through equality of opportunity (particularly in terms of education and health care) rather than outcomes, and even this is dependent upon the economy generating a surplus sufficient to the task. Blair goes on to argue:

> The driving force behind the ideas associated with the Third Way is globalisation because no country is immune from the massive change that globalisation brings ... what globalisation is doing is bringing in its wake profound economic and social change (Blair, 1999a) (see also Blair, 1996, ch. 12, and 1999d)

For some, Blair's reaction to globalisation is essentially correct; these changes mean that it is no longer possible for individual nation states to 'buck the market' and carry out the redistributive policies which characterised the period between 1945 and the mid-1970s. However, others would question the particular interpretation that New Labour offers of globalisation and the straitjacket it places on the actions of national governments (see Hirst and Thompson, 1996). The charge here is that New Labour offers a particularly restrictive interpretation of globalisation in order to justify a particular orthodox neo-liberal economic stance and not engaging in redistributive politics that might alienate financial markets. Moreover, even some supporters of the Third Way (e.g. Giddens, 1998, pp. 28–33) recognise that globalisation is a far more complex concept than New Labour orthodoxy would appear to allow for. Giddens (1998, p. 31) argues:

> Is the nation-state becoming a fiction … and government obsolete? They are not, but their shape is being altered. Globalization 'pulls away' from the nation-state in the sense that some powers nations used to possess, including those that underlay Keynesian economic management, have been weakened. However, globalization also 'pushes down' – it creates new demands and also new possibilities for regenerating local identities.

He goes on to point out that 'Globalization is quite often spoken of as if it were a force of nature, but it is not. States, business corporations and other groups have actively promoted its advance.' (ibid, p. 33). The charge against New Labour is precisely that they present globalisation as if it were a force of nature to which there is only one possible response – their response. The interpretation of globalisation offered by writers such as Hirst and Thompson (1996) and Giddens (1998) would suggest that there is more room for manoeuvre than New Labour allows for and one might infer from this that it serves a dual purpose. Firstly, such a narrow interpretation of globalisation's effects justifies New Labour's caution and non-interventionism in the running of the economy other than to improve its competitiveness (e.g. supply-side interventions). As Blair's quotes above exemplify, the first priority is economic growth; greater social justice can then follow on. Secondly, this interpretation of globalisation may be seen as part of a strategy designed to reduce the electorate's expectations of what governments can actually do in the modern world.

Does this therefore mean that on economic policy New Labour is simply Thatcherism Mark II? Marquand (1998) has argued that compared to the exclusionary politics of Thatcherism, New Labour is inclusionary. Does this spill over into economic policy? Driver and Martell

(1999, p. 73) take up these general arguments in a review of economic policy and conclude:

> On the fundamentals, New Labour has accepted that Old Labour was wrong and Mrs Thatcher was right, and it has moved on to Tory economic ground. It is on the details, the competence and unity of the government, and the freshness and imagination of ministers to carry out what they promise, that Labour is confident that it is different. Labour's stress on community, inclusion and the interests of the many and not just the few sets a different tone to that of the Conservatives.

It would seem that with regard to economic policy it is in matters of detail, style and emphasis, rather than substance where New Labour differs from its Conservative predecessors. The opportunity to develop a distinctive New Labour approach to the economy might have been possible had the idea of the stakeholder economy been developed (see Blair, 1996, part IV); however, this idea was never really genuinely embraced and did not figure in the governmental programme of New Labour. Moreover the version considered by New Labour lacked the radicalism and thoroughgoing critique of contemporary Anglo-Saxon capitalism contained in versions such as that proposed by Hutton (1995).

New Labour's Moral Emphasis

Like its Conservative predecessor New Labour has placed considerable emphasis on notions such as duty, responsibility and obligation, arguing that these are vital counterparts to notions of rights/entitlements and that too often in the post-war period the latter have been emphasised at the expense of the former. This emphasis on obligations has been linked by Blair to what he describes as 'a big idea left in politics' – community (Blair, 1996, p. x, and see also ch. 22). For him, community 'expresses the mutuality of both interests and obligations that rise above a narrow view of self-interest' (ibid, p. 218); however, it also has implications for the relationship between society and the individual. This involves a new notion of citizenship which:

> gives rights but demands obligations, shows respect but wants it back, grants opportunity but insists on responsibility. So the purpose of economic and social policy should be to extend opportunity, to remove the underlying causes of social alienation. But it should also

take tough measures to ensure that the chances that are given are taken up. (ibid, pp. 218–219)

In addition Blair argues that this new relationship between individual and society requires 'new principles of public intervention and action. Economically, it requires the creation of a genuine partnership between the public and private sector' (ibid, p. 220). Clearly these views have major implications not only for economic policy but also for social policy and the welfare state. As Gordon Brown, Chancellor of the Exchequer, pointed out:

> Our approach is to build a new and modernised welfare state around principles – that in addition to its traditional and necessary function of giving security to those who cannot work, for those who can work the welfare state should promote work, make work pay and give people they skills they needed to get better jobs. (Brown, 1999)

Such a view clearly reflects New Labour's emphasis on the need to ensure equality of opportunity and that citizens are morally obliged to take advantage of such opportunities as their part of the new contract between citizen and society.

New Labour's morality, at least in the form espoused by Tony Blair, has its origins in the British Tradition of Christian and Ethical Socialism (Blair, 1996, ch. 7; Dennis and Halsey, 1988). This perspective, while stressing notions of fraternity, liberty and equality, also emphasises morality and 'a theory of personality and society which places moral motivation as the mainspring of individual conduct and social organisation. Socialism can only ever be built on moral character' (Dennis and Halsey, 1988, p. 11; see also Blair, 1999b). For many, morality and politics are best kept apart, particularly given John Major's experience with the 'back to basics' campaign. However, for others the issue revolves around the particular interpretation of Christian morality which Blair attempts to develop in support of the acceptance of free markets and their outcomes whilst espousing notions of community and individual responsibility (see Barratt Brown and Coates, 1996, esp. ch. 2). The problem here is that so-called free markets, and the decisions taken by individuals and organisations in those markets, are rarely based upon morality and a concern for the welfare of others. Thus according to Barrett Brown and Coates (1996, p. 26), 'To talk of community while welcoming "the rigour of competitive markets" is frankly double talk and runs counter to all the social teaching of the Christian churches.'

The Dilemmas of a New Politics

One of Tony Blair's frequently stated aims is to create a new politics based around what he terms a radical coalition (Blair, 1996, ch. 2) and an associated political consensus that is inclusive, a Labour version of one-nation politics. He argues:

> The fundamental shift I've worked for all my political life to bring about is this: to build a new coalition in British politics between those who have and those who have not; between those who know the necessity of strong economic and business competence and those with a strong sense of compassion and obligation to others. In a phrase, to re-unite the economic and social parts of political motivation. That is what I mean by one-nation politics. A country with shared values where opportunity and responsibility to each and from each combine. (Blair, 1999c)

Blair identifies this project with what he defines as the 'forces of progress' that he hopes will dominate the politics of the twenty-first century which 'will not be about the battle between capitalism and socialism but between the forces of progress and the forces of conservatism' (Blair, 1999b). In order to carry this project forward, Blair argues that what is required is that a struggle be waged by the forces of progress against conservatives of both left and right, including those in his own party who represent the divisive class-based politics of the 1970s and 1980s (Blair, 1999b and 2000). As part of this strategy Blair has expressed a willingness to collaborate with those politicians who are the heirs to the great nineteenth-century reforming Liberal tradition, in particular the Liberal-Democrats. It appears that on entering office Blair seriously considered inviting the then leader of the Liberal-Democrats, Paddy Ashdown, to sit in Cabinet; however, this proposal encountered serious opposition from within the party and was dropped. Nevertheless, the Liberal-Democrats do sit on a Cabinet committee concerned with constitutional reform, although to date this has produced little in the way of significant proposals for reform. Similarly, despite setting up a committee, chaired by the Liberal-Democrat peer Lord Jenkins, to consider options for introducing a form of proportional representation at general elections, there seems little possibility of such a system being introduced for the next general election. Indeed, New Labour is acutely aware that a system of proportional representation could potentially reduce its ability to govern effectively by denying any future government a working majority.

This dilemma reflects a central paradox confronting New Labour: the desire to be inclusive and integrate as wide a range of political forces as possible into the coalition described as the forces of progress whilst at the same time retaining a tight rein on the processes of governance. Moreover, in order to carry their project forward Blair and his allies have to retain the support of the majority of the Labour Party, particularly the Parliamentary party. Whilst New Labour continues to win elections with a sizeable majority this support is likely to continue. However, should the party stumble at the next election, and its majority be significantly reduced, those voices in the Labour Party who argue that the party has become detached from its core voters will no doubt speak with a renewed vigour. In such a situation it would be interesting to see just how deep-rooted the Blairite modernisation of the party had been and to what extent those associated with New Labour could retain control of the party. However, given the internal problems currently dogging the Conservative Party it seems highly unlikely that they could mount a credible challenge at the next election, thus guaranteeing Labour a second term in office. The key to Blair's ability to carry his project forward during a second term will be the size of Labour's majority (see Dunleavy, 2000). Whilst no one expects a majority of 150 seats, should that majority decline significantly below 100 then there may be renewed challenges to Blair's authority and the associated political project.

Finally we should also note that as part of the Blair project to modernise Britain and create a new political landscape the government has embarked on what Marquand (1998, p. 20) has described as 'the most far-reaching programme of constitutional reform attempted in this country this century'. In particular, devolution and the reform of the House of Lords hold out the promise of significantly altering the shape of British politics in the twenty-first century. Yet there are dangers here for New Labour; having proceeded with devolution for Scotland and Wales, although to different extents in each country, one wonders whether this will be the end of the process or merely the beginning of a new one. Certainly in Scotland there appears to be a significant demand for greater devolution of powers, and Labour's poor showing in recent polls would seem to suggest that there is a momentum building up which the Scottish Nationalist Party could exploit to press for Scottish independence were it to gain control of the Scottish Parliament. And of course where Scotland leads Wales may decide to follow.

Moreover, there are likely to be 'spill-over effects' into England as some of the more peripheral regions (e.g. the North East and South West) begin to demand more regional autonomy; already the creation of

Regional Development Agencies and the setting up of non-elected Regional Chambers has seen demands that the latter be directly elected and given greater powers. After initially appearing rather lukewarm towards further devolution of powers to the English Regions, Blair recently appeared to modify his stance when he admitted 'The logical conclusion of the growing pressure for regional change in England is to create more accountable regional government.' (*The Guardian*, 29 March 2000, p. 13). Whilst the meaning of the phrase 'more accountable regional government' may be open to interpretation it does seem likely that during a second Labour term there will be a strengthening of the electoral underpinnings of Regional Chambers, although whether this will take the form of direct or indirect elections will remain a contested issue. Whatever the outcome of these developments it does appear that New Labour has set in motion processes that it may be unable to control and which will challenge the centralised nature of the British state and politics and therefore the ability of any national government to effectively govern Britain.

With regard to the House of Lords we have witnessed the instigation of a reform process that is best described as a partial reform, a halfway house in which the vast majority of hereditary peers have lost the right to sit in the Lords alongside life peers. The outcome of the Wakeham Commission appears to have satisfied few people, and as a result there is no widely accepted strategy for the future shape and constitution of the Lords. However, if greater democratic accountability for Scotland, Wales and the English regions is granted then it will be increasingly difficult for central government to deny the Lords a more democratic element in its selection process. This would increase the Lords' political legitimacy and, ironically, create an additional challenge to the ability of the dominant parliamentary party to govern in an uncontested manner. Once again it may be that New Labour has released a genie that it cannot control.

Conclusion

Perhaps it is still too early to identify a distinct set of New Labour ideas that constitute a coherent political and ideological formation underlying the actions of the Blair government. After all, it was only during Thatcher's second term of office that it became possible to talk of a coherent body of thought and action that underlay Thatcherism and even then most commentators accepted that there were a number of inconsistencies and contradictions between ideas and actions. However, it does seem to us that New Labour has altered the political landscape of Britain; in part it has built upon the achievements of its Conservative predecessor and exploited some of the unintended processes it unleashed. Nevertheless New Labour cannot simply be portrayed as Thatcherism Mark II; it is a much more complex political phenomenon than such an interpretation allows for. For instance while New Labour still looks across the Atlantic for inspiration it does so from the Democrats rather than the Republicans and, perhaps more important, it has adopted a much more positive stance towards Europe. But it should be noted that Blair does not appear to be particularly sympathetic towards European forms of Social Democracy and does not seem to wish to portray his reforms, or the Third Way, as an attempt to renew social democracy in the overt manner advocated by Giddens (1998).

While New Labour has undoubtedly accepted key elements of the Thatcherite economic and social agenda its rhetoric is much more inclusive and less divisive and there does appear to be a genuine desire to tackle problems of inequality and poverty through a strategy of providing equal opportunities for all, although whether it will be prepared, or able, to provide the resources necessary to put such a strategy into practice is another matter. This in turn reflects a rather different understanding of morality and citizenship, which whilst superficially bearing a certain resemblance to that of Conservatives does appear to offer a genuine alternative based around the notion of an inclusive community; although even here it has been argued that Blair's notion of community is an essentially 'authoritarian' one based around a form of populism and governmental moralism. What all of this does indicate is that New Labour is a much more complex political animal than many of its critics allow for. Thus we find ourselves in agreement with Kenny and Smith (1997) and Driver and Martell (1999) who portray New Labour as representing both a continuity with, but also a departure from, Thatcherism – in other words, post-Thatcherite. As New Labour develops, particularly during a second term in office, it may be that it becomes less pragmatic and more confident about asserting its own identity and therefore articulates a more clearly defined political and ideological project that will be embodied in the policies it pursues. However, even then, like its predecessor Thatcherism, New Labour will still display inconsistencies and contradictions between its thought and actions, but perhaps that is inherent in the nature of politics and government.

2

Policy, Management and Implementation

ANDREW MASSEY

Introduction

In the opening statement of the much-delayed White Paper, *Modernising Government*, its Cabinet Office authors affirmed:

> Government Matters. We want it to deliver policies, programmes and services that make us more healthy, more secure and better equipped to tackle the challenges we face. Government should improve the quality of our lives. (Cabinet Office, 1999)

Prime Minister Blair's own Foreword to the document emphasised his mission to modernise the way in which government works 'in line with the Government's overall modernisation programme'. Yet the fact that it took nearly two years to produce this substantive policy statement on public policy and administration illustrates that far from there being a high priority for deep-rooted reform, for example along the lines of the devolution of powers to Scotland, Wales and Northern Ireland, the new Labour government was content to accept the status quo and concentrate on better policy coordination. In part this results from the continuing impact of the substantial reforms implemented in this field by the preceding Thatcher and Major governments.

Over a century earlier, the reforms begun by the Northcote–Trevelyan Report of 1854, eventually provided the politically impartial service that is taken for granted in Westminster-style democracies. The Report supplied the reasoning which allowed Gladstone and his successors to summon the resolve required to attack and remove the nepotism and

16

corruption of the Georgian and early Victorian public service (Hennessy, 1989). The Major government's White Paper, *Continuity and Change* (Cabinet Office, 1994), could proudly echo Northcote and Trevelyan's sentiments with its opening sentence: 'For many years the British Civil Service has had a high reputation, nationally and internationally, for its standards of integrity, impartiality and loyal service to the Government of the day' (1994, p. 1).

It was the concerted attempt by the Conservative administrations between 1979 and 1997 to combine those core values of impartial and loyal service with the ideals of efficiency, effectiveness and economy, that was to witness the most radical reforms of the civil service since the Victorian era. In tracing the line between these reports it is possible to chart the approach of British governments over the last twenty years towards the machinery of government, that is, the administrative apparatus used by governments to aid the formulation of their policy and manage its implementation.

As with the other policy fields discussed in this book, the aims for this chapter are to:

1. summarise and explain the major patterns and developments which took place in British Public Administration between 1979 and 1997, and which constitute the inheritance of the new Labour administration;
2. examine the emerging and actual policies which Labour have embarked upon since the election;
3. briefly discuss the way in which these emergent trends may develop over the life of Labour's first Parliament.

The Administrative Inheritance

The period of Conservative government under Margaret Thatcher and John Major was one of profound change for the structures and processes of public policy. The United Kingdom shifted from what Hughes has referred to as an era of 'Public Administration', to one of 'Public Management' (1998). Others, in accepting this premise, have referred to the fundamental reforms implemented over this period as representing the death of the old public administration paradigm and its replacement by New Public Management (NPM) (Campbell and Wilson, 1995). For the purposes of this chapter, traditional public administration may be described as:

an administration under the formal control of the political leadership, based on a strictly hierarchical model of bureaucracy, staffed by permanent, neutral and anonymous officials, motivated only by the public interest, serving any governing party equally, and not contributing to policy but merely administering those policies decided by the politicians (Hughes, 1998, p. 22).

The work of theorists from several countries underpin its foundations and these include (from Britain) Lord Haldane, (from Germany) Max Weber, and (the former US President) Woodrow Wilson. At its core, traditional public administration seeks to ensure there is a clear line of accountability from appointed public officials to elected politicians. The officials, although directed by politicians, must act objectively according to established rules and procedures, scrupulously distinguishing between their personal interests and those of their office. It has even been argued that the higher ranks have been guided by a Platonic notion of 'The Public Good', however that may have been defined (O'Toole, 1990, pp. 337–52).

Although some variant of this traditional public administration model was adopted by many countries, the model was most often found in those societies which also established either the 'Westminster' or 'Washington' model of politics generally; in short, it is largely (but not exclusively) a liberal-democratic model. From the mid-1970s the model came under attack from differing political perspectives. Some saw it as being elitist and bureaucratic, ensuring that far from serving the elected politicians, the permanent bureaucrats formed a powerful and self-serving coterie of their own. They were accused of thwarting the policies of elected politicians in order to advance their own welfarist and corporatist agenda (Smith, 1999; Denham, 1996; Considine and Painter, 1997). Furthermore, the old system was seen to concentrate too much on process and the interests of producers, giving insufficient attention to outcomes and the needs and demands of consumers and citizens, leading to inefficiencies in the delivery of services and ineffectiveness in terms of their outcomes.

Although the political Left was critical of the elitist and authoritarian nature of the system, it was the critique of the Right that was to prove most damaging, especially that group of theorists known as the 'Public Choice' school, which originated in the USA but whose influence manifested itself in reform movements across the world. It was the sustained assault of these new managerialists which was to prove decisive in the decision by many countries to reform their public sector and none was more determined and committed than Margaret Thatcher during her tenure of office.

Between 1979 and 1997 the Conservative governments of Margaret Thatcher and John Major established a new approach to the public sector in Britain which has become known as New Public Management (NPM) (Pollitt, 1990).

- NPM pays greater attention to results or outputs and the personal responsibility of individual officials or managers (Hughes, 1998, p. 52);
- there is a move from tall hierarchies to flatter more flexible and devolved management structures, with flexible terms of employment (Farnham and Horton, 1999);
- institutional and individual objectives are clearly defined and include the establishment of key performance indicators against which to measure delivered outputs (Hughes, 1998; Horton and Farnham, 1999);
- there is greater attention to economy, efficiency and effectiveness; this includes a greater commitment to procedures such as market testing and compulsory competitive tendering (Hughes, 1998; Elcock, 1991);
- this in turn is linked to a general commitment to reducing the role of the state in the disposal of GNP and the provision of services in favour of privatised companies and the establishment of a market in areas previously viewed as the preserve of natural monopolies or public administrators (Hughes, 1998; Massey, 1993).

Whilst the UK was not alone in this managerialist revolution, its impact upon the public sector and the determination of successive governments to enforce the implementation of what amounted to a cultural revolution therein was prolonged and intense. As Prime Minister, Blair has embraced this inheritance. All parts of the state have been affected by a process which has restructured both the institutions and the procedures by which they operate. The machinery of central government, public bodies, and local government have all undergone a continuous process of reform (Massey, 1999, pp. 1–29).

The Thatcher/Major reforms of central government, like that in other sectors has continued to concentrate on better value for money, in the form of efficiency and effectiveness, 'downsizing' and 'delayering', as well as:

decentralisation and devolution, and greater concentration on 'core businesses' outputs and outcomes. A key thrust has been delegation of authority from the Treasury and Cabinet Office to departments; from departments to accountable units such as Agencies, and from personnel units and senior managers to line managers. (Cabinet Office, 1998a, pp. 12–17)

As the cutting-edge of these reforms, privatisation and market testing have greatly reduced the numbers of civil servants. Other initiatives, such as the establishment of 'executive agencies within departments' (as part of the 'Next Steps' reforms), have also dramatically reconfigured the public sector. The most far-reaching reforms under the Tories were:

- the Efficiency Scrutinies, begun in 1979;
- the Financial Management Initiative, begun in 1982; *FM* ⏌
- the launch of the Next Steps initiative in 1988;
- the introduction of the Citizen's Charter and Market Testing in 1991;
- Fundamental Expenditure Reviews in 1993;
- the initiatives implemented as a result of the 1994 and 1995 White Papers on the Civil Service, *Continuity and Change* (Cabinet Office, 1994) and *Taking Forward Continuity and Change* (see Cabinet Office, 1998a and b; Smith, 1999; Massey, 1993, 1995a and b; Campbell and Wilson, 1995; Hughes, 1998).

The Efficiency Scrutinies began soon after the 1979 election, with the establishment of the Efficiency Unit under Sir Derek (later Lord) Rayner, on loan from the retailer Marks and Spencer's. To emphasise his access to the Prime Minister and the weight she gave to his advice, Rayner was initially located at No. 10 Downing Street in an office near to Margaret Thatcher, then later moved a short way along the road to the Cabinet Office (Massey, 1993; Pollitt, 1990). The short, narrow audits of small pieces of departments' business he pioneered sought to establish ways of saving money within departmental budgets and were used effectively to this end across Whitehall. The key to their success lay in the fact that Rayner used young 'high-flying' officials from within the departments themselves to conduct the scrutinies, which was combined with the unrivalled support given to him and the recommendations of his team by Margaret Thatcher. The limitations of this approach became apparent fairly quickly, but the way had been prepared for a more fundamental process of reform; this took the shape of the Financial Management Initiative (FMI).

The FMI evolved into a revolutionary initiative, and from it almost all other reforms may be traced, either wholly or in part. The overall objective of the FMI was 'to improve management in the Civil Service by ensuring that all managers knew what their objectives were and how their achievements would be assessed' (Cabinet Office, 1998a, p. 13). All departments, and all constituent parts of departments, including those parts which were to eventually become Executive Agencies, were to establish and publish (internally to begin with):

- well-defined responsibilities and procedures for making the best use of their resources;
- the necessary information, training and advice to exercise their responsibilities effectively;
- managers were to be given much greater responsibility for managing their own budgets;
- output was to be more carefully measured wherever possible, and the cost-effectiveness of their work considered;
- civil servants became more directly accountable for their work;
- each department was to work within a limit for its total running costs (Cabinet Office, 1998a; Pollitt, 1990; Massey, 1999, pp. 18–19).

The success of the FMI in delivering genuine managerial (and financial) reform led the then government to look at the next reforming step it might take. This was to become known as The Next Steps initiative.

Margaret Thatcher launched the Next Steps initiative in February 1988, following a report entitled *Improving Management in Government: The Next Steps* (also known as the Ibbs Report, after the then Head of The Efficiency Unit). It advocated that departments move towards identifying coherent areas which could be grouped together into one operational unit under a single official who was to be accountable directly to his or her Minister for delivering specific objectives, results and services. This official was to be designated the Chief Executive, a title which resonates with the private sector approach to delivering services that the Conservatives aspired to for the public sector. Each agency's objectives are set out in a Framework Document which 'sets out the aims and objectives of the agency, and its expected output and outcomes in terms of both quantity and quality, with explicit performance indicators' (Cabinet Office, 1998a, p. 14).

Next Steps brought about major changes in the way the civil service is managed and also in the management culture of the executive parts of the civil service. It has ensured that departments and agencies

> look critically at functions of Government and apply the 'prior options' tests to them, i.e. can a function be abolished, privatised or contracted out. An agency is only established where these options are ruled out by ministers (Cabinet Office, 1998a, p. 14).

The following points also apply:

- a belief that the centres of departments should concentrate on strategic management rather than day-to-day 'hands on' control;
- appointing the right Chief Executive, from within or outside the Civil Service, for the job to be done;
- encouragement of the full use of managerial freedom and incentives by both departments and agencies, with maximum possible delegation of their operation to local management.

Whilst some of the claims regarding a full 'cultural revolution' are open to question, it is certainly true that the agencification and marketisation instituted by Next Steps have brought within their wake the greatest transformation of the modern Civil Service since its establishment following the Northcote–Trevelyan Report (Hennessy, 1989; Smith, 1999; Massey, 1995b and 1999).

It may be seen that this is a reform in terms of both structure and accountability. With the insertion of a Chief Executive into the hierarchy between Ministers and the rest of the agency, there is now a reformulation of ministerial accountability and civil service anonymity, as the examples of the Prison Service and Child Support Agency (amongst others) demonstrate (Massey, 1995b, pp. 16–29; Greer, 1994). Next Steps recognises the interrelation of policy and management, 'but attempts to remove large amounts of routine executive activity that does not have a day-to-day impact on policy via the political system. Ministers exercise strategic oversight except when policy failure and exceptional circumstances intervene' (Massey, 1995b; and 1999, pp. 5–20). The main thrust of the policy is that to the greatest extent practicable the executive functions of government are carried out by units clearly designated within departments and referred to as Agencies. The main characteristics of Agencies are that:

- they operate within a rigorous framework with clear targets set by ministers for the task to be done, the results to be achieved and the resources to be provided;
- the day-to-day responsibility for running the organisation is delegated to a Chief Executive;
- they have the management tools and freedoms they need to do the job (Massey, 1999, p. 19).

The total number of permanent staff working in Executive Agencies and on Next Steps Lines on 1st October 1997 was 362,000, 77per cent of all permanent staff. Upon the accession to power of Britain's first Labour government for 18 years, it was clear the institutional map of the British public sector had been transformed in the intervening period. Although it would not be true to argue that the UK had shifted completely over to the New Public Management, it would be fair to suggest the era of the traditional form of Public Administration had passed.

Policy Under New Labour

From the period of John Smith's short tenure as leader, the Labour Party had accepted many of the Conservatives' reforms of the public sector. It became clear in the Party's public pronouncements and off-the-record briefings that its leadership welcomed the FMI and embraced Next Steps. As it has re-branded and marketed itself as New Labour, it is obvious that in the field of public sector reform it has few quarrels with its Conservative predecessors. Upon his appointment by the Queen as Prime Minister, following the 1997 election, Tony Blair was not about to reverse any of the Tories' substantive public sector reforms; he was and remains committed to consolidating them and ensuring their implementation under his administration. Any structural change is to be as a result of those limited aims and the unseen or unintended affects of devolution.

The situation that has emerged under New Labour has been clarified by the *Modernising Government* White Paper (Cabinet Office, 1999). Labour is seeking to evolve the concept of 'joined-up government' and to put it into practice. That is, the government is attempting to develop a greater coordination of government efforts across Whitehall and beyond in order to overcome the almost 'federal' nature of much departmental behaviour, while at the same time insisting that this is done in such a way that the impact of the state upon individual citizens is more coherent, understandable and accessible. This is despite an explicit commitment to a more federal approach in the relationship of the constituent parts of the United Kingdom to each other. The different parts of the Blair agenda in this field may be summarised as:

- coherence through 'joined-up government' as outlined in various documents, but put most cogently in *Modernising Government*;
- an attempt to reformulate the role and relationship of the Non-Departmental Bodies (or quangos);
- Devolution to Scotland, Wales and Northern Ireland;
- a re-launch of the Citizen's Charter as 'Service First';
- the development of a greater regional emphasis in the governance of England through the establishment of Regional Development Agencies (RDAs).

The Blair Agenda: New Approaches, Same Goal

In the 1997 Next Steps Review, the first under New Labour, the government explained that the initial target of extending Next Steps to cover 75per cent of the Civil Service in ten years had been achieved. The emphasis was turned, therefore, from agency creation towards improving performance, identifying four key action areas:

- Ministers are to be encouraged to take a closer involvement with target setting and attainment for the agencies over which they exercise authority;
- the greatly increased use of information technology and other modern management techniques by agencies to ensure they use best practice as demonstrated in comparable private and public sector organisations;
- to ensure cooperation and coordination across institutional boundaries to provide seamless delivery of service, the so-called 'joined-up' government;
- Ministers will work to dispel confusion over their accountability for agencies in that whilst the managerial delegations would be maintained (and in places deepened), ministerial accountability to Parliament for the performance of agencies will remain unchanged (*Next Steps Review*, Cabinet Office, 1997; Massey, 1999, pp. 20–21).

Achieving many of these goals involves the use of advanced information technology in order to improve access to government and facilitate the flow of information to citizens from the many public sector organisations with which they have to deal. The government's other main focus here is on performance through greater efficiency, achieved in part through the expansion of the Benchmarking process and the incorporation of the Business Excellence Model into the work of agencies and elsewhere (Samuels, 1998).

The second major area where Blair's government accepted, but repackaged Tory policies, was with the relaunch of the Citizen's Charter under the title *Service First*. The Citizen's Charter was launched by the then Prime Minister, John Major, in 1991 as a 10-year programme to raise the standard of public services and make them more responsive to users. There are now 40 main Charters, covering all the key public services, setting out the standards of service that people can expect to receive, with over 10,000 local charters covering local service providers, such as GP practices, police forces and fire services (Massey, 1999, pp. 15–25). It may be seen that although they came into office with limited aims in this policy area, Ministers 'hit the ground running' in that they already knew they were going to continue travelling in the same general direction as their Conservative predecessors. Even though new White Papers may have been inordinately delayed from time to time, the first two Chancellors of the Duchy of Lancaster (the relevant Cabinet Minister) produced a coherent set of policies outlining the government's objectives as they evolved in the first two years of Blair's administration.

For example, in November of 1997, the first Labour Chancellor of the Duchy of Lancaster, Dr David Clark, issued a consultation paper entitled *Opening up Quangos* (Cabinet Office, 1997), which showed the way the government was seeking to progress. The paper, and its follow-up report, did not suggest any radical departures for the public sector, but placed an emphasis on ensuring that quangos should be more open to women, people from ethnic minorities and others traditionally missing from public service in numbers proportionate to their demographic contribution to society. Clark's paper also sought to progress the issues of open government (which itself formed another paper) within the public sector, the role of quangos, their structure, complaints procedures, relationship to other bodies at central, regional and local level, and so forth. In short, the paper anticipated many of the notions the government would grow into fruition with *Modernising Government* (Cabinet Office, 1999).

As well as the devolution of substantial powers to new institutions in Scotland, Wales, and Northern Ireland (a subject beyond the scope of this chapter), the government also quickly moved to fulfil its election pledge to establish new regional bodies in England, which when they were established in April 1999, were called Regional Development Agencies. The Department of the Environment, Transport and the Regions' paper of April 1998, *Regional Development Agencies' Regional Strategies*, argued in its Foreword:

> We are looking to the RDAs to deliver more effective, more integrated regeneration programmes, to take forward at the regional level many of the priorities of the White Paper 'Our Competitive Future: Building the Knowledge Driven Economy' and to develop a framework for improving the regional skills base. The regional strategies to which this guidance relates will give focus and coherence to this work, and to the work of others working in and for our regions.

Their powers to do this emanated from the Regional Development Agencies Act 1998 (Section 7 (1)) which:

> requires a regional development agency (an 'agency') to formulate and keep under review a strategy in relation to its purposes and to have regard to the strategy in exercising its functions. Section 4 of the Act sets out the purposes of an agency which are:
> (a) to further the economic development and regeneration of its area,
> (b) to promote business efficiency, investment and competitiveness in its area,
> (c) to promote employment in its area,
> (d) to enhance the development and application of skills relevant to employment in its area, and
> (e) to contribute to the achievement of sustainable development in the United Kingdom where it is relevant to its area to do so.
> (Regional Development Agencies' Regional Strategies, Department of the Environment, Transport and the Regions, 1998, Introduction).

Thus, it may be seen that from its earliest days in office, the Blair government's agenda for public policy and administration was concerned with the boundaries of governance and the coordination of policy formulation and delivery across those boundaries, a horizontal and vertical process leading to a matrix approach.

Furthermore, the moves to work across sectors, and the establishing of the People's Panel, demonstrate the government's continuing commitment to shift the emphasis of government further towards delivering coherent service provision to meet the perceived expectations of citizens. As part of this, the Comprehensive Spending Review published in 1998 set new priorities for public spending and identified key issues that the government is seeking to tackle across organisational boundaries. An example is Sure Start, where:

> the aim is to work with parents and children to improve the physical, intellectual, social and emotional development of young children. Cross-departmental groups, involving people with an interest in health, education, the local environment, juvenile crime and family welfare as well as local government and the voluntary sector, were set up to devise and implement Sure Start. They have come up with an initial programme of 60 pilot projects. (*Modernising Government*, Cabinet Office, 1999, p. 17)

The move to break down vertical institutional barriers in order to deliver coherent policies, insulated from the predations of individual government departments jealously guarding 'their' territory, has therefore been a key reform. Other initiatives to address cross-cutting policies and provide 'joined-up government' include:

- The Social Exclusion Unit, a cross-departmental team based in the Cabinet Office set up to tackle in a coherent way the wide range of issues which arise from the inequalities in society.
- The Women's Unit, which supports the Minister for Women in representing the needs of women within government through research, specific project work, and longer-term work on institutional change.
- The Performance and Innovation Unit, which reports directly to the Prime Minister on selected issues that cross departmental boundaries, and proposes policy innovations to improve the delivery of the government's objectives.
- The crime reduction programme, which relies on coordinated working across central and local government, drawing on their expertise in policy development, implementation and research, to identify and deliver effective measures for reducing crime.

- The UK Anti-drugs Co-ordinator, Sir Kenneth Helliwell, was appointed in 1997 to coordinate the government's approach to drugs problems and to ensure greater effectiveness and better use of resources.
- The Home Office, the Lord Chancellor's Department and the Crown Prosecution Service have moved to the joint planning and managing of the criminal justice system (CJS) as a whole, including the publication for the first time of integrated plans (all from *Modernising Government*, Cabinet Office, 1999, p. 17).

In addition to this, it became clear from early 1999 that the government had begun to concentrate on better ways of developing and delivering policy by improving the legislative process. For example, it has put into place new procedural ways of achieving greater consultation over draft legislation and formal pre-legislative scrutiny of all draft Bills in Parliament (ibid., p. 20).

It may be seen, therefore, that the management of government business is being reformed by adding to the Conservative emphasis on focusing on outcomes. Each of these initiatives heavily emphasises the end-user, or delivery of services to citizens in an efficient and (above-all) effective way. There is a growing list of examples of areas where action has taken place. These include:

- the establishment of a Civil Service Management Committee of Permanent Secretaries, and ensuring they use a more corporate approach to achieving the cross-cutting goals needed to drive cultural change in the civil service;
- using the new Centre for Management and Policy Studies to deliver joint training to Ministers and officials which will allow them to discuss the way policy is, and should be, made and to address particular areas of policy;
- the attempt to modernise evaluation standards and tools (ibid., p. 20).
- In addition to this, the 'Government is also introducing a series of steps aimed at removing unnecessary regulation and ensuring that future regulations are limited to measures which are necessary and proportionate' (ibid., p. 21).

By July 1999 the Press Office of the second Labour Chancellor of the Duchy of Lancaster, Dr Jack Cunningham, could boast of some progress:

People will be able to access on-line Government services and information and carry out their business with Government on-line much more easily in future by using a single 'gateway' point of access... The commitment is one of 62 listed in a detailed Action Plan for the first two years of the Modernising government Programme launched ... following the publication of the Modernising government White Paper in March, the Action Plan details specific commitments in a wide range of key areas. Action to come includes:

- By December, the government will run a trial of a single electronic 'gateway'. This will open up a range of one stop shop services, such as providing information about a change of address to different parts of government in one go.
- Government websites will give more information and be more convenient to use. (Cabinet Office, Press Release, 27 July 1999)

The emphasis on ease of use and effective delivery is clearly seen to be carried forward into the implementation phase of the policy process.

The *Modernising Government* White Paper and subsequent ministerial pronouncements also marked the establishment of an attempt to use national programmes the government has described as being 'Citizen-focused', which again emphasises the end-user of public services. These are managed centrally by government departments or agencies and examples include the new NHS Direct and Employment Service Direct. As well as these broad national schemes, delivered in the new 'joined-up' way, the government has also established some specific 'group-focused programmes', such as those concerned with the needs of particular groups. Examples include the Better Government for Older People pilots, the New Deal for the Young Unemployed, or the Service Families Task Force (*Modernising Government*, p. 21). These last examples are also being coordinated with area-based programmes. They are designed to tackle the problems of particular areas or localities experiencing the difficulties of economic deprivation following, for example, the end of mining or some other heavy industry within the local region (ibid).

It needs to be emphasised that the government requires all these examples, which have cut a swathe across the social, economic, geographical and political terrain of the UK, to be 'joined-up' in a way that has rarely been successfully applied in countries lacking some kind of National Plan. The idea of some *dirigiste* plan is one that is itself an approach replete with unhappy experiences for the last Labour Prime Minister who attempted it in the mid-1960s (Smith, 1979; Middlemas,

1979). The difference this time is that New Labour is seeking to act as an empowerer and coordinator, encouraging others to ensure they 'join-up' their work. For example, local authorities are to implement a community planning process so that they and other local bodies can adopt a common and coordinated approach to local needs. New procedures at central, regional and local level will oversee barriers to coordination and establish ways to overcome them. These include an attempt to align the boundaries of all public bodies, moving away from the anarchic situation whereby when Labour came to power over 100 different sets of regional boundaries were used in England alone. In order to reiterate the importance of public accountability and end-user friendliness, running like a golden thread through all of this, the government has extended the Parliamentary Ombudsman's jurisdiction to cover an extra 150 public bodies and re-emphasised the importance of the auditing authorities at all levels of government. The public's indirect access to the Ombudsman is also to be reviewed and probably extended.

The revamped mechanisms for delivering these policies include the aforementioned Comprehensive Spending Review, with its coordinated set of objectives for public spending, and new Public Service Agreements for public sector organisations which set out firm targets for improving services over a three-year period. As part of the attempt to disseminate best practice in service delivery, the government launched the Public Sector Benchmarking Project:

> to spread use of the Business Excellence Model across the public sector. The Model is widely used by leading private sector companies, but for the public sector this project is the world leader in scale and ambition. It is helping to spread best practice across boundaries, not just within the public sector, but between public and private users of the Model and internationally. Take-up of the Model has already reached 65% of central government agencies and 30% of local authorities. Over 90% of users report that their rate of improvement has increased as a direct result. (*Modernising Government*, 1999, p. 39)

In conclusion to this section, it may be seen that at the same time as the previous government was attempting to improve economic competitiveness and expand deregulation of the economy, its privatisation of natural monopolies, such as gas, electricity, water, railways and telecommunications, coincided with the extension of citizens' rights and producer obligations via Citizen's Charters. This meant that society required a system of oversight and regulation to protect it from the abuse of monopoly privilege and position, a process that occurred simultaneously with the deregulation movement. It is clear that some aspects of reform, therefore, could conflict with one another, and the programmes of privatisation and greater competition provide an example (Moran and Prosser, 1994, pp. 35–49; Middleton, 1996, pp. 638–9; Foster and Plowden, 1996, pp. 82–101).

Modernising Government seeks to correct some of the illogicalities and inconsistencies that have developed over the years – for example the clash between competition and privatisation programmes, or the fact that the successful Market Testing programme cut across the establishment of Next Steps agencies, with parts of agencies being contracted out, making the agencification process less coherent and stable (Foster and Plowden, 1996, ch 6 and 8). The move to marketisation, agencification, greater devolution and regionalisation all tend to fragment the policy process and the coordination of service delivery. 'Joined-up government' addresses this by seeking to ensure that services are designed to respond to the needs of the user, that is, individual citizens.

Potential and Future Developments

To some extent, the history of public administration and public policy is a history of attempts at coordinating government. The use of the traditional model to enforce the implementation of political decisions via hierarchies of officials, bound by rules, regulations and limited spans of control, reflected the requirements of our Victorian and Edwardian predecessors to curtail the excesses of a system riddled with nepotism and corruption. The move towards flatter hierarchies and a more business-oriented approach reflects the New Labour concern with a desire to match need with delivery, and demand with provision, in an efficient and effective manner; leavening these activities with a liberal dose of accountability through accountancy (Massey, 1999). The government of Tony Blair has accepted the legacy of Conservative Premiers Thatcher and Major in the field of policy and administration, embraced it and sought to extend the logic of that inheritance. Hence, the emphasis on consolidation and coordination across sectors.

The Conservatives implemented a cornucopia of reforms and initiatives across the public sector, some of which, like Next Steps and Market Testing, began to pull against each other, leading to inconsistency and muddle. There are the seeds for some similar inconsistencies germinating in New Labour's rose garden. The first of these is concerned with devolution. Leaving aside the political illiteracies inherent to the unfair federal settlement in favour of Scotland, the establishment of the RDAs in the English regions is fraught with difficulties (Gay, 1998; Bradbury and Mawson, 1997; Mawson and Spencer, 1997). The existing Government Offices of the regions have sought to coordinate and finesse all manner of central policies and European funding, as well as inward investment for their respective regions; they will continue to play a major role in this. The role of the RDAs however remains unclear. If they seek to challenge central government policy, as applied to their region, they will be overruled. As quangos, their line of accountability is clear and it is to the Secretary of State for the Environment, Transport and Regions. To attempt to set them up as some kind of coordinating body is all well and good, but aside from the probability of replicating Government Office work, they do not have the authority to coordinate the activities of other Departments' quangos or NHS trusts and they will not easily acquire it. It is hard to see how they will develop, other than as debating bodies for their constituent local authorities and small businesses (Mawson and Spencer, 1997).

Of the more substantive reforms, those pertaining to central government, there is also likely to be a mixed result. Developments in IT will allow the one-stop shops and other more open-access initiatives to develop piecemeal. But there remains a real difficulty of attaining coordination across powerful entrenched bureaucracies. Take just one example listed in this chapter, the attempt to coordinate the criminal justice system. In the process of attempting to ensure 'joined-up' government in the CJS there has been inadequate attention paid to the resource issues involved. Not only does the Crown Prosecution Service remain under-resourced, but local largely county-based police forces have a financial incentive to become tardy in carrying out the orders of lower courts in different parts of the country regarding things like following up on arrest warrants. Chief Constables have to set priorities for the use of their scarce resources and there are many calls made on their officers, of which the concerns of the CJS is but one. There is no mechanism, beyond laboriously chasing up every single one of the thousands of arrest warrants issued annually, to ensure Chief Constables are carrying out their duties in this respect. These are petty concerns, but they reflect the nuts and bolts of the daily reality of governance for citizens. In a large, pluralist country, the 'joins' of 'joined-up' government are always going to show across a large number of policy areas when those policies are implemented.

Those reforms most likely to succeed are those most deeply rooted in the system and which also have technological innovation on their side. Agencification, marketisation, contracting out, benchmarking, one-stop shops and cross-cutting policies are all examples of activities that were in place (or being touted) prior to Labour's election, in one form or another, and which are also part of a wider global context of their implementation. Like privatisation twenty years ago, in time hindsight will make them seem inevitable. The extent to which there will be joined-up government in practice, however, rests upon the ability of central units, such as the Prime Minister's Office, the Treasury and the Cabinet Office, to force through the changes. The experience of the last twenty years suggests that only those reforms which have the total and unremitting support of the Prime Minister in Cabinet will succeed. Those that lack this level of sustained commitment will fail. Governments of all persuasions like to try and 'make a difference', but the constraints of the global economy, Britain's dwindling power relative to the rest of the world and the harsh realities of economic constraint will ensure that Blair, like Thatcher and Major before him, will have only a limited success in a limited number of policy areas.

3

The Europeanisation of British Policy-Making

STEPHEN COPE

This chapter examines the impact of the European Union (EU) upon policy-making within British government. Since joining the European Community (EC) in 1973, which later became part of the EU, membership has had very far-reaching implications for the way that public policy is made in Britain. Unfortunately much of the political debate surrounding Britain's membership of the EU is centred either on the perceived loss of national sovereignty (Holmes, 1996), or on the perceived awkward relations between Britain and the EC/EU (George, 1994). Kaiser observed that a 'great deal of scholarship on Britain and Europe after 1945 has been preoccupied with the question as to why and at which junction Britain "missed the bus" with the destiny of ever closer political union in Western Europe' (1996, p. 204); and Young argued that the study of relations between Britain and Europe amounted to a 'story of fifty years in which Britain struggled to reconcile the past she could not forget with the future she could not avoid' (1998, p. 1).

Though the 'loss of sovereignty' and 'awkward partner' theses are important aspects in understanding Britain's relations with Europe generally and the EC/EU specifically, they often fail to fully appreciate the complexity of relations between a myriad of policy-making actors within the EU and the consequent mutual impacts upon both the EU and British government. This chapter focuses upon the interplay of such actors in the way that public policy in Britain is made, and argues that there has been increasing Europeanisation of policy-making which neither necessarily means that national sovereignty is eroded nor that Britain's relations with the EU is peculiarly problematical (particularly when compared to relations between other member states and the EU).

The chapter is divided into four sections: the concept of Europeanisation, Europeanisation in historical context, Europeanisation as policy-making, and the Europeanisation of British government.

The Concept of Europeanisation

Europeanisation is a shorthand term denoting the increasing influence of the EU upon its member states and also non-member states (particularly those aspiring to become member states, such as many Eastern European states). However, Europe is much more than the EU, despite it becoming a magnet for most European states. There exist other processes of Europeanisation pushed by others outside the EU – such as the Council of Europe, Organisation for Security Cooperation in Europe (OSCE) and Western European Union (WEU) – but the EU remains by far the most dominant regional actor within Europe, and is an increasingly significant actor worldwide. Indeed the EU represents the most advanced form of regionalisation in the world, and its 'construction ... ranks among the most extraordinary achievements in modern world politics' (Moravcsik, 1999, p. 1). The EU has become an increasingly important site within which many 'history-making decisions' are taken (Peterson, 1995, p. 72), and also within which public policy is framed in Britain.

For this reason alone, this chapter views Europeanisation as the creeping adaptation of national policy-making systems towards the EU. Europeanisation, whether state-sponsored harmonisation or market-driven convergence, represents 'an incremental process reorienting the direction and shape of politics to the degree that EC political and economic dynamics become part of the organizational logic of national politics and policy-making' (Ladrech, 1994, p. 69). As a result, the EU and its constituent member states need to be seen increasingly as a distinct, though somewhat disjointed, political system in which policies are made (Andersen and Eliassen, 1993, p. 10). The EU 'incontestably represents a new level of government' (Wallace, 1983, p. 406), and is 'pioneering a form of transnational governance' unrivalled elsewhere in the world (Giddens, 1999, p. 80). The EU is now a firmly established part of the multi-level governance of Britain that constitutes a key set of policy-making actors, processes and structures shaping the making of public policy in Britain. For example, 'over 80 per cent of British environmental policy originates in the EU', forcing British government 'to adopt much higher environmental standards than would otherwise have been the case' (Jordan, 2000, p. 262).

Europeanisation in Historical Context

The origins of the EU can be traced back to the aftermath of the Second World War. Several Western European states – West Germany, France, Italy, Belgium, the Netherlands and Luxembourg – committed themselves to specific forms of economic and political cooperation as a way of rebuilding their war-torn economies and preventing further war between themselves. These founder member states signed the Treaty of Paris in 1951 establishing the European Coal and Steel Community (ECSC) and the Treaties of Rome in 1957 establishing the European Economic Community (EEC) and the European Atomic Energy Community (Euratom), which were merged together in the 1960s to form the EC. Their motives were a mix of economic and political factors. First, and economically, the treaties, particularly the Treaty of Rome setting up the EEC, can be regarded as 'a hard commercial deal, a set of rather specific bargains between the signatory states, at the core of which was the central bargain between the French and the Germans' (Taylor, 1996, p. 13). The EEC committed member states to establishing a common market whereby tariffs on trade between member states would be gradually abolished and to setting a common external tariff on trade between member and non-member states. The West German government wanted a common market for its manufactured goods, and the French government for its agricultural products; the common external tariff, along with the Common Agricultural Policy (CAP), were largely protectionist measures insulating member states from outside competition. Second, and politically, the treaties were attempts to allay French fears about further German military designs and to realise West German hopes for long-suppressed political expression. In the words of Taylor (1996, p. 14):

A grand purpose of the Treaty of Rome, as with the Paris Treaty before it, was to bind West Germany, and to meet continuing French concerns about their security in relations with Germany. The German government saw the framework of the European Community as the place where they could define themselves as a state, find a new sense of identity to replace that which had been so tarnished by the Third Reich, and adapt to their new constitutional and legal mechanisms – to rediscover Germany as a nation and as a state. In return for this grant the French were to be given a more secure environment. From the beginning, therefore, the European Community was as much about state creation as about integration.

Furthermore, the US government was also keen to support economic and political cooperation between Western European states in the belief that a more politically coherent, economically strong and ideologically friendly Western Europe would 'contain Soviet influence' (Carr and Cope, 1994a, p. 53). Indeed the US government hoped that Britain would join the EC from its inception, not least because it believed that the British government could safeguard American interests more effectively inside than outside the EC. However, Britain declined its invitation to join the EC, arguably suffering from 'delusions of grandeur' and preferring instead to maintain its relations with the US and its empire over those with Europe. The British government was also wary of the political designs of the EC with its treaty commitments towards 'ever closer union'.

However, the position of the British government not to join the EC soon began to be questioned as a result of a combination of political and economic pressures – continued American pressure upon British government to join, Britain's diminishing world role and declining empire, growing pressure from domestic business wanting better access to larger EC markets, and dismay at EC economies outperforming the British economy. After two failed attempts to join the EC in the 1960s, both vetoed by a suspicious French government, Britain successfully applied for membership, and, along with Denmark and Ireland, became a member of the EC in 1973. Since joining Britain's relations with the EC have frequently been troubled, and it has been dubbed 'an awkward partner' (George, 1994). A root cause of Britain's sometimes stormy relations with the EC is undoubtedly its late entry; it joined a club late, thus having to accept rules – the EC's *acquis communautaire* – that it had no influence in making and some of which did not work in Britain's favour (for example, the workings of CAP and the formula for calculating member states' budgetary contributions towards the EC). Edward Heath, the former Prime Minister who negotiated Britain's successful application to join the EC, stated (Engel, 1998, p. 13):

> It was the period between 1950 and 1972 which shatters me, 22 wasted years. We gained nothing and they [the founder member states] arranged everything to suit themselves.

Since its establishment, the EC has both 'widened' and 'deepened'. It has expanded from the six founding member states to the present 15 member states – Greece, Portugal and Spain joined in the 1980s, and Austria, Finland and Sweden in the 1990s, with a growing queue of mainly Eastern European states seeking membership. The EC has also expanded its policy briefs, now embracing agricultural, social, environmental, economic, monetary, foreign, security and policing policy. In particular, the Maastricht Treaty, signed in 1992, established the EU comprising three pillars – namely, the EC, Common and Foreign and Security Pillar (CFSP), and Justice and Home Affairs (JHA) – which together represent a significant integrationist push towards both economic and political union (Carr and Cope, 1994b). As a consequence of such 'widening' and 'deepening', there has been a significant, and increasing, Europeanisation of policy-making within member states (and also aspiring member states).

The 'widening' and 'deepening' of the EU can be best explained by the growing interdependence (and acceptance of such interdependence) within Europe and also between Europe and the rest of the world. The development of the EU can be seen as a response of managing such interdependence. The EU originated in attempts by member states to engage in relatively limited forms of cooperation (e.g. coal and steel production, agriculture), but these moves, providing economic and political benefits for participating member states, led to further moves to cooperate in interconnected policy sectors. This neo-functionalist account of European integration explains, for example, why moves creating a free-trade area within the EC led to moves to launch a single currency within the EU, and why moves creating a large EC-wide market in which goods, services, capital and persons can move about freely led to moves (albeit embryonic) to develop a common foreign policy and a common policing policy. These 'spill-over', and 'deepening', effects of policy cooperation are manifestations of policy interdependence, in that what happens in one policy sector affects other connected policy sectors. Furthermore, the effects of successive moves towards policy cooperation between member states within the EU 'spill over' onto non-member states, often prompting them to seek membership of the EU, where inside they can at least exercise more influence over the forms of cooperation than if they remained outside the EU. For example, most members of the European Free Trade Association (EFTA), a free trade association largely set up in 1960 to rival the EEC by countries (including Britain) not wishing to sign up to the EEC's commitment towards political union, have left to join the EU, recognising that their national interests can be protected and indeed furthered better inside than outside the EU. In the EU's drive towards economic and monetary union, most member states (though not Britain) signed up to the launch of the single currency in January 1999, which is managed by the European Central Bank (ECB) setting a common interest rate for all those in this 'euro-zone'. If the launch is successful, then, there will be considerable pressure upon those non-participating member states (including Britain) to sign up to the single currency project, as they will be able to exercise more (if only limited) influence over this project. These 'spill-over', and 'widening', effects of policy cooperation are manifestations of state interdependence, in that what happens in one state, or grouping of states like the EU, affects other states.

As well as the EU being regarded as a way of managing increasing interdependence between policy sectors and states, a further more recent push towards European integration, particularly in its post-Maastricht drive towards both economic and political union, has come in the form of the perceived challenges of globalisation (Giddens, 1998, pp. 141–2). The EU simultaneously has sponsored and has been shaped by the processes of globalisation. Business, particularly big business, within the EU is highly dependent on free trade worldwide to buy imports and sell exports, and consequently the EU has been at the fore-front generally in pushing for the liberalisation of world trade. As a result of increasing globalisation, states and societies have become more interconnected and thus more interdependent. National govern-ments are increasingly unable to make public policy singlehandedly, and are increasingly dependent on others to make policy. For example, it is increasingly difficult for governments to manage their national economies and pursue significantly distinctive economic-policy goals in isolation. Therborn argued (1995, p. 191):

> The importance of states began to decline in the 1980s, when capi-talist states began to drift in the high seas of global financial markets, when the EC gathered momentum in the second half of the decade. The change was consummated in the early 1990s, when the multina-tional states of the USSR and Yugoslavia broke up into chaos, as well as into new, fragile states, and when private financial operators brought down the monetary system of Western Europe states.

In the early 1990s many central banks of EU member states, includ-ing the Bank of England, struggled and even failed to manage exchange rates of national currencies within the prescribed bands of the Exchange Rate Mechanism (ERM) against a tide of considerable speculation in foreign exchange markets. The ERM, launched in the late 1970s as part of the European Monetary System (EMS), was itself an attempt at 'establishing a zone of monetary stability in Europe at a time of inter-national monetary instability' (George, 1996, p. 25). However, the chastening experience of the ERM crises in the 1990s, including the humiliating exit of sterling from the ERM, prompted many member states, led by Germany, to pursue economic and monetary union further in the belief that member states collectively can manage the single currency more effectively within increasingly globalised financial markets largely devoid of capital controls. Though individual member states may compromise on their preferred policy stance, collectively they will exercise more influence over economic and monetary policy than if they acted singlehandedly. The recent development of the EU therefore can be seen partly as a manifestation of globalisation – regionalisation is an increasing response to increasing globalisation (Gamble and Payne, 1996; Ross, 1998; Starie, 1999).

Europeanisation as Policy-Making

The increasing Europeanisation of policy-making within member states of the EU has led many (particularly the so-called 'Europhobes' and, to a lesser extent, 'Eurosceptics' in Britain) to argue that the autonomy of national governments has been severely constrained as a result of membership of the EU. This view generally misunderstands how policy is made within the EU. Policy-making in the EU rests on the critical axis between the Council of Ministers and the European Commission – and to a lesser extent the European Court of Justice – with the directly elected European Parliament exercising increasing though still limited influence. The structure of the EU 'contains elements of supranationalism and elements of intergovernmentalism' (George, 1991, p. 16). Of the three pillars of the EU only the EC can be regarded as both intergovernmental and supranational; the CFSP and JHA pillars are intergovernmental, with the Council of Ministers (and the European Council) firmly in control of policy-making. The EC consists of a mix of intergovernmental and supranational policy-making processes and structures. It is intergovernmental in that the Council of Ministers and the European Council represent the national interests of member states, which can (or more often, threaten to) exercise a veto if 'very important interests ... are at stake'. It is supranational in that the European Commission, the European Parliament and the Court of Justice, all relatively detached from national politics, exercise some influence over policy-making, and in that for some prescribed matters (mainly single market matters where there is a high degree of consensus) a form of majority voting applies in the Council of Ministers, thus negating the use of a national veto, and the European Parliament enjoys co-decisionmaking powers with the Council under the terms of the Maastricht Treaty.

The Council of Ministers performs key legislative functions within the EU (Hayes-Renshaw and Wallace, 1997). It is the main policy-making body within the EU, consisting of one political representative (usually a senior minister) drawn from each member state. The Council is an intergovernmental body representing the interests of member states. Ministers serving on the Council of Ministers are 'concerned about the impact of any decisions made in Brussels on the people back home and about the impact of those decisions on any upcoming elections' (Peters, 1992, p. 79). The principal role of the Council of Ministers is to legislate after receiving proposals from the European Commission (and also opinions on these proposals from the European Parliament, as well as those from the Economic and Social Committee and Committee of the Regions where legally required). However, for some proposals the Council must legislate on the basis of qualified majority voting (where votes cast by each member state are weighted according to population size) and the European Parliament may effectively veto the Council's decision. The European Council, comprising the political leaders of member states, generally gets involved to resolve disputes that cannot be resolved in the Council of Ministers, thus acting as a 'super-Council'. The Council of Ministers, according to Middlemas, 'is not necessarily more than the sum of its member governments' previous positions, acting as they do in the service of party-defined perceptions of their national interests' (1995, p. 273).

The European Commission performs key executive and bureaucratic functions within the EU (Cini, 1996). Though formally obliged to be independent, Commissioners are 'national champions who defend national positions in the Commission' because they are appointed by and maintain close links with their national governments (Ludlow, 1991, p. 90), though their appointment (including that of the President) needs the approval of the European Parliament. The Commission puts forward proposals to the Council of Ministers for decision, giving the Commission considerable influence in brokering policy and setting the policy agenda. The Council (and in some cases, the European Parliament) can request the Commission to draw up proposals for its deliberation. The Commission, however, does not generally put forward proposals if there is little chance of them being accepted by the Council of Ministers; it thus consults widely with national governments and others before drafting proposals to ensure their political feasibility. It also oversees the process of implementing EU law, which is binding upon member states, and may refer matters to the Court of Justice and impose fines if a policy is not implemented. Generally the Commission proposes and the Council disposes (Kirchner, 1992, pp. 4–7).

The Council of Ministers and the European Council are essentially intergovernmental structures, in which national governments strike intergovernmental bargains and veto proposals. The European Commission, the European Parliament and the Court of Justice are largely supranational structures, in which the accommodation of competing and conflicting positions of national governments is mediated by relatively detached institutions to produce common policies. However, given the key role of the Council of Ministers within the EU, national governments thus 'continue to play a dominant role in the decision-making process' (Keohane and Hoffmann, 1991, p. 13). The EU is thus an arena on which national governments defend and promote their interests, though their interests are mediated and sometimes modified by a supranational process of policy-making, involving 'a cumulative pattern of accommodation in which the participants refrain from unconditionally vetoing proposals and instead seek to attain agreement by means of compromises upgrading common interests' (Haas, 1964, p. 64). Policy-making in the EU is largely characterised by the striking of intergovernmental bargains between member states within supranational processes and structures of policy-making. For example, the Amsterdam Treaty, signed in 1997, introduces 'tightly constrained' forms of flexible integration, allowing some core member states to further cooperation between themselves that cannot be vetoed by nor applied to non-core member states (Dinan, 1999a, p. 303). Such flexibility represents an intergovernmental agreement by all member states to pursue differentiated integration within the EU, allowing some member states to integrate further and others not to. The EU is more about the pooling of national sovereignty than the loss of national sovereignty. Milward argued that the EU represents a 'European rescue of the nation-state' that 'marked some limits of the state's capacity to satisfy by its own powers and within its own frontiers the demands of its citizens' (1992, p. 447). Member states of the EU, constrained by increasing global interdependence, 'pursue integration as one way of formalizing, regulating and perhaps limiting the consequences of interdependence, without forfeiting the national allegiance on which its continued existence depends' (Milward, 1992, p. 19).

The Europeanisation of British Government

This concluding section specifically focuses upon the consequences of EU membership for British government and addresses the extent to which policy-making in British government has become Europeanised, reflecting a 'process of increasing convergence of national policies towards the EU "model" ' (Lodge, 2000, p. 89). The argument contained here is that there is an increasing process of Europeanisation within British government, that to a certain extent has been pushed further since the election of the Labour government in May 1997; but that this Europeanisation has both enhanced and constrained the policy-making capabilities of British government.

Though EU law (such as treaty provisions, directives and regulations) is binding upon member states, and such law is enforced by national courts and ultimately the Court of Justice, there is no significant loss of national sovereignty but instead a pooling of national sovereignties within the EU. Many key decisions within the EU are largely made on an intergovernmental basis, and consequently the British government can more effectively defend and promote its perceived national interests working with other member states inside the EU than if it singlehandedly made such decisions outside the EU. Even outside the EU the British government would be constrained by decisions made within the EU (such as interest-rate decisions made by the ECB), while exercising no influence over such decisions. The EU is a very significant policy-making site where policy deals can be struck, necessarily involving policy compromises, but where member states generally perceive a net gain in their policy-making capacity. National policy-making is thus framed within such intergovernmental policy bargains.

For example, by joining the EC in 1973 (introducing the common market) and by signing the Single European Act later in the 1980s (introducing the single market), the British government committed itself to removing many trade barriers used to protect national industries. As a consequence, the Labour government could not bail out Rover as a result of BMW's decision made in early 2000 to sell off or close down the Longbridge car factory in the West Midlands, because such state subsidies would be regarded as a trade barrier and would be vetoed by the European Commission administering the EU's trade policy. However, though constrained in this specific case, the British government has guaranteed access for British companies to the world's largest trading bloc, thereby enhancing its historically-rooted policy favouring free trade that benefits much of British business. This example illustrates the weakness of the 'loss of sovereignty' thesis, in that the thesis fails to recognise the largely intergovernmental nature of policy-making within the EU. Though a national government may be constrained by such policy trade-offs, these constraints are more manifestations of increasing economic and political interdependence than the imposition of rules from a distant place. As Chryssochoou argued, the EU 'is not about the subordination of states to a higher central authority, but rather about the preservation of those state qualities which allow the segments to survive as separate collectivities, whilst engaging themselves in a polity-formation process that increasingly transforms their traditional patterns of interaction' (1999, p. 26). Similarly Bulmer and Burch observed that 'the impact of the EC-EU on the activities of British government has been profound' while noting 'the sheer resilience of British traditions' (1998, pp. 624–6). Intergovernmental policy-bargains within the EU both constrain and enhance the policy-making capabilities of member states, but providing national policy-making elites calculate a net gain in their influence, then it is difficult to see quite how national sovereignty has been substantially weakened but easy to see how it has been pooled and consequently strengthened – it is no coincidence that nearly every European state has either joined or wants to join, with only Greenland (part of Denmark) having left the EU. Moravcsik concluded that the EU is 'so firmly grounded in the core interests of national governments that it occupies a permanent position at the heart of the European political landscape' (1999, p. 501).

Given Britain's late entry into the EC and the ingrained nature of intergovernmental bargaining within the EU, it is not surprising that Britain's relations with the EC/EU have sometimes been problematic. For example, in 1963 and 1967 the French government vetoed Britain's application to join the EC tabled by the Conservative government (under Harold Macmillan) and continued by the subsequent Labour government (under Harold Wilson). In 1975, two years after the Conservative government (under Edward Heath) took Britain into the EC, the Labour government (under Harold Wilson) held a referendum on Britain's membership of the EC, which led to a majority vote in favour of continued membership. In the early 1980s the Conservative government (under Margaret Thatcher) was locked into an acrimonious dispute over its 'excessive' budget contributions towards the EC, which was resolved in 1986 by reducing its annual contributions. In 1989 the Thatcher government, alone amongst member states, refused to sign the (known as the 'Social Charter'). In 1991 the Conservative government (under John Major) negotiated significant opt-outs of the 'Social Chapter', providing legislative force to the 'Social Chapter', and of Economic and Monetary Union (EMU), committing member states to a single currency, both of which were part of the Maastricht Treaty. On 'Black Wednesday', 16 September 1992, the Major government was 'forced' to withdraw sterling from the ERM, costing taxpayers up to £4 billion (Stephens, 1996, pp. 226–60). In 1996 the European Commission banned exports of beef from Britain following the BSE (or 'mad cow disease') crisis that emerged in the 1980s. These, and other, examples lend support to the 'awkward partner' thesis, but this thesis is too simplistic on two counts. First, it emphasises the disagreements between Britain and the EC/EU, and downplays the many times that Britain and the EC/EU have agreed (such as the launch of the single market programme in the 1980s, and the commitment to expand the EU to embrace many former communist Eastern European states in the 1990s). Second, the thesis is a little parochial and fails to take sufficient account of conflicts between the EC/EU and other member states. For example, in 1965 the French government effectively walked out of the EC, and only returned to the fold on the understanding – under the terms of the 'Luxembourg Compromise' of 1966 – that a member state can exercise a veto in the Council of Ministers if its vital national interests are threatened by a proposal from the European Commission. In June 1992 Danish voters narrowly rejected the Maastricht Treaty in a referendum, prompting the Danish government to renegotiate significant opt-outs to the Treaty that was subsequently endorsed in a second referendum in May 1993. More recently the EU is largely cold-shouldering the Austrian government because of the inclusion of members of the neo-fascist Freedom Party within its coalition government.

Relations between Britain and the EC/EU have certainly been problematical, but not inherently nor peculiarly problematical. Furthermore, the issue of Britain's relations with the EC/EU is one that transcends party lines, and is essentially a cross-party political issue. Both Conservative and Labour governments wanted to take Britain into the EC in the 1960s. In the 1970s the Conservative government took Britain into the EC and the subsequent Labour government held a referendum on Britain's continued membership of the EC. In the 1980s the Conservative government signed the Single European Act which introduced qualified majority voting in the Council of Ministers (thus removing the national veto for certain prescribed, mainly single market, matters), but took an increasingly 'Eurosceptical' stance in its dealings with the EC/EU (sometimes for domestic consumption). In the 1983 general election campaign the Labour Party pledged that 'British with-drawal from the Community is the right policy for Britain' (Labour Party, 1983, p. 33); but in the run-up to the 1997 general election, Tony Blair, the leader of the Labour Party, wanted Britain 'at the centre of Europe' and argued that 'the drift towards isolation in Europe must stop and be replaced by a policy of constructive engagement' (Young, 1998, p. 485). Viewed historically, this new-found commitment in favour of the EU expressed by the Labour government perhaps needs to be treated with some caution, because new governments often seek to have more constructive dealings but only to later confront significant problems in their dealings with the EC/EU; John Major, the Prime Minister of the previous Conservative government, wanted Britain at 'the very heart of Europe' and promised 'closer co-operation' with the EC (Young, 1998, p. 424), only to find he was leading an increasingly 'Eurosceptical' gov-ernment and indeed 'Europhobic' party. Young warned that 'there are plenty of signs that the Blair government may not look too different from its Conservative predecessors' (1997, p. 153).

Gamble and Kelly noted that one of the 'hallmarks' of the new Labour government is its 'positive attitude towards the European Union' (2000, p. 1). On taking office, for example, the government soon signed up to the 'Social Chapter', of which the previous Major govern-ment opted-out; and it worked with the European Commission in seek-ing to remove the export ban on British beef in the face of French (and German) continued boycotts. However, in 1997 the Blair government negotiated an opt-out of the Amsterdam Treaty commitment to abolish internal border controls, thus retaining national control over asylum, immigration and visa policies. Despite this mixed, albeit brief, record of opting-in and opting-out, according to Hix, 'new Labour has a greater chance than perhaps any previous British government of being "at the heart of Europe"' (2000, p. 67), largely because of an emerging new social democratic consensus within the EU. With many governments within the EU now led by centre-left parties (particularly those in France and Germany), there is a strong view that Britain's relations with the EU will significantly improve (Gamble and Kelly, 2000, pp. 20–22; Starie, 1999).

The 'litmus test' for the Blair government's relations with the EU will undoubtedly be its policy on the single currency. The single currency project is the culmination of EMU enshrined in the Maastricht Treaty in the early 1990s, though economic and monetary union has long been on the EC's agenda (Dyson, 1994; Tsoukalis, 1996). The single currency, as the third and final stage of EMU, was launched on 1 January 1999;

11 out of 15 member states immediately signed up to the plan to replace their national currencies with the euro, which is managed by a formally independent central bank, the ECB based in Frankfurt, charged with a low-inflation mission in setting interest rates. The previous Major government opted-out of this stage of EMU mainly for political reasons; this opt-out has been reasserted by the Blair government adopting 'the wait-and-see strategy of the Conservatives' (Gamble and Kelly, 2000, p. 18), though it did grant operational independence to the Bank of England in its first week of office as required by the Maastricht Treaty to fulfil EMU. However, the Labour government has committed itself to join the single currency project, subject to a popular referendum to be held after the next general election, if certain economic conditions are met. The government 'has opted to play down the political significance of the euro' (Krieger, 1999, p. 165). It prefers to hide behind economic arguments, arguing that Britain's economic cycle is out of line with those of its counterparts in the EU and that consequently joining the single currency on its launch would involve significant initial economic shocks (Krieger, 1999, pp. 165–6). However, there are three political arguments that need to be won before adopting the euro. First, the Labour Party is not overwhelmingly enthusiastic about the euro, which explains why the government has delayed its embrace of the euro (Gamble and Kelly, 2000). Second, the Blair government will only hold a referendum when it will be sure of winning. Though much of economic and political elite opinion is largely in favour of the single currency, popular opinion is not (Hix, 2000). Third, much of the mass media (particularly the tabloid press), seen as central in winning over popular support, remains unconvinced about or even hostile towards the single currency. Arguably these political obstacles, rather than the economic obstacles, are key to whether and when Britain joins the single currency project.

The single currency is the most significant issue facing British government with enormous economic and political implications at stake. Following Featherstone, EMU is 'the most ambitious and far-reaching' project yet launched by the EC/EU, and 'is thus the biggest single current component in the process of "Europeanization" ' (1999, p. 311). EMU is more than economic and monetary union; it is also about political union. If successful, it will very significantly deepen the process of Europeanisation, both enhancing and constraining what British governments can do in making policy, from monetary to fiscal policy, economic to social policy and foreign to security policy. Krieger argued (1999, p. 47):

The post-Maastricht agenda for increased economic and monetary union, focused on the introduction of a single currency, will fundamentally influence the UK's ability to compete internationally and sustain its own model of economic development.... Economic and monetary integration, therefore, has potentially quite significant repercussions for standards of living and distributional politics at home.

Europeanisation is 'the given reality' (Young, 1998, p. 515), and the Blair government, with its greater 'sense of Euro-realism' (Young, 1998, p. 514), will almost certainly go further down the road of Europeanisation, not least because there are no other roads to go down. It is not about the imposition of rule from Brussels, but about the framing of negotiated public policy within the multi-level governance of Britain within the EU.

Part II

Substantive Policy Areas

4

UK Economic Policy: The Conservative Legacy and New Labour's Third Way

Rob Thomas

'Policy is a matter of trial and error – some would say errors by the authorities and trials of the private sector.'
(Mervyn King, an Executive Director and Chief Economist of the Bank of England) (King, 1994, p. 263)

A glance at the economic indicators for 1997 (Table 4.1 contains data on the main UK economic indicators for the period 1979 to 1998) will give the impression that the economic 'baton' handed on by the defeated Conservative government was made of gold. The aims of this chapter are to consider whether it was pure or 'fools' economic gold and then to explore the direction of New Labour's 'leg' of the economic relay.

The economic 'baton' had been in Conservative hands for 18 years and much had been learned from the experience at both the theoretical and the policy implementation levels. These lessons are the focus of the second section of this chapter because they form an important part of the historical context of New Labour. In the third section the theoretical basis of the Labour government's approach to economic policy is explored before considering its record. The discussion which is the basis of the final section is concerned with issues that the government will have to confront in the near future.

Table 4.1   UK economy 1979–1998 – main economic indicators

Year	% change in real GDP	Unemployment (%)	% change in retail prices	Balance of payment current account (£b)	PSBR/ PSNCR (£b)
1979	2.7	4.1	13.4	–0.5	12.6
1980	–2.0	4.8	17.9	2.8	11.8
1981	–1.2	8.0	11.9	6.7	10.5
1982	1.8	9.5	8.6	4.6	4.9
1983	3.7	10.5	4.6	3.5	11.6
1984	2.0	10.7	5.0	1.5	10.3
1985	4.0	10.9	6.0	2.2	7.9
1986	4.0	11.2	3.4	–0.9	3.1
1987	4.6	10.2	4.1	–5.0	–1.7
1988	5.0	8.2	4.9	–16.6	–12.4
1989	2.2	6.2	7.8	–22.5	–9.8
1990	0.6	5.8	9.5	–19.0	–1.9
1991	–2.1	8.0	5.9	–8.2	8.8
1992	–0.5	9.7	3.7	–9.8	30.3
1993	2.3	10.3	1.6	–11.0	43.9
1994	3.9	9.3	2.4	–1.7	38.7
1995	2.7	8.1	3.5	–3.7	31.5
1996	2.6	7.4	2.4	–0.6	22.7
1997	3.5	5.6	3.1	6.1	1.1
1998	2.1	4.7	3.4	1.5	–7.3

Source: Office of National Statistics, *Economic Trends Annual Supplement 1998* (London: The Stationery Office, 1999).

However, we begin with an overview of the theory of economic policy in order to understand the basic principles – and difficulties – of economic management.

Targets and Instruments – the Problems of Economic Management

The aim of economic management in a democratic society is to maximise (or, in a more diluted form, increase) the economic well-being of its citizens. Defining the term 'economic well-being' or economic welfare is not straightforward and it is therefore a difficult concept to measure (Parkin, Powell and Matthews, 1998, pp. 543–5; Sloman, 2000, pp. 440–1). Thus, governments, economists and the media tend to concentrate on certain measurable macroeconomic objectives or targets in the belief that achieving the targets leads to an increase in economic welfare.

The main targets as listed in the economics texts (e.g. Sloman and Sutcliffe, 1998, p. 440) are:

- a stable price level – the reduction/prevention of rising prices (inflation)
- growth of the economy's output of goods and services – 'economic growth'
- low unemployment
- a favourable balance of payments.

Different governments will give different priorities to the above objectives, though since 1945 the main ones have been low unemployment or price stability (Kennedy, 1996, p. 123). To achieve the targets, government has available to it policies or 'instruments':

- fiscal policy – taxation, government expenditure and the balance between the two
- monetary policy – control of the amount of money, interest rates, hire-purchase terms
- direct controls – import quotas, price and income controls.

Received economic 'wisdom' is that to manage an economy, a government needs as many instruments as it has targets; then it can concentrate each instrument on a specific target (see Griffiths and Wall, 1997, pp. 684–9). However, matters are not that simple in practice and it is as well at this stage to consider the general reasons why economic management has proved so difficult (for a more detailed analysis, see Kennedy, 1996, pp. 124–30).

1. An economy is not a machine; the same policy input will not necessarily produce the same output each time. What is required is an understanding of how the economy will react, but the theory of the macroeconomy has gone through various changes and there remain disputes as to how the economy works (Begg, Fischer and Dornbusch, 1994, ch. 32).
2. Economic management decisions must be made on the basis of the available data. When published, the data is out of date by a month or several months, may be subject to revision, affected by a random event or the definition may have been changed (see Curwen, 1997c,

pp. 346–8, for changes in eligibility rules which affected the measurement of unemployment).

3. There are time-lags in the government's economic decision-making and implementation process.
4. The full impact of a policy change will take time but experience shows the time it takes is not precisely predictable.
5. Thus, it is necessary to anticipate (or forecast) what will happen at least twelve months ahead. Unfortunately, such forecasting has been unreliable (Kennedy, 1996, pp. 127–30).
6. There can be 'side effects' to economic policy changes. It is accepted that giving priority to the attainment of one target (say, reducing inflation) can mean not hitting another target (acceptable rate of economic growth).

Notable by its absence from the above list is the role of (and blame to be placed on) politicians. That political parties will tend to favour policies based upon economic theory that fits with their political ideology is no surprise (Sloman, 2000, p. 382), particularly as economists do not always agree on the appropriate theoretical model. However, democratic governments may need to be more pragmatist that idealist when faced with strong opposition either in Parliament or in the country. This has led to the implementation of inappropriate policies (Curwen, 1997d, pp. 522–3) and to the argument that the boom-to-slump business cycle is exacerbated by the political cycle: government expanding the economy in order to raise income prior to an election (the 'feel-good' factor), but then having to stop the expansion after the election because it has an adverse effect on inflation and/or the balance of payments (Vane and Thompson, 1992, pp. 133–5).

The Conservative Legacy

The 1979 Conservative government portrayed itself, and was accepted, as introducing radical changes in the management of the economy (Lawson, 1992, pp. 20–1; Britton, 1991, p. 44). Furthermore, much of the theoretical underpinning remained in place for subsequent Conservative governments and has been accepted by New Labour. Therefore, this section begins with a review of the theoretical base before considering the ways in which policy was amended in the light of experience.

The Theoretical Underpinning

The economic policies of Margaret Thatcher's first administration had been forged during the years in opposition when the ideological under-pinning was combined with a shift in macroeconomic thinking (the most noted influence being that of the Chicago School, especially Milton Friedman, though Lawson (1992, pp. 13–14) also records the contribution of Friedrich Hayek). On coming to power in 1979, priority was given to the reduction of inflation, thus ending the post-Second World War consensus that low unemployment was the principal target of policy.

> The new strategy effectively abandoned Keynesian short run demand management aimed at full or high employment. Instead, emphasis was placed on improving the long run supply side performance of the economy. (Maynard, 1991, p. 137)

Thatcher's first period in office is often remembered for the intro-duction of 'monetarism' – a 'rather disparate set of ideas' (Congdon, 1999, p. 19), the central tenet of which is that controlling the money supply in an economy will reduce the rate of inflation. Theoretical dis-agreements concerning the role of money in an economy and, more especially, the experience of the UK in the early 1980s, caused money supply control to be effectively abandoned in 1983 (Lawson, 1992, ch. 36). Its legacy, however, was that government became more aware of the need to control government borrowing. Pre-1979, the so-called Keynesian approach to economic management had accepted govern-ment budget deficits as necessary when manipulating the total amount of demand using fiscal policy. That the resultant borrowing could lead to an increase in the money supply was recognised but it was not until money supply control came to the fore that the need for fiscal restraint was reinstated.

Later Thatcher administrations turned to targeting the exchange rate, either formally via a fixed exchange rate or informally by having an unofficial target ('shadowing' another currency). To work effectively as an anti-inflation policy, the exchange rate target must be set in relation to the currency of a country that has low inflation. If the domestic econ-omy experiences a rise in prices then, with an unchanged exchange rate, its exports become less competitive; recognising this, exporting firms will keep price increases in check (resisting pay increases not matched by productivity rises) and the impact will spread to lower prices domestically. If domestic firms are not successful in restraining prices, exports will fall, the balance of payments will worsen and this will put downward pressure on the exchange rate. To maintain the exchange rate, government will raise interest rates so that domestic financial assets are more attractive; funds initially held in foreign currencies will be converted into the domestic currency in order to buy the assets, thus increasing demand for the domestic currency and thereby preserve the exchange rate. The higher interest rates will act to reduce the inflation.

The disadvantages of such targeting lie in the loss of control of domestic monetary policy with interest rates being geared to the exchange rate not necessarily to the domestic situation. Also, if there are time-lags in the adjustments described in the previous paragraph, exchange rate speculation may build up, forcing interest rates higher to maintain target.

To support its concentration on controlling inflation, the 1979 Conservative government stressed the need to consider the medium and long term when enacting monetary and fiscal policy. Keynesian 'myopia', as encapsulated by the mid-1970s Labour government 'fine tuning' the economy via frequent policy changes, was rejected and replaced by a financial planning horizon of four years incorporated in the Medium Term Financial Strategy (MFTS).

There were two further reasons for the change. One was the adoption of 'rules' (rather than 'discretion') for policy to overcome some of the policy management problems (see the previous section). The other was the role of expectations in economic theory. It does not require an act of faith to accept that the behaviour of people, firms and the government is influenced by what they expect to occur in the future. The implication for economic policy is simply, 'a government had better mean what is says' (Sloman, 2000, p. 618) – the government should set out its economic policies and stick with them so that it gains credibility. People and firms will then adjust their expectations in accordance with the policies and their actions will become more predictable.

So far the story has been in terms of money and finance. This is not by chance, because the underpinning economic theory draws a distinction between the monetary sector and the real (or production of goods and services) sector of an economy. Prior to 1979, fiscal policy was used to manipulate the level of total (or aggregate) demand for goods and services. Then, with total (or aggregate) supply adjusting to meet aggregate demand, the output of goods and services would change – so fiscal policy was concerned with the real sector. Monetarism downgraded fiscal policy to a secondary role in combating inflation (via the MTFS), and gave it a different function in respect of the real sector.

From the beginning, Thatcher's administrations promoted the efficacy of the market (or price) mechanism; that is, left alone, the market forces of demand for and supply of goods and services will set prices that reflect the preferences of individuals and firms in the economy. In this way, the level of economic welfare will be raised because individuals and firms, given their resources, achieve what they want. Thus, the economic role of government is to reduce/remove barriers, including the tinkering of government itself, to the operation of these market forces – so-called supply-side economic policy. Here was another major shift away from the Keynesian approach: no longer was aggregate supply seen as simply reacting to changes in aggregate demand; rather, policy was to be directed at improving the operation of the supply side.

Supply-side policy comprises a range of actions (Sloman, 2000, p. 635) including those relating to fiscal policy:

- reducing government spending to release more resources to the private sector
- lowering taxes to increase incentives
- removing the monopoly power of trade unions
- encouraging flexibility of pay and working practices
- reducing entitlement to certain welfare (or transfer) benefits
- encouraging investment and enterprise
- promoting competition via deregulation and privatisation
- removing barriers to the free movement of capital.

It was claimed that the unleashing of market forces would generate increases in productivity (usually measured by output per person employed) that would lead to greater competitiveness in the world economy and higher incomes domestically.

Such was the 'grand (economic) design' of the Conservative governments of Thatcher and subsequently Major. The implementation of it, however, brings to mind that phrase, 'there's many a slip 'twixt cup and lip'.

The Policy Experience, 1979–97

The objective of this section is to review the period in terms of the lessons learned rather than provide a blow-by-blow account of the economic events (for further reading, see Griffiths and Wall, 1997, pp. 693–703). For analytical purposes, the section will consider three main policy areas, namely, monetary policy, fiscal policy and the non-fiscal aspects of supply-side policy.

Monetary policy. The process for implementing money supply control was firstly to adopt a strategy for slowing down its rate of growth over a period of time. The 1980 Budget introduced the first Medium Term Financial Strategy (MTFS) which incorporated a set of declining target ranges for a broad definition of money (exactly what constitutes money is open to debate because in developed economies there are financial assets – 'near-monies' – which are not what is normally regarded as money for making transactions but which can be converted into money very quickly) called sterling M3 (£M3).

Disenchantment with a strict monetarist policy set in fairly quickly with £M3 growth being above the target range in the first two financial years despite reductions in government borrowing (as a percentage of national income). Also, interest rates were pushed higher in an attempt to control £M3 but this was a factor in the appreciation of the exchange rate – both of these impacted adversely on the UK economy which was already experiencing a downturn.

Having said that, the policy did eventually work in terms of its objective: the rate of inflation began to fall from its peak in May 1980 and economic growth was restored in 1981. Thus, it may seem strange that having stayed with the policy through the difficult times of the early 1980s, by 1983 money supply control was being questioned and £M3 targeting was formally suspended in 1985 – 'just when the policy was working it was changed, and not for the better' (Naisbitt, 1991, p. 191). The reason seems to lie with Nigel Lawson succeeding Geoffrey Howe as Chancellor in 1983, the former having a preference for an exchange rate target due to the 'puzzles and confusions' of the working of the monetary system (Lawson, 1992, ch. 33).

In 1987, Lawson got his way and the decision was taken to 'shadow the Deutschmark' within a range of between DM2.75 and DM3.00 as a prelude to eventually entering the Exchange Rate Mechanism (ERM) of the European Monetary System (Lawson, 1992, pp. 731–2). Again, the difficulties inherent in simplifying policy by reliance on one intermediate target became rapidly apparent. Interest rates had to be changed in line with the needs of the exchange rate and, with sterling becoming stronger on the back of the so-called 'Lawson boom', rates were reduced; in addition, interest rates were further lowered after the Stock Market crash of October 1987. This loosening of monetary policy occurred at a time of relatively rapid economic growth that rekindled inflationary pressure. Although not targeted, the money supply aggregates rose above their MTFS monitored ranges so that in 1988 the Chancellor was forced to abandon the exchange rate policy and raise interest rates.

The experience can hardly be said to have inspired confidence in adopting an exchange rate target but the Chancellor remained committed to such an approach (Lawson, 1992, p. 800). Despite the resignation of Nigel Lawson in 1989, the Conservative government did return to an exchange rate target in 1990 when it placed the pound sterling in the ERM of the European Monetary System. The two-year episode has been well documented (for example, Curwen, 1997b, ch. 11) and ended with sterling's membership of the ERM being 'suspended'. As the sterling exchange rate against the major currencies subsequently floated down, the UK economy revived and blossomed, adding to the questions raised about adopting an exchange rate target and having some bearing on the debate about the desirability of the UK joining the Single European Currency.

The policy void left after the withdrawal from the ERM was filled by a pragmatic approach. The inflation target remained and was reinforced by the specification of a target range. Monetary policy was to be enacted via interest rates that were set in monthly discussions between the Chancellor and the Governor of the Bank of England following the deliberations of a group of independent economic advisers.

Fiscal policy. The operation of fiscal policy during the Conservative administrations also went through changes in respect of managing aggregate demand: from the initial phase, under the MTFS, as a supporting player in the drive to control the money supply, to a more neutral, sound finance, approach in the late 1980s. The one constant was the supply-side emphasis.

Fiscal policy came to be summed up in the Public Sector Borrowing Requirement (PSBR) which is a measure of the amount by which government expenditure exceeds revenue. This statistic had been introduced in 1968 but under the Thatcher governments came to be an intermediate target. When monetarism ruled in the early 1980s, the PSBR target contained in the MTFS was set on a decreasing trend in accordance with the need to control the money supply. One of the reasons for rejecting monetarism was that the relationship between the PSBR and the money supply was open to question (Congdon, 1999, p. 20). Towards the end of the 1980s, Chancellor Nigel Lawson had shifted the objective to achieving a balanced Budget for the medium term; 'hence-forth a zero PSBR will be the norm' (1988 Budget speech as quoted in Lawson, 1992, p. 811). This continued to be the objective under subsequent Conservative Chancellors though the recession of the early 1990s blew the government's finances off course temporarily.

Linked to this aspiration for fiscal prudence were the supply-side objectives. Limiting government spending was an aim in itself and also necessary if taxation was to be reduced and the Budget to be balanced. Government spending proved to be an intractable problem despite the efforts of several Chancellors. During the period of Conservative administrations, government spending as a proportion of GDP varied with the business cycle; overall there was a tendency for the proportion to decline primarily due to sharp falls in the mid-1980s and mid-1990s (Parkin, Powell and Matthews, 1998, pp. 633–4).

Evaluating success in reducing taxation depends on the measure used. Supply-side economics stresses the disincentive effects of high direct (or income) taxes. Income tax rates were reduced when the Budget finances permitted (as in the 1988 Budget) or when an election was looming (as in the 1992 Budget); between 1979 and 1997, the highest rate of tax was reduced from 83 per cent to 40 per cent and the standard rate fell from 33 per cent to 23 per cent. However, the tax burden (total taxation as a proportion of GDP) was not significantly reduced – 'it took from 1979–80 to 1992–93 for the tax burden to fall back below that prevailing at the time the first Thatcher government was elected' (Curwen, 1997a, p. 167).

Non-fiscal supply-side policies. Two main aspects of supply-side policies are discussed in this section: firstly, industrial and competition policies which sought to improve performance in product markets; and secondly, labour market polices aimed at increasing flexibility. Both sets of policies were the result of the individualist, market-based ideology of the Thatcher governments finding an economic underpinning in supply-side economics.

Industrial policy was not just about privatisation but the disposal of public sector assets tended to take the headlines. The justification was in terms of opening up the nationalised industries so that market pressures could operate to increase technical efficiency and lower prices for consumers. Turning the nationalised industries into private companies, it was claimed, would free them of government control and provide a profit incentive for both managers and shareholders (Curwen and Hartley, 1997, pp. 479–81). It also raised funds for the Treasury (as in the emotive 'selling the family silver' accusation) and made the government's financial accounts look better, especially as the revenues from privatisations were counted as negative expenditure (see Lawson, 1992, pp. 238–9, for the justification). Allied to the sales of nationalised industries, the government also attempted to introduce market forces into areas of the public sector that could not be sold. Competitive tendering or contracting-out of services such as cleaning and catering in local government, the NHS and parts of central government was introduced. The objective was the same as for privatisation except that instead of selling the whole organisation, such as the NHS, parts of it were placed in private ownership.

Judging the impact of these changes in isolation is fraught with difficulties. As well as the usual 'what would have happened if?' question that bedevils such assessments, the issue is further complicated in that some of the major privatisations merely changed the ownership of a market monopoly; the company created by the privatisation was the major supplier of the product nationally or locally – such was the case with the privatisations of gas and water. Thus, the government established regulatory bodies (OFGAS, etc.) to set maximum prices for these monopolies, and assessing the success of privatisation is influenced by the evaluation of the operation of the regulatory bodies. Not that Nigel Lawson is in any doubt: the title of chapter 18 in his book is 'Privatization – 1: The Jewel in the Crown' (Lawson, 1992, p. 197), whereas, for Griffiths and Wall (1997, p. 199), 'It has not been convincingly demonstrated that the form of ownership of an organization is the most important influence on its performance. Of much greater importance would seem to be the degree of competition and the effectiveness of regulatory bodies.'

Competition policy covering the private sector had been set prior to 1979 and the subsequent Conservative governments had little to add. The Monopolies and Mergers Commission and the Office of Fair Trading were retained and their powers enhanced by the 1980 Competition Act to include such anti-competitive practices as predatory pricing and price discrimination; public sector bodies and nationalised industries were also brought within the terms of the law. Otherwise, the main impetus to changes in competition policy came from the European Community, particularly the development of the single market and its requirements for intra-Community trade free of restrictions and distortions.

The other main strand of supply-side policy was directed at labour markets. We have discussed the need for reductions in direct taxation in order to improve incentives; other aspects of labour market policy were legislation to reduce the influence of trade unions, and exhortation, legislation and incentives to increase flexibility.

Trade unions were a *bête noire* of the Conservative party. The 1970–4 Conservative government of Edward Heath had, in the eyes of Conservatives, failed in its attempt to legislate and stand up to the unions. Margaret Thatcher's administrations took a cautious approach to reform of the unions, introducing pieces of legislation aimed at specific aspects of union activity and organisation (Lawson, 1992, pp. 436–7; for a detailed analysis of the legislation, see Farnham and Pimlott, 1995, ch. 10). Whilst many opponents believed the motive for the reforms was ideological, the Conservative governments tended to justify the legislation on economic grounds – the removal of a monopoly in the labour market: unions have the potential of using their market power to raise the wage and level of employment above the market clearing levels. They are therefore a barrier to the operation of the market mechanism. Isolating the impact of the 1980s legislation as against the influence of other factors, such as wider changes in the structure of employment, privatisation and decline of inflation, is not easy (Brown, Deakin and Ryan, 1997), but the more obvious outcomes were a marked decline in trade union membership (from over 13 million in 1979 to 8 million in 1995: Bland, 1999) and an almost continuous fall in the number of strikes and days lost due to strikes (Blyton and Turnbull, 1998, p. 296).

Flexibility in labour markets has several dimensions, the main ones being: the ability of firms to increase or decrease their labour forces in accordance with demand for their products (numerical flexibility); the capacity of labour to move between different jobs either within the same firm or between firms (functional flexibility); and pay flexibility in relation to economic circumstances. The reform of trade unions had implications for flexibility of pay and in reducing union-induced restrictive practices relating to crew sizes and demarcation. However, the legislative focus in respect of flexibility, was on changing the employment rights of the individual (Farnham and Pimlott, 1995, ch. 9) and on increasing the provision of education and training. Empirical assessment of whether labour market flexibility increased during the 1980s must take account of both quantitative and qualitative dimensions. In 1994, Beatson concluded that, 'on balance it can reasonably be concluded that the British labour market has become more flexible' (Beatson, 1995, p. 56). For Curwen, the test was more generalised, noting that, 'flexibility should enable the economy to respond to demand relatively early in the economic cycle, and there is evidence for this in that output began to rise only four quarters after the 1992 trough in GDP whereas it took eight quarters after the 1981 trough' (Curwen, 1997c, p. 340).

Conservative Government Economic Policy, 1979–97: The Lessons

By 1997, the Conservative government could claim to have 'got it right' in that the economic management lessons had been learned albeit at a cost of high unemployment during and after two deep economic recessions. The main economic indicators (see Table 4.1) were pointing in the right direction with relatively low inflation, falling unemployment, reasonable economic growth and a balance of payments current account that could be easily financed. The government maintained its stance on controlling inflation, and interest rate manipulation seemed to be the best instrument for achieving the target. Fiscal balance was being restored so that the PSBR was falling and the supply-side reforms had given the economy vibrancy in terms of speed of adjustment to sudden changes.

What the government seemed to lack was economic credibility having attained a buoyant economy almost by default – by being forced to leave the ERM and the economy benefiting from the subsequent 20 per cent plus depreciation of the currency.

Other problems remained. The once trumpeted increase in productivity (as measured by output per person employed or per person hour worked) was not maintained. Figures from the Organisation for Economic Cooperation and Development show that whereas the percentage average annual rate of change in UK business sector productivity during the period 1960–73 had been 2.8 per cent, the comparable figure for the 1979–97 period was 1.2 per cent (OECD, 1998a, annex table 59). In terms of international comparisons, UK productivity may have caught up a little but the productivity gap continued – 'the UK currently lies bottom of the G7 league table in terms of output per capita' (McKinsey Global Institute, 1998, p. v). As Oulton (1995, p. 53) asked, 'How could all those years of supply side reforms produce such an apparently disappointing result?'

Secondly, the benefits of economic growth during the Conservative administrations were not shared equally.

For one thing that can be stated without fear of contradiction is that the income distribution has grown wider. This rise in inequality appears to have begun towards the end of the 1970s, and to have been particularly speedy in the second half of the 1980s. There has at least been some slowing in that rate of increase during the 1990s, though no clear sign of a major reversal. (Goodman, Johnson and Webb, 1997, p. 274)

New Labour's Third Way

In the run-up to the 1997 general election, New Labour was careful to portray itself as heir to the successful economic policies but ready to change those which it deemed not to have worked. For the purposes of comparison, this section will adopt the same structure as in the previous section.

The Theoretical Underpinning

New Labour's positioning of itself in the political context has come to be called 'The Third Way' (Blair and Schroeder, no date). The economic aims of this approach are:

- locking in economic stability as a platform for long-term sustainable growth;
- raising productivity through promoting enterprise and investment;
- increasing employment opportunities with a better deal for working families; and
- building a fairer society, with a better deal for families and children.

(HM Treasury, no date)

The economic policy base underlying this approach is that of 'endogenous growth' – a theory of long-run economic growth generated by technological progress that comes from investment and innovation. The theory is set in the context of a market-based economy, but as against the free market model with little government intervention favoured by the Thatcher administrations, endogenous growth theory sees a role for government in stimulating investment and innovation by supporting basic research, promoting entrepreneurship and taking a more favourable view of monopoly in high-growth sectors. Thus, the theory emphasises the role of market forces in order to give the freedom and the incentive to innovate but also gives the state a major role in the supply of public capital – the government is seen as an investor (Shapiro, 1994).

Amongst the questions to be raised about the theory is whether investment generates economic growth or if the direction of influence is the other way round with investment being the result of growth (Brittan, 1993). Statistical studies may find a close relationship between the two, but do the studies adequately identify which is influencing which? For firms to invest either in plant or machinery or via innovation, there must be the incentive of expected profit from meeting demand in the economy; demand which comes from economic growth.

Also, as we move towards New Labour's economic policies in practice, it should be noted that endogenous growth theory 'cannot be used to justify minimum wage rates, strong labour unions, housing subsidies or large welfare payments' (Barro, 1994).

The Policy Experience, 1997–9

Monetary policy. Once elected, Chancellor Gordon Brown – perhaps mindful of the problems caused to previous Labour governments by events in financial markets – moved quickly to assert its monetary policy. It maintained the previous Conservative government's target for low and stable rate inflation of 2.5 per cent (to be precise, the target is set in terms of the 'underlying' rate of inflation which is the retail price index measure of inflation excluding mortgage interest payments). What it changed was the way in which monetary policy is enacted; the UK central bank, the Bank of England, was given operational independence in achieving the target. A Monetary Policy Committee (MPC), which includes independent economists, was established to decide changes in the rate of interest in order to achieve the target. The deliberations of the MPC are published and if the inflation target is missed by more than one percentage point the Governor of the Bank of England must explain in writing why the target was not achieved.

The debate about the desirability of an independent central bank centres on the degree of independence and its ability to control inflation without having a marked deflationary impact on the domestic economy (Heather, 1997, ch. 18). For the Chancellor's Economic Advisor, Edward Balls, the issue was that of credibility: credibility through a precommitment to a target, so removing the opportunity for the government to cheat; credibility through maximum transparency because the deliberations of the MPC are published (Balls, 1998). This view relates to the role of expectations and the need for people, firms and government to have as much information as possible upon which to base their view of the future. Thus, the change in the role of the Bank of England and the operation of monetary policy is based on the same approach as that of the previous Conservative governments except that they rejected the notion of an independent central bank (Lawson, 1992, pp. 867–73).

Fiscal policy. Another aspect of credibility identified by Edward Balls (1998, pp. 122–5) is credibility through sound long-term policies. Whilst this relates to monetary policy, it is an important base for understanding New Labour's fiscal policy. The inclusion of the 'long-term' continues the Conservatives' rejection of the Keynesian approach of using fiscal policy to manage aggregate demand in the economy – though, as fiscal policy includes expenditures that are influenced by the state of the economy (e.g. on social security), it will still have an important impact on aggregate demand.

Hence, New Labour's fiscal policy is subject to two rules: the 'golden rule' that over the economic cycle, the government will not borrow to finance current expenditure but only to fund investment; secondly, in order to ensure that such borrowing does not run out of control, the 'sustainable investment rule' is that public debt (the total amount of borrowing) as a proportion of GDP will be maintained at a stable and prudent level over the economic cycle (Labour Party, 1997a, p. 13).

> the new fiscal rules introduced by the present Labour government resemble a number of old fiscal rules which prevailed before the so-called 'Keynesian era'. They cannot be easily related to the received concerns of macroeconomics. (Congdon, 1999, p. 23)

The rules reduce the importance of the PSBR as an indicator and it has been renamed the Public Sector Net Cash Requirement (PSNCR). With the golden rule implying a Public Sector Current Balance of zero, the second rule signals that the PSNCR will remain small (Congdon, 1999, p. 21).

The other aspects of credibility discussed by Edward Balls (1998) also operate in respect of fiscal policy with the provision of more information (including a Pre-Budget Report in November each year) and ensuring that the information is clearly presented (Balls, 1998, p. 131). However, Gordon Brown has adopted one tactic of previous Chancellors when presenting the annual Budget: previewing changes in one Budget that will not come into operation during the relevant financial year but are delayed until the one after or the one after that. Arguably this gives people and firms time to prepare for the changes; or it can be interpreted as a way of disguising tax rises so that they do not receive much attention when declared, as they are not immediately relevant nor are they noticed much when introduced because they were announced long before.

Staying within the rules (and ready for the end of the first two years in office during which it had promised to work within the department spending limits set by the previous Conservative government (Labour Party, 1997a, p. 13)), the government published a Comprehensive Spending Review in 1998. As well as projecting an increase in total expenditure, the Review reallocates spending between departments reflecting the priorities of the government (more on this below in relation to supply-side policies). In a departure from the annual 'bun fight' of government department spending, the Review presented the plans on a three-year basis – though three years do not constitute the long-term.

However, the government's oft-claimed 'prudent' approach to fiscal policy has been called into question by the IMF following the Budget 2000 statement:

> it would be desirable for fiscal policy to take some burden off of the monetary policy and move to a modestly tighter rather than modestly easier stance. That is not happening. And I would characterize that as regrettable, but not catastrophic. (Mussa, 2000).

Supply-side policies. The supply side remains an important government focus under Labour though the emphasis given to the various dimensions of the supply side have changed. Market forces are acknowledged and acclaimed (Blair and Schroeder, which includes the statement, 'The weaknesses of markets have been overstated and their strengths underestimated') but in the context of the 'Third Way': policies to promote opportunities for work and enterprise liberally sprinkled with terms such as 'fairness' and 'social justice'.

The commitment to market forces means that Labour has not rejected privatisation nor tried to reverse the process. In fact, the Blair administration has plans for further privatisations, or asset sales as they are more correctly labelled because they involve part privatisations (Comprehensive Spending Review speech by Gordon Brown as reported in the *Financial Times* on 15 July 1998, p. 12). The regulatory agencies have not been subjected to major change except in so far as the changes in competition legislation have affected them. In short, New Labour has accepted much of its inherited industrial policy.

Not so with competition policy where the government moved quickly to introduce the 1998 Competition Act (which came into force in March 2000), aiming to bring UK policy in line with Articles 85 and 86 of the Treaty of Rome. In respect of commercial practices that restrict or distort competition, the Office of Fair Trading (OFT) can investigate (including the entry and search of premises), and if found illegal (an appeal can be made to the Competition Commission which replaced the Monopolies and Mergers Commission), the companies involved can be fined up to 10 per cent of their annual UK turnover. The other main part of the Act deals with monopoly (or 'abuse of a dominant position' – Office of Fair Trading, 1999). Here again, the OFT carries out the examination, this time based on market share and whether there is abuse of market power; appeal is to the Competition Commission.

> It is generally agreed by commentators that the policy is correct to concentrate on anti-competitive *practices* and their *effects* rather than simply on the existence of agreements or on the size of a firm's market share. After all, economic power is a problem only when it is abused. (Sloman, 2000, p. 357, emphasis as in original)

Encouragement of enterprise and of innovation through research and development has been a priority: from changes in the tax system (including a 10p corporation tax rate for growing businesses) to additional funding for investment in science plus the promise of a research and development tax credit system. However, the changes need to be put into the context of the challenge facing the UK: 'On a frequently used measure of output per worker or labour productivity, the UK has a [productivity] gap of 36 per cent with the US, around 25 per cent with France and about 15 per cent with Germany' (HM Treasury, 2000, p. 37). Similar comparisons in respect of skill levels in the UK workforce lead to the same conclusion – the UK lags behind its main competitor nations. Education and training policies are a very important part of Blair's interpretation of the Third Way, not only on grounds of social justice but also as a way of improving the flexibility and adaptability of the UK labour force (Blair and Schroeder). Sceptics may feel that it is the 'vote catching' potential that is important to New Labour but, as noted above, the proponents of endogenous growth view education and training as a valid public sector investment. Whatever the interpretation, education was singled out in the Comprehensive Spending Review for extra funding, whilst training schemes in the form of 'New Deal' and 'Welfare to Work' (the latter funded by a £5.2 billion windfall tax on the excess profits of the privatised utilities) aim to provide opportunities for training which leads to jobs.

Whilst Blair is not for turning on the importance of labour market flexibility, critics point to policies that contradict the government's public stance. Most notably, the introduction of a national minimum wage (NMW, in April 1999) impairs the ability of pay to fall so that all those willing to work can obtain jobs (as envisaged by the market mechanism), with the result that unemployment is increased. The rates set by the Low Pay Commission were at the lower end of the expected range and initial analysis of the impact suggested 'the predicted job losses did not occur ... Hardly anyone we talked to last year mentioned job loss as a consequence of the NMW' (Income Data Services, 2000).

Critics can also point to New Labour's signing of the European Union's Social Chapter (Major's government had opted out of this part of the Maastricht Treaty) as having the potential for introducing further restrictions on flexibility in labour markets. Working time regulations and changes in other employee rights under the Employment Relations Act 1999 and the Employment Rights and Human Rights Acts 1998 are the more obvious of the limits being placed on the right of managers to manage; interestingly, in its election manifesto, New Labour placed these policies in the section on strengthening family life (Labour Party, 1997a, p. 25). However, the Blair government has retained the 1979–93 legislation on trade unions except in restoring a right of trade union recognition.

New Labour's Economic Policy, 1997–2000

If a week is a long time in politics then you would think that three years would be sufficient for an assessment; not so with the economic assessment. It has been pointed out above that changes in economic policy take time to work their way through the economy before the full effect is felt (with supply-side policies, it is envisaged that the effect is in the long run). Thus, the economic experience in the first year of a new administration is largely influenced by the policies of the previous government; the exception is where there is some dramatic change elsewhere in the world economy.

As already noted, the main economic indicators were moving in the right direction in 1997 so that New Labour inherited a relatively buoyant UK economy. As well as disproving the notion that a healthy economy is a sufficient condition for election victory, it gave the incoming Labour administration time to re-order priorities and undertake the changes in economic policy that it had promised.

Not that one should conclude that Labour had an easy start. Soon after its election, the 'Asian crisis' commenced with the collapse of the so-called 'tiger' economies of Thailand, Indonesia, Malaysia and South Korea. The importance of the crisis for the UK lay in a loss of export markets, the threat to inward investment by companies from these countries and the associated currency problems related to these economies (later the currency difficulties spread to Russia and certain Latin American countries). Initially, the expectation was that the UK would suffer a recession in its economic growth which would have threatened the Chancellor's plans for the public finances. There was a slowdown but recession was avoided. The extent to which government policy was responsible for warding off the recession is unclear but the strength of the economy and the economic credibility of the government may well have played important roles.

Within the grip maintained on public finances, the government has sought to affect the distribution of income. Using a model of household finances, the Institute of Fiscal Studies estimates that changes in the tax and benefit system (up to and including the Budget 2000 changes) have seen lower income households gain relative to those with higher incomes. 'The post-tax income of an average household in the bottom decile [lowest ten per cent] of income distribution is 8.8% higher … and the richest 30% of households experience a fall in post-tax income' (Institute of Fiscal Studies, 2000).

Future Policy Challenges

The task facing Europe is to meet the challenges of the global economy while maintaining social cohesion in the face of real and perceived uncertainty. Rising employment and expanding job opportunities are the best guarantee of a cohesive society. (Blair and Schroeder, no date)

The government's answer, not unexpectedly, lies in the Third Way's supply-side policies and sound, long-term economic policies. That it seems to be working during a period of increasing prosperity is not too surprising; whether it will continue to work if the economy suffers from prolonged low or negative economic growth is another question (Coman, 1998).

One issue that is inescapable is that of the Single European Currency (the 'Euro'). New Labour has taken a cautious approach to whether the UK should abandon the pound sterling and become a member of 'Euroland' (as the 11 member states which joined the Single Currency in 1999 are known). The Prime Minister and the Chancellor have placed the issue in the economic domain and established five criteria that will be used to judge whether the UK should apply for membership (HM Treasury, 1998a). Of these criteria, the one relating to the convergence of the UK economy with those of Euroland has been emphasised – the objective being to ensure that the UK is not at a disadvantage in terms of being in an economic downturn when other countries are experiencing economic booms. The debate goes deeper, however, and can be seen by analogy to the regional problems of the UK: each region of the UK, like each member state in Euroland, is subject to the same currency and to the same monetary policy. A region does not have the ability to adjust its relative economic position by altering the exchange rate between itself and other regions in the UK; similarly with the Euroland states. Thus, the relevant question is not so much about initial convergence; rather, what happens when having joined, an economy changes and loses its relative economic position? How will the Euroland states help each other in the absence of exchange rate adjustment? (Friedman, 1997). Another inescapable issue is the impact of information technology. The government incorporates its response largely in the supply-side measures already mentioned, especially training and re-training plus via the education system. In addition, there are implications for the operation of monetary policy. Reminiscent of the problems caused by financial deregulation in the 1980s (Coakley and Harris, 1992, p. 55), policy-makers will need to be aware of how new technologies are changing the ways in which people and firms behave.

5

Welfare to Work? New Labour and the Unemployed

DAN FINN

In the period before the 1997 general election the then Labour opposition mounted an effective assault on the government for its failure to tackle major social and economic problems. Despite falling unemployment and relative economic success Labour politicians argued that seventeen years of Conservative rule had produced a legacy of 'dependency' and social exclusion, where one in five families of working age had no one in a job, alongside a labour force which too often lacked either basic skills or the capacity to develop the new skills needed to compete effectively in the labour market.

   In its election manifesto, and in government, New Labour has put welfare reform, improving employability, and 'making work pay', at the heart of its strategy for modernising Britain. These objectives can be seen at work across a whole range of complex policy areas, from changes in the tax and benefit system, the introduction of a minimum wage and new rights at work, through to reforms to education and training aimed at creating a system of lifelong learning. The objectives are also at the centre of the 'New Deals' for the unemployed. Indeed, in 1997 the Prime Minister declared that the 'greatest challenge' his government faced was 'to refashion our institutions to bring the new workless class back into society and into useful work' (PM, 1997, p. 4). The main objective of what he called his 'Welfare to Work Government' is to 'attack unemployment and break the spiral of escalating spending on social security' (LPM, 1997, p. 7). This is to be achieved by securing high and stable levels of growth and employment and by creating a modern welfare state that provides effective assistance to enable people to move from benefits into work.

This chapter briefly outlines how Conservative governments responded to and managed mass unemployment between 1979 and 1996. It then assesses how New Labour redefined its traditional commitment to full employment and reversed its earlier opposition to compulsory training and employment programmes. It outlines the various New Deal employment and advice programmes that have been introduced and describes how the Labour government is integrating these initiatives into what it describes as a new 'work based' welfare state. Finally, it assesses the early impact of the New Deals and outlines the problems that will have to be overcome if the government is to convince the unemployed that it is creating worthwhile opportunities rather than a temporary respite from the dole.

The End of Full Employment: Conservative Governments and Labour Market Programmes

During the 1970s successive British governments attempted to maintain full employment, with decreasing success. The election of the first Thatcher government in 1979 marked a radical break with the policy consensus of the postwar era. The most dramatic aspect of this change was the approach to unemployment where the implementation of monetarist fiscal policies provided the technical rationale for redefining the objective of economic policy – away from maintaining high levels of employment to 'squeezing' inflation out of the system through control of the money supply.

The consequences of this new approach to economic management, which were exacerbated by the decision to maintain sterling at a high exchange rate, were that in its first two years in office the Thatcher administration presided over what rapidly became described as the deindustrialisation of Britain. The number of people employed in manufacturing industry fell by a million, and between 1979 and 1982 overall unemployment increased from 1.2 million to over 3 million.

Although the 1979 Conservative government was initially hostile towards large-scale labour market programmes it changed its stance as unemployment increased to levels not experienced since the 1930s. In the wake of the riots that erupted in many inner-city areas in mid-1981 it expanded programmes for the young unemployed and by the end of the year was proposing to spend £1bn a year on a new Youth Training Scheme for all unemployed school-leavers. Over the following decade special employment and training programmes for both the young and older unemployed were to play a key role in the government's strategy for managing the social and political consequences of mass unemployment and for massaging the unemployment count (Finn, 1986).

The expansion of labour market programmes in the 1980s was matched by a qualitative change in their objectives. Training programmes, job subsidies and temporary job creation became explicitly linked to the general strategy of reducing wage expectations and increasing work incentives. One consequence was that pay levels in temporary employment programmes were cut and training allowances were set at levels just above benefit entitlement. In combination with poor supervision of workplaces and inadequate training, successive schemes found it difficult to shed the widely held public perception that too many placements were of low quality and used people as 'cheap labour'. Negative perceptions were exacerbated by the large number of participants who failed to move into regular work, feeding images that the programmes were a 'revolving door' that only led back to the dole queue (see, for example, DE, 1990).

The Active Benefit System and Welfare Dependency

From the late 1980s the British approach to the unemployed was much influenced by a growing international consensus about the need to move from what was called a passive to an active benefit system, and by the US debate on welfare dependency and 'workfare' (OECD, 1994; King, 1995). In Europe the emphasis was on modernising welfare systems by shifting resources away from the simple payment of income support or unemployment benefit, which compensated people for unemployment, towards advice, training and employment programmes which actively supported job search and skill building. In the USA, by contrast, the key proposition, originally articulated by right-wing think-tanks, was that the welfare state had become too lax, and that by giving income benefits without stronger work obligations the state had undermined work incentives, created dependency, and encouraged the emergence of an underclass (Murray, 1990; Mead, 1997).

By the early 1990s, Conservative governments had embarked on a series of reforms which more directly linked the benefit system to its active labour market programmes. The aim was to improve the 'supply-side', by 'activating' the unemployed and getting them into whatever jobs were available as soon as possible, rather than putting them 'on hold' in large-scale schemes (OECD, 1998b, p. 86). More expensive training and employment programmes were replaced by large-scale, but cheaper, compulsory job search programmes. The central objective was to restructure the rules and administration of the benefit system to reinforce the work ethic, increase work incentives and stimulate job search in ways that were better integrated with the new opportunities being created through economic change and flexible labour markets.

Most significantly, after the introduction of compulsory 'Restart' job search review interviews in 1986, which unemployed people are required to attend at least every six months, benefit assessment, eligibility testing, and programme participation became increasingly integrated. By the early 1990s unemployed people were required to demonstrate active job search, attend regular Restart interviews with Employment Service (ES) advisers to review their efforts, be offered assistance and, after 1990, those out of work for over a year were likely to be required to attend short job search courses (Finn and Taylor, 1990).

This was the context in which Britain's unemployed were redefined as 'jobseekers' by the 1996 Jobseekers Act (HMSO, 1994). To be eligible for the new Jobseekers Allowance (JSA) unemployed individuals had to be available for work for up to 40 hours a week and were now required to enter a binding Jobseekers Agreement specifying the steps they intended to take to look for work. Benefit rules were changed to ease the transition into low-paid jobs and the legislation gave officials a new discretionary power enabling them to issue a 'Jobseekers Direction' requiring an individual to look for work in a particular way, to take other steps to 'improve their employability' or to participate in job search programmes or training schemes.

The new regime created a 'work first' approach aimed at getting the unemployed into a job as soon as possible. Although it was acknowledged that most unemployed people were genuine about looking for work, policy-makers now suggested that too many of them were ineffective in their job search or were too selective about the jobs they wanted, especially amongst the long-term unemployed. The new powers given to ES officials by JSA were also aimed at enabling and (through performance targets) requiring them to put pressure on another group amongst the unemployed who it was suggested observed the rules but had no intention of getting work or who were already working in the informal economy.

By 1996/97 the scale of the active benefit regime was significant and was clearly contributing to the marked falls in unemployment that the Labour government was to inherit (Sweeney and McMahon, 1998). In that year the ES carried out over 3.3 million new claims interviews, nearly 3.3 million Restart interviews, and just under another 1.2 million advisory interviews. As a direct result of these interventions over 147,000 people were placed directly in jobs; nearly 150,000 people started on employment and training programmes that took them off the unemployment register; and over 440,000 people started on (predominantly) job search programmes where they remained on the register. Another 65,000 made a transition to another benefit and there were over 162,000 other 'sign offs' directly attributable to the impact of the interviews (DfEE, 1998c, Table 3.5).

New Labour and Unemployment

In the 1990s, the leadership of the Labour Party gradually transformed its approach to unemployment and the welfare state. Following its election defeats in 1987 and 1992 Labour redefined its commitment to securing full employment. By 1995, the then Shadow Chancellor of the Exchequer explicitly rejected the use of direct job creation or Keynsian demand management to stimulate employment growth, indicating instead his 'iron commitment to macroeconomic stability and financial prudence' (Routledge, 1998, p. 222). The new objective was to create 'economic and employment opportunities for all', and in November the Shadow Chancellor set out the key elements of Labour's proposed 'New Deal for Britain's Under-25s' (LP, 1995a, p. 1; LP, 1995b).

This change was paralleled by a new stress on the 'responsibilities' as well as the rights of the unemployed. Labour continued to criticise what they described as the Conservatives' unpopular low-quality workfare programmes, but in preparing themselves for office they dropped their previous opposition to JSA and to compulsory employment and training programmes. Instead Labour proposed to radically reform 'a welfare system which encourages dependency and traps people in unemployment' and would balance the new responsibilities of the unemployed with new rights (LP, 1995a, p. 56).

The Labour government believes that it can now best tackle unemployment and poverty by improving the 'employability' of the unemployed, and others of working age on benefits, and by making work pay. This not only helps individuals compete for and obtain the jobs being created through the flexible labour markets of a modern economy, but it is also suggested that it will enable the labour market to operate more efficiently and help reduce wage pressures. This in turn should enable the economy to operate at a higher level of overall employment and output without creating inflationary pressures (Layard, 1996).

The 'welfare to work' strategy is not just about the abstract creation of opportunities and incentives. The government has recognised the need to couple policy change with organisational reform, and the introduction of its new programmes is linked with radical changes in the bureaucracies and institutions charged with delivering and administering the existing systems. The reasons for the perceived inadequacies of the existing systems are contested, but at least part of the problem has been attributed to the 'top down' inflexible nature of policy formation and implementation; to the fragmented structure and role of the traditional welfare bureaucracies and national Employment Service (ES); and to the absence of competition and market forces. Monolithic national service agencies are now being required to work in partnerships, and public sector monopolies, in the delivery of employment and training services, are being dismantled. These organisational reforms are linked with the introduction of new management techniques and a new generation of front-line employment advisers who have the task of turning abstract incentives and opportunities into real day-to-day choices.

The New Deals

In 1997, Labour's first 'welfare to work' budget raised over £5 billion through a 'windfall' tax on the profits of the privatised utilities, most of which has been committed to finance a variety of New Deal programmes between 1998 and 2002. Although programmes have been introduced for the full range of working-age people living on benefits, over half of the proceeds of the tax, just over £2.55 billion, has been specifically allocated to the 'flagship' New Deal for the younger long-term unemployed (see Table 5.1).

The overall objectives of the New Deals are:

- to increase long-term employability and help young and long-term unemployed people, lone parents and disabled people into jobs; and
- improve their prospects of staying and progressing in employment.

The New Deals for the unemployed consist of a complex mix of mandatory advice, employment and training programmes. They normally commence with an advisory process aimed at helping an individual find work, followed by a more or less resource-intensive range of employment and training options which aim to improve individual employability. There is a 'follow through' process of advice and support

Table 5.1 'New Deal' expenditure: 'windfall tax'

New Deal for the young unemployed (18–24)	£2,550m	70%
New Deal for the older long term unemployed (25+)	£530m	15%
New Deal for the over 50s	£50m	1%
New Deal for lone parents	£190m	5%
New Deal for disabled people	£210m	6%
New Deal for partners of the unemployed	£60m	2%
New Deal for childcare	£40m	1%
Total	**£3.63bn**	**100%**

Note: The 'windfall tax' actually raised just over £5.2bn, but £1.3bn was invested in a New Deal for schools, with smaller amounts allocated to initiatives such as the University for Industry. In March 1999 there was also an unallocated reserve of £290m.
Source: Budget Economic and Fiscal Strategy Report, HM Treasury, HMSO, March 1999.

for those who fail to get a job. Individuals who fail to take up a place or leave early without good cause will have their benefit reduced. In particular, the government has emphasised that there is 'no fifth option of an inactive life on benefit' for the younger unemployed (PM, 1997, p. 7). If an eligible young person rejects a New Deal option without 'good cause' they are initially subjected to a two-week benefit sanction, a second refusal results in a four-week sanction, and a third refusal can result in a loss of benefit for up to six months. Ministers argue that what they are offering in the New Deal is 'tough but fair' and suggest that while sanctions 'will only directly affect a small minority' the 'tough' approach will act as a cultural 'teaching agent' which will 'indicate how people should behave and what their responsibilities are' (Field, 1997a, p. 62).

The New Deals are national programmes with coverage for all those eligible. In addition, the government is also testing new approaches to targeting additional assistance, often linked to the New Deals, at those areas which have high levels of long-term and persistent unemployment. In particular the government is testing out the concept of 'benefit transfer', where in 14 'fully fledged' Employment Zones up to 48,000 of the long-term unemployed will be able to combine the resources that were available for benefits, training and job search into a 'personal job account' which can then be used flexibly to obtain the most appropriate support for the individual. The government has made it clear that it expects the partnerships running the zones to build 'synergy' between their activities and other government interventions, such as the 'New

Deal for Communities', aimed at tackling the problems faced by poor neighbourhoods and areas with multiple social and economic problems.

New Deals have also been created for working-age people living on state benefits who were previously regarded as 'economically inactive'. For example, from 2000 the wives or dependent partners of those unemployed people who are eligible for the young persons' New Deal, and who do not have childcare responsibilities, have been required to register and regularly sign on as unemployed and participate in ES programmes and, when eligible, enter what is called the 'New Deal for Partners'. Initially this approach will only apply to small numbers of partners, those aged 18 to 24, but the intention is to gradually extend this approach to the older age groups. In a context where both partners in most British families of working age now have jobs, the aim is to end the assumption of 'spouse dependency' in the benefit system which reflects an outdated family structure where male 'bread winners' worked and women stayed at home.

Finally, there are voluntary New Deal programmes for lone parents and for people with disabilities. Lone parents who make their first claim for state benefits or whose youngest child starts school are invited to their local Jobcentre, to be given advice, directed as to where they might get jobs or upgrade their skills and be advised about any childcare support that can be obtained. The programme for people with disabilities has been less prescriptive, and between 1998 and 2002 organisations working with the target group are testing new advisory services, and a limited range of more intensive support, aimed at enabling people claiming disability benefits to return to work.

In effect, through the New Deals the Labour government is integrating the active benefit regime it inherited into the broader process of welfare reform through which it intends to 'rebuild the welfare state around work'. In this new era 'it is the Government's responsibility to promote work opportunities' and 'the responsibility of those who can take them up to do so' (HMSO, 1998a, pp. 23, 31). The critical assumption is that welfare dependency and unemployment can be substantially reduced both by improving the employability of working-age benefit recipients and by connecting them more proactively to the labour market.

The 'One' Service

The government intends to radically extend its new approach and to 'activate' the benefit system for all working-age lone parents, carers and those claiming disability benefits. The approach is being tested in twelve pilot areas where what is described as the 'One Service' – a 'single work focussed gateway to the benefit system' – integrates the delivery of the previously separate benefits claimed through the ES, the Benefits Agency and Local Authorities. This 'One' gateway has three key objectives:

- to increase the sustainable level of employment by getting more benefit claimants into work by putting them in touch with the labour market through the intervention of a personal adviser;
- to ensure that individuals experience customer service that is efficient and tailored to their personal needs; and
- to change the culture of the benefits system and the general public towards independence and work rather than payments and dependence.

The aim is to provide a seamless and more coherent service for claimants where they will be able to access information on work, benefits and other services in one place. Most significantly, in the pilot areas, since April 2000, new legal obligations have been placed on *all* people of working age who now have to attend an initial work-focused interview, and subsequent recall interviews, as a condition for receiving benefit. There are safeguards to ensure that only those who can benefit from the advice are called to interview and only unemployed JSA claimants can be required to take a job or participate in a particular programme (HMSO, 1998b).

The government intends to extend the 'One Service' throughout the country and in 2001 replace the BA and ES with a unified Working Age Agency. When implemented nationally it is estimated that just over two-thirds of those using the 'One Service' will be traditional unemployed JSA claimants. Nearly one in five will be people with disabilities or health problems, and around 7 per cent will be lone parents. The remainder will be other working-age claimants such as carers and widows.

Participation in the New Deals and the Impact on Unemployment

By December 1999, two years after the first dozen 'pathfinder' areas began recruitment, over 404,000 young unemployed people had started on the New Deal and 126,400 were still in the programme. Of these nearly half were still in the initial Gateway stage and 36 per cent were in one of the options. Nearly one in four of those on the options were in subsidised jobs, a third were on placements in environmental projects or in the voluntary sector, and just over 40 per cent were in full-time education or training. Nearly one in five of all those still on the New Deal were in the 'follow through' period back in unemployment although the ES was expected to continue to try to place them in jobs (DfEE, 2000a).

Of the 277,800 young people who were no longer in the programme, two-thirds, or 185,250, had been placed in unsubsidised jobs; 12 per cent had started to claim other benefits; 18 per cent had entered other known destinations (for example, full-time education); and the destination of over a quarter (28 per cent) was unknown. Data on retention showed that nearly 50,000 of those who were placed in unsubsidised jobs had left them within 13 weeks.

During the first year particular concern had been expressed about the large number of young people whose destinations were unknown. However, follow-up research with a sample of this group found that 57 per cent of those contacted had actually left to take up a job, though only 29 per cent were in work at the time of interview. Another 25 per cent had left because of illness or caring responsibilities, and another 12 per cent were no longer looking for work (NCSR, 1999). The findings did not suggest that significant numbers of these young people were at risk of exclusion; instead they indicated that some young people were only tentatively engaged with the labour market and were likely to move in and out of jobs quickly and take intermittent advantage of the help and support offered by the New Deal and other programmes.

The numbers participating in the New Deal for those aged over 25 and out of work for over two years built up from 13,300 in July 1998 to 216,000 starters at the end of December 1999, of whom 86,000 were still in the New Deal. Most of those who were participating in the programme (82 per cent) were still in the three-to-six month advisory period, with the others moving into subsidised jobs (5 per cent), work-based training (8 per cent), or other full-time education or training (3 per cent). Of those who had left the New Deal nearly 20,000 had gone into unsubsidised jobs; 15,630 had started to claim other benefits and 62,640 had returned to claim Jobseekers Allowance; 6,360 had entered other known destinations; and the destination of 14,540 ex-participants was unknown.

Results from the New Deal for Lone Parents reflected its voluntary nature, with about 20 per cent of those who were asked to attend an initial interview taking up the offer. Between October 1998 and December 1999 over 116,000 lone parents attended the interview, with just under 90 per cent agreeing to participate further. Of those who participated, 35,190 had found jobs and just over 9,000 had taken up education or training opportunities. Of those involved, 95 per cent were women (DfEE, 2000b).

In terms of the direct impact of the New Deals on unemployment, by February 2000 the number of 18–24-year-olds unemployed who had been claiming JSA for over six months had fallen to just under 52,000. This compared with 169,500 in May 1997, when the New Labour government was elected. The fall in the number unemployed for over a year was even more dramatic, from 85,500 to 7,200. Using the more rigorous international (ILO) definition of unemployment, on data collected from the Labour Force Survey (which includes those who are unemployed but not eligible for JSA), the number of young people unemployed over six months had fallen to 117,000 in the November–January 2000 quarter from 221,000 in the February–April 1997 quarter (ONS, 2000, tables 9 and 11).

These dramatic falls in unemployment were less marked for the older age groups. They also owed much to the strength of the economy, where continuing jobs growth led to marked falls in the durations and numbers of unemployed in all the groups claiming JSA. The overall statistics also masked the uneven impact of the decline, with the areas with lowest unemployment experiencing the greatest reductions, and those that started with high unemployment the least reductions. This reality helped fuel criticisms of the New Deal, with some analysts suggesting that in the areas of highest unemployment the new approach could begin to look very much like the failed programmes of the past. Without jobs to go to, the programme could simply waste resources and merely churn 'people into and out of temporary projects and work placements, with no lasting reduction in unemployment' (Turock and Webster, 1998, p. 325; Peck, 1998).

By contrast, government ministers have pointed out that large numbers of the long-term unemployed live close to areas which have job vacancies, especially in London, and that the New Deal is aimed at tackling the attitudinal and physical barriers that prevent them from competing for those jobs. They also point out that in those areas which are undergoing structural economic change there are other programmes aimed at regenerating their economies and additional resources are being made available through Employment Zones and the New Deal for

Communities. Indeed, by the beginning of 2000, with overall registered unemployment at its lowest level for over twenty years, and with record numbers of people in work, Ministers claimed that the New Deals and other welfare-to-work initiatives had already started to have a positive impact on the operation of the labour market.

An independent assessment, carried out by the Trades Union Congress, warned against reading too much into this data, either positively or negatively, stressing that the direct effects of the New Deal will need a longer period to assess properly and will be difficult to measure (TUC, 1999, p. 4). Nevertheless they suggested that the government should be prepared to introduce temporary job creation programmes in the areas likely to be hardest hit by any future increase in unemployment. Overall, however, they acknowledged that the government was adapting the New Deal to the changing realities of local labour markets and was also working hard to ensure that employer support for and involvement in the New Deal was sustained.

Implications of Existing Evaluation Evidence for the New Deals

Preliminary results from more rigorous evaluations of the New Deal, which will be assessing the net additional impact of programmes over the next five years, were first released in early 2000. A government-commissioned report from the National Institute of Economic and Social Research estimated that in its first year the New Deal for Young People had reduced youth unemployment, relative to what it would otherwise have been, by 30,000: equivalent to a reduction in long-term youth unemployment of nearly 40 per cent. This did not appear to be at the expense of other unemployed people. The report also suggested that while the overall future net impact of the programme on the economy was likely to be small, the programme would be self-financing as the extra economic activity it generated would lead to higher government revenues (Anderton *et al.*, 2000). However, the authors acknowledged that their findings were tentative and the programme was at an early stage. Others were more critical, suggesting that they had 'guestimated' the precise results the government would wish to see.

While it is difficult to draw conclusions from this early evidence, it is possible to draw out the implications that evaluation evidence from programmes in other countries and from earlier British studies has for the likely success of the New Deals.

Essentially, there are two fundamental propositions that underpin the Labour government's welfare-to-work strategy. The first is that a more active benefit regime, coupled with time limits and employment and training programmes, will help reduce wage pressures, stimulate the economy and lead eventually to more jobs. The second assumption is that on an individual level the new approach will improve the employability and/or earning capacity of people currently living on benefits.

The first proposition is at the core of the 'supply side' strategy. For its main proponent, Professor Richard Layard, job substitution is not a major concern, because if the long-term unemployed can be got into jobs in place of other job seekers who are more readily employable, then a generally more employable group of unemployed people has been created. As the economy grows they will find jobs more easily and the economy will be able to operate with a lower natural rate of unemployment (Layard, 1996).

Unfortunately, the macroeconomic evaluation evidence in this area is bedevilled by a number of complex data and technical difficulties, and the results, according to one OECD review, are inconclusive, with 'some studies appearing to show robust effects of active policies in terms of lowering the natural rate of unemployment or real wage pressures, others appearing to show zero or insignificant correlations' (Martin, 1998, p. 13). After reviewing much of the available evidence the author concludes that 'the jury is still out'; a conclusion supported by another major review which suggested that the 'question was unresolved' (Meager, 1998, p. 36).

Although there is no consensus around the macroeconomic proposition, many of the economists and policy-makers accept that there is still a strong case for investment in labour market programmes, on the grounds of equity, social cohesion and efficiency. In this context, British programme evaluation evidence has more positive implications for the change of direction represented in the New Deals.

Control group and qualitative local studies show that the net impact of programmes on individual job prospects can be significant, especially where they are more effectively customised to individual and local labour market needs. Higher-quality evaluations, using sophisticated comparison techniques, illustrate that earlier programmes which contain elements of the New Deal approach, especially those either directly linked with real employers or offering training, had an impact on employment prospects and earnings over quite long periods (see, for example, Payne, 1991; Payne *et al.*, 1996; Dolton and O' Neill, 1996; White and Lakey, 1992; White *et al.*, 1997). However, as White and his colleagues emphasised, the best results were found with programmes that were 'selective, small scale and resource intensive', and they warned that if they were expanded in a simple way this could reduce their success rate (1997, p. 37). A vital challenge for the New Deals, and the related Employment Zones, will be their capacity, through the local delivery mechanisms that have been established, to build on the positive impact and potential that these earlier programmes have demonstrated is possible.

A more challenging issue involves tackling what has been described as the 'revolving door'. Although control-group evaluations show that the better designed and resourced programmes of the late 1980s and early 1990s had a significant net impact on job prospects, and that those who participated in work-based training were more likely to obtain more secure and better-paid work, the evidence also showed that large numbers of participants in even the best programmes were likely to return to unemployment. This 'revolving door' effect may reflect labour market realities but it did great damage to the credibility of training and employment programmes, and managing and minimising its impact will be one of the major tests facing Labour's New Deals. In this context, particular emphasis is now being placed on improving job 'retention' strategies, to ensure that New Deal participants keep the jobs they enter; on the 'follow through', to get effective assistance to those who come to the end of their placements without a job; and to 'progression', where skill training and follow-up support can enable those who do take entry-level jobs to make progress to higher-paid and more secure employment (NDTF, 1999).

If the New Deals and welfare-to-work programmes are delivered flexibly, and as intended, they could help to improve the employability and job prospects of those living on benefit, especially the younger unemployed. However, closing the 'revolving door' and translating worthy policy objectives and theoretical design into day-to-day practice is fraught with difficulties. Despite an imaginative 'continuous improvement' response to operational problems and ministerial assurances about job creation and availability throughout Britain, much of the success of the New Deals will depend on continued economic growth and the macroeconomic strategy which the government has committed itself to. Although New Labour has expressed confidence about its approach it may be that its critics will be proved right, and that without a stronger commitment to job creation in areas of high unemployment the positive impacts of the New Deals could be undermined when the economic cycle changes and unemployment begins to increase (Turock and Webster, 1998; Peck, 1998).

6

UK Environmental Policy under Blair

JOHN BRADBEER

One notable feature of political and public policy processes over the last quarter-century, has been the addition of the environment to the set of significant concerns. This has occurred gradually and often almost imperceptibly. The environment has only rarely been a matter of party political conflict but its political and policy importance is attested by the establishment of environment ministries by governments across the industrialised world. This chapter sets out to examine the environmental policy inheritance of the Blair government, to seek pointers as to how environmental policy might develop under New Labour and to identify some more troublesome longer-term problems. As some of the themes considered here have been examined before (e.g. Bradbeer, 1990 and 1994; Gray, 1995; Lowe and Ward, 1998b), the treatment here is of broad principles of policy.

The Inheritance: United Kingdom Environmental Policy since 1980

There are five significant but often interrelated themes. The European Community had begun to develop its own environmental policy but few could have seen how crucial the European dimension would prove to be in the subsequent development of UK environmental policy. By the early 1990s, the environment had arrived as a matter of real public concern and governments were also faced with substantial environmental problems. Although not very clear in 1980, the UK had lost its position as an innovator and leader in environmental policy. Indeed, by the late 1980s, Britain was widely regarded as the 'dirty man of Europe' (Rose,

1990). Environmental policy in Britain has emerged by a mixture of piecemeal and evolutionary change, punctuated by occasional bursts of innovation. There were perhaps fewer bouts of innovation until the early 1990s and rather more after. Finally, there has been the effective nationalisation of the spatial scale of environmental policy in the sense that national institutions rather than local ones now take the major responsibility for setting and administering policy.

The Europeanisation of UK Environmental Policy

In 1981 the European Community gave the environment its own Commissioner and Directorate General (DG XI) within the Commission. More environmental Directives followed, and the environment as a policy issue took on a definite European dimension as so many problems were clearly trans-boundary in their manifestation.

Lowe and Ward (1998b, p. 3) comment on environmental policy that 'an agenda which had been driven principally by domestic factors and issues has been thoroughly Europeanized'. The impetus from the EU has come for a number of reasons and in a variety of ways. First, since 1980, the EU has been more enthusiastic about environmental policy development than the UK. In particular, Conservative governments from 1979 to 1990 laid great emphasis on the need to deregulate economic activity and saw in environmental policy a major and unwarranted imposition of regulation. Partly in response to the growing number of environmental Directives being issued and partly because the European Commission, unlike the UK government, appeared to be sympathetic to environmental issues, UK environmental interest groups made Brussels the target of intensive lobbying. EU initiatives have also extended the scope of environmental policy far beyond its traditional limits in the UK. A good example of this was the Bathing Water Directive (EC76/160) which was received in the UK with what could only be described as disbelief. Far-reaching changes have also occurred because of a very different European approach to environmental pollution control. The European approach has favoured the setting of uniform effluent standards and their application in a formal but open regulatory system. By contrast, the UK has historically favoured a case-by-case approach that is informal, discretionary and essentially private. The UK has also generally avoided uniform effluent standards and considered as critical the ambient environmental quality after discharges have been made. As Jordan (1998) argues, the UK's traditions have been challenged by EU environmental policies and the environmental regulatory system has changed in ways that would have been far less likely but for EU membership.

The relationship over environmental matters between the EU and the UK has been complex. Lowe and Ward (1998b) see three phases in this relationship:

- 1973–1983: lack of interest and insularity on the UK's part and a rather tentative evolution of environmental policy in Europe
- 1983–1992: defensiveness by the UK and its effective isolation on environmental matters as the EU increased the tempo of environmental policy-making
- 1992–: slow convergence as the UK takes a more accommodating stance and the pace of EU environmental policy-making slackens

They also comment that the state of the relationship depended on the issues under discussion and on the attitudes to Europe of the UK's Secretary of State for the Environment. It is no coincidence that the most difficult periods occurred when the strongly Eurosceptic Nicholas Ridley and Michael Howard were in office and that something of a rapprochement occurred under John Selwyn Gummer. One of the most difficult periods occurred in 1989–92, when the dynamic and charismatic Carlo Ripa di Meana was the Environment Commissioner.

The Environment as an Issue of Public Concern and Political Importance

The environment has partially challenged the *issue attention cycle* of Anthony Downs (1972). By the early 1980s, levels of environmental concern were appreciably higher than those in previous decades and interest had been fanned by some major incidents. By the end of the decade all the major media had permanent environment correspondents. Programmes and articles on the environment were no longer for the green minority and served further to raise public awareness and concern. Environmental interest and pressure groups themselves benefited greatly from this increased media interest. They were able to extend their membership and financial base among a better-informed public. Simultaneously, groups such as Friends of the Earth and Greenpeace were able to feed an increasingly receptive media with environmental interest stories and campaigns.

Such has been the growth in public concern for the environment that Eurobarometer Surveys have shown since the late 1980s that environment is a major issue, nearly as important as unemployment, health and education. This has been as true of the UK as of the 'greener' states such as Denmark, Germany and the Netherlands. As a result of this, and no doubt confirmed by private polling, both the Conservative and Labour parties have felt it necessary to have a range of environmental policies. While party manifestos for the 1992 and 1997 general elections contained sections on the environment, it has to be conceded that neither election saw much campaigning on environmental issues.

However there remains the paradox that the environment has not really become a major issue between the parties. It would not be accurate to describe party attitudes to the environment as bipartisan but they do reflect a view that portrays the environment as essentially a technical issue. Debates are couched in terms of technical means rather than those about environmental goals and their relationship to economic and social justice. Should the environmental debate develop in this way, then party differences are likely to grow.

From Leader and Innovator to Laggard in Environmental Policy

With hindsight, it is clear that by 1980 the United Kingdom had lost its position and reputation as a leader and innovator in environmental policy. The late 1980s saw the UK being called, not necessarily unfairly, the 'dirty man of Europe'. Britain's reputation had been built by the Labour government of 1945–50 with its wide-ranging legislation in the fields of land-use planning, nature conservation, pollution control and environmental management. However, thirty years later, it was clear that other countries had made great strides in environmental policy. In 1969 the United States passed its National Environmental Protection Act, still one of the most far-reaching pieces of environmental legislation anywhere, and in 1973 the Netherlands produced its first National Environmental Policy Plan. The UK had to wait for some two decades before attempting anything similar.

By the 1970s there was a certain amount of complacency and insularity in UK environmental policy and administration. Two further factors played a part in the loss of the UK's reputation. In the period 1970–82, economic problems loomed large and environmental projects suffered badly in successive rounds of public expenditure cuts. A notable casualty of this process was the 1974 Control of Pollution Act, many of whose provisions were suspended for over a decade as the attendant costs were deemed too great. As Downs (1972) had noted in the issue attention cycle, when the full costs and the sacrifices necessary to act on issues of concern are realised, then interest usually evaporates.

A second aspect was a form of capture by anti-environmental interest groups. Road transport, industrial and farming interests put powerfully to government their cases that environmental legislation was unnecessary, would be expensive to implement and would almost certainly destroy jobs. Some environmental policy was made specifically to satisfy such interest group demands, and none more so than the dismemberment of the Nature Conservancy Council in the 1990 Environmental Protection Act.

Piecemeal and Evolutionary Change

Given that government departments rarely get more than two major pieces of legislation passed in each Parliament, it is hardly surprising that in many areas of policy, change is gradual, piecemeal and evolutionary. What change there is frequently relies on ministerial discretion contained in the primary legislation. This certainly seems to be the case for environmental policy, and authorities such as Blowers (1987), McCormick (1991) and O'Riordan (1991) have argued that even the environmentally indifferent Conservative governments of the 1980s proceeded in this way. For the environment, where there was little party political pressure for action and which was seen as a technical issue, continuity was always likely. Continuity in environmental policy has reflected its status as an essentially non-political issue. The opposition can usually be relied upon to offer some degree of cooperation for measures that are presented as technicalities and necessary to remedy defects or omissions in previous legislation. Change requires legislation, and for relatively minor policy fields such as the environment, legislative time is not a priority.

The Royal Commission on Environmental Pollution (RCEP) established in 1970, survived the cull of the quangos of the early 1980s. It has considerable authority, derived in large measure from the eminence and expertise of its mainly scientific members. The RCEP has now produced twenty-one reports and set out a broad environmental agenda for government. It has returned several times to key issues such as transport and water quality and has been able to sustain concern for such problems. Governments have always issued formal responses to the RCEP's reports and in many cases have brought forward legislation along the lines foreshadowed in them. The RCEP helps to maintain a legislative interest in the environment and to prod governments into action.

The Nationalisation of Environmental Policy

The last quarter of a century has seen an increased Europeanisation of UK environmental policy as EU Directives have come to play as important a part in environmental policy as domestic initiatives. Nationalisation of environmental policy has occurred in the sense that the administrative locus has shifted progressively from local government to Westminster. This has happened for three contrasting reasons:

- The spatial extent and scale of environmental problems have increased since the 1960s. At that time many environmental problems were local in scale and relatively few involved an international dimension. Since then more problems have at least an international, if not a global dimension. Inevitably the locus for action has moved to the national government scale.
- The growing number of EU environmental Directives require enactment into national law. Again this is the responsibility of the national government, even when the implementation may be devolved to local government. The Whitehall administrative machine has also jealously guarded its rights to deal with the EU and has tried, if not always successfully, to deny these to local government.
- There has been an actual removal of powers from local government and a corresponding concentration of responsibilities for environmental policy with national government or commercial enterprises. In part this reflected a deep hostility to local government in Margaret Thatcher's governments. However there has also been a longer-term drift of powers and responsibilities from local government, well illustrated in the case of the water industry.

The Emerging Environmental Agenda under New Labour

The full characteristics of environmental policy of the Blair government remain to be seen. Reform and modernisation of environmental policy do not appear to be at the heart of its project. It is therefore likely that environmental policy will once more develop with a mixture of continuity, opportunistic change, occasional panic responses to crises and a few more deliberate changes. Before examining some possible environmental policy problems and developments, it would be useful to identify the forces for continuity and change.

Forces for Continuity in Environmental Policy

The distinctive administrative and policy style of Britain tends to favour continuity and incremental change, especially for an issue like the environment that is not regarded as central to party political debate. Furthermore, the probable environmental problems of the next few years are likely to be those of the recent past. The persistence of problems, administrative structures and personnel all favour a large degree of continuity. Taking major new policy initiatives usually requires new powers and sometimes the creation of new agencies, both of which take up scarce parliamentary time. The pattern of the last quarter-century has been for governments to enact only one or two major pieces of environmental legislation in each parliament. There is little reason to expect a Blair government, especially in a first term, to be any different.

Forces for Change in Environmental Policy

Apart from unexpected events and crises, forces for change in environmental policy are likely to come from five sources:

- *public opinion:* Opinion polls have shown that there is widespread support for measures to protect the environment and that the environment is usually seen as being of only little less importance than the economy, health, education and social welfare. Whether this enthusiasm for the environment will extend to paying higher taxes or even paying new 'green' taxation remains to be seen; one should be circumspect about opinion polls about the environment which do not ask respondents whether they would feel differently about their preferences if they meant higher prices and taxes. Nonetheless, a populist government such as that of Tony Blair will not be able to afford to neglect public concerns about the environment.
- *environmental interest groups:* Over the last two decades, the environmental movement has become much more skilled at lobbying government, and the EU, and in placing environmental interest stories with the mass media. The media have become much more interested in the environment and prepared to run stories on it. Skilled campaigns, such as that mounted by Greenpeace over the *Brent Spar* oil installation, can compel multinational companies and governments to change their policies. The environmental interest groups have also attained a new respectability and are now given more access to government.

- *the EU:* Many of the changes in the UK's environmental policy since the mid-1980s have stemmed from EU Directives. While the pace of formulating new EU environmental policy has slackened since the early 1990s, it has not stopped altogether, and the present trend is towards consolidation through Framework Directives. Evaluation of the extent and impact of environmental policy in the light of the Amsterdam Treaty is also likely. More distant, but potentially having far-reaching effects, would be the reform of the Common Agricultural Policy. This will almost certainly be driven by financial considerations, especially the implications of EU expansion into eastern Europe, but any moves away from a productionist agricultural policy would have environmental benefits. Fears of rural communities about the effects of withdrawal of large sums of money from the CAP could also be a trigger for funding rural environmental protection and restoration programmes.

- *the Royal Commission on Environmental Pollution:* Since its creation, it has played an important role in shaping the UK's environmental policy. It has good access to government and has rarely shrunk from posing awkward questions, even if concealed in its considered prose. Its last four reports on energy, transport and environmental standards have yet to be acted upon and delineate a challenging agenda.

- *Labour Party concerns:* The Labour Party made few explicit environmental commitments in its manifesto but certainly tried to cultivate an environmentally friendly image. Labour governments of the past have generally been more innovative on environmental issues, not least because they have not shared the Conservatives' distaste for state intervention and tighter regulation. Furthermore, John Prescott at the new Department of Environment, Transport and the Regions, is one of the major figures in the Cabinet. Although he is not regarded as a close ally of Tony Blair, he may be (arguably) a 'greener' member of the Cabinet and has been allowed a fairly free hand at a post he seems to have relished being given. Labour's promised Transport Bill was not in the Queen's Speech for the second Parliamentary session, although aspects were added to the legislative programme subsequently. This suggests that John Prescott will have difficulties in sustaining an environmental agenda. What would happen if he were to be given another portfolio leaves one pondering the fate of the Department of Economic Affairs in the 1964–70 Wilson governments, after the departure of George Brown.

Some Major Environmental Policy Issues

Countryside and agricultural issues. One of the first protests against
the Blair government was the Countryside March in London in 1998.
Although the protesters had a diverse set of grievances, many of them
concerning hunting, one common element was a fear of the threat to the
countryside posed by new development. Through Planning Policy
Guidelines, Secretaries of State for the Environment have wide existing
powers to shift the emphasis in planning and land-use issues. A major
problem currently facing John Prescott is a 1996 estimate that England
will need 4.4 million new houses by 2011 and that perhaps as many as
60 per cent will have to be on greenfield sites in the countryside. Here
two aspects of his wide ministerial brief could work together.
Geographers and planners as long ago as the 1960s posed the question
'must we all live in south-east England?' Regional policy throughout
the 1970s was intended to promote a negative answer by restricting
development in the south-east and positively encouraging it elsewhere.
The Conservative governments of the 1980s were hostile both to
regional policy and any strategic dimension in urban development. This
ensured that much new economic activity was located in the south-east
and generated a growing demand for housing there. It is hard to see any
resolution without some recourse to regional policy. A real grievance of
the farming community was the collapse in agricultural incomes in the
mid-1990s in the wake of the BSE crisis, restructuring of the CAP and
during mid 1997/8, the rise in value of the pound sterling. The case to
redirect agricultural spending away from subsidies to large farmers on
the best agricultural land to smaller farmers on land that is poorer in
agricultural terms but richer in environmental value, is strong. Whether
the CAP will be so restructured remains to be seen but clearly some of
the funds used to subsidise unwanted and ecologically damaging food
production could have great benefits if directed to environmental conservation in the countryside.

The growing recreational use of the countryside has been a feature of
British life since the 1960s, but legally recognised public access to
much of the countryside remains limited. Labour promised to improve
this and in February 1998 the consultative paper *Access to the
Countryside in England and Wales* was published. This reaffirmed the
commitment and sought to achieve it by voluntary agreement, although
not ruling out the prospect of further legislation if necessary. The
Countryside Marchers vigorously opposed even these limited measures,

while at the same time groups such as the Ramblers Association feared that the government would not greatly widen public access at all.

The size of Labour's majority has meant that it now has for the first time since 1945 a significant number of MPs who represent seats that are quite rural. The wider rural agenda may be advanced by the merger in 1999 of the Countryside Commission in England with the Rural Development Commission but this will further emphasise the distinction in England between rural landscape and economy on the one hand and nature conservation and environment on the other.

Nature conservation. The problems confronting nature conservation have been not those of legislation and administrative structure but rather those of political will and financial resources to enforce strictly existing policy. There is effectively a two-tier conservation policy with the more important sites, National Nature Reserves (NNRs), being either owned or held on long leases by the major state conservation bodies, English Nature, Scottish Natural Heritage and the Countryside Council for Wales. However, this system is not without its problems, as was seen in 1996 when the Braunton Burrows NNR in Devon was de-designated by EN when it failed to reach agreement on a new lease and concomitant management plans with the landowner. When a leading nature conservation site suffers this fate, the system as a whole loses credibility. The lower-tier sites are the Sites of Special Scientific Interest, usually in private ownership, and theoretically, if not practically, protected by policy. In the period 1991/2 to 1995/6, Phillips (1998) estimated that 400 SSSIs were damaged by agricultural activity and even EN, charged with the task of protecting them, admitted that 45 per cent of England's SSSIs are in 'unfavourable conservation' condition. Present protection revolves around a complex system of notification and compensation to landowners for compensation for benefits forgone by leaving SSSIs untouched that was introduced with the 1981 Wildlife and Countryside Act. Such a regime has done little to protect SSSIs and does nothing to encourage and reward positive conservation management. In a consultative paper, Labour has promised to redirect funds to promote the positive conservation management of SSSIs and to afford them further protection through a greater recognition in the planning process.

While the UK has made good progress in designating Special Areas for Conservation (SACs) under the EU Habitats and Species Directive, those SACs that are not NNRs lack full protection. The voluntary conservation sector, especially the Royal Society for the Protection of Birds and the various County Wildlife Trusts, has sought wherever possible to secure these sites through purchase.

Pollution control. The last decade has seen considerable change both in the structure and approach to pollution control. Some of the changes have come from recommendation of the Royal Commission on Environmental Pollution, some from EU Directives and others emerged as the unexpected and unintended outcomes of the privatisation of the water and energy industries. This latter development has served to make far more open to public scrutiny the environmental standards demanded and the methods used to regulate the industries. Integrated pollution control has become the goal to be attained, and the best-practicable-means approach traditionally favoured has given way to a more technology-forcing best-available environmental option. Both integrated pollution control and best-available environmental option have been recommended by the RCEP and emphasised by EU Directives.

The 1995 Environment Act created a single pollution control agency in England and Wales, the Environment Agency (EA) from the National Rivers Authority and Her Majesty's Inspectorate of Pollution (the Scottish Environmental Protection Agency was set up at the same time). The EA, with its budget of £550 million a year and a staff of around 10,000, is now one of the most powerful such bodies in Europe. The challenges facing it and the government will be to make this new structure work effectively and, in particular, to promote the precautionary principle and anticipate pollution problems. Also, this new structure and its staff inherited from the old will have to abandon the traditionally informal, consultative and secretive pollution control regulation and move to a regime that is more formal, standardised and open to public scrutiny.

Energy, transport and the environment. This is one of the most complex issues facing the DETR, involving not just questions of transport and environment but also fiscal policy. Furthermore, environmental questions are only some among many to be addressed by transport policy. Some of the most pressing environmental problems concern the pollution generated by burning fossil fuels. Acid rain comes from the soluble oxides of sulphur and nitrogen being absorbed by precipitation and which becomes more acidic as a consequence. Of even greater severity is the emission of greenhouse gases, most notably carbon dioxide, which contribute to global warming.

The UK, along with other industrialised nations, made commitments to cut greenhouse gas emissions at the Rio Earth Summit in 1992 and again in Kyoto in 1997. Some progress has already been relatively painlessly made, as economic restructuring has taken a disproportionate toll of old and relatively energy-inefficient plant. The 'dash for gas' of the newly privatised electricity generators has also helped considerably, as less carbon dioxide is emitted per kilowatt of electricity generated by gas as opposed to coal-fired power stations.

Transport accounts for about a quarter of the UK's greenhouse gas emissions. Recent efficiency gains in energy use in transport have largely been cancelled out by growth in traffic and by greater distances being covered. For transport to contribute to meeting the UK's targets of cutting greenhouse gas emissions, radical measures will be necessary. The RCEP in its eighteenth and twentieth reports has underlined this and criticised government for its relative inaction. A few figures suffice to show the scale and difficulties that will be entailed. Just over two-thirds of freight movement in Britain is by road but the carbon dioxide emissions per tonne-kilometre of large heavy-goods vehicles are three to four times higher than for rail transport, while lighter trucks and vans can emit between ten and twenty times as much. Yet only 6 per cent of Britain's freight is moved by rail and rail freight facilities have been closed and redeveloped. The private car is about 30–40 per cent less efficient in terms of carbon dioxide emissions per passenger-kilometres than public transport by road or rail and yet accounts for over 75 per cent of passenger movements. While cuts in road building programmes may save money and please countryside campaigners, they will do little to effect the necessary changes in transport use.

Changes in taxation to promote energy efficiency in general and especially in transport, would do much to contribute to the necessary cuts in greenhouse gases. Here the government faces conflicting pressures. Green taxes on fuel, on car parking and forms of road charging would be popular with the Treasury as it seeks ways of sustaining government income without going back on election pledges not to raise income tax rates. As indirect taxes, however, they would tend to bear heaviest on the poor, especially if VAT were to be raised on fuel or a carbon tax imposed, as the poorest live in the least energy-efficient housing and spend disproportionately more on domestic fuel than the wealthy. As significant to New Labour as it woos the middle classes, taxes on motoring would be unpopular and would certainly test the public's enthusiasm for protecting the environment.

Greening government. Following the 1990 White Paper *This Common Inheritance* and the Rio Earth Summit in 1992, the government committed itself to a cabinet environment committee and to annual reviews of the environment and progress towards sustainable development. Each department has had to have a designated 'green minister' to ensure coordination and compliance. Labour has moved to strengthen this structure. John Prescott now chairs the cabinet's environment committee. The DETR has issued guidelines to departments on how to conduct their environmental reviews of policy and actions, which have also been elevated in status to equal those required on financial, regulatory and health impacts and consequences. Labour has also introduced a new House of Commons Environmental Audit Select Committee to hold the green ministers to account.

While structural change of ministries and agencies takes parliamentary time, it is paradoxically easier to do than to make real changes in policy implementation. The challenge facing the Blair government is to change the environment from being a self-contained, distinct and often marginal concern of government to one that is at its very heart and fundamental to all aspects of policy. This will in turn involve a shift from a focus on the relatively 'easily' solved environmental problems (i.e. those susceptible to technological solutions) to the more difficult and longer-term problems requiring changes in lifestyle.

Future Environmental Problems

Over the last quarter-century the environmental movement has succeeded in popularising two phrases that could be taken as defining the medium-term environmental agenda. 'Think globally, act locally' has served to remind that environmental problems were among the first to be experienced and recognised as global, predating by some years the idea of globalisation in the social and economic spheres. It also underlines the interconnections between places at a variety of geographical scales. The second phrase, 'think and act holistically', urges societies to see the environment as a whole, rather than as a series of distinct resources and also to treat it not as an inert thing that surrounds humans but as a complex and delicate web that sustains all life, human and non-human.

The spatial scale of environmental policy poses several problems. In the UK, changes in administration over the twenty years have reduced the power and discretion of local government. For environmental issues, this has worked against real community action to care for local environments and to manage them sustainably. Labour has promised to restore more powers to local government and embarked upon major change with devolved assemblies in Northern Ireland, Scotland and Wales. The impact that these measure will have on the environment remains to be seen. On the one hand, more local control should see concern for local environmental problems turned into effective action and will allow greater scope for contextually specific policies. On the other hand, more administrations and jurisdictions could make the integration of environmental policy much harder.

Similar questions arise in the UK's relationship with the EU. Subsidiarity and harmonisation could prove to be two principles pulling in opposite directions. Harmonisation has led to growing standardisation of environmental policy at the national level but may neglect the greater variations within countries. Subsidiarity in environmental policy would point to large-scale, general principles being established at the EU level and discretion in both lesser policy development and implementation being devolved to the regional or even sub-regional level within countries. This is something that current debates about national sovereignty signally fail to address. In the recent past the EU has forced Britain and other countries to confront their deficiencies in environmental policy and more subsidiarity could weaken this trend.

At the national scale there are many vital issues concerning the full integration of environmental concerns with all aspects of government policy. The role of DETR remain crucial. As Carter and Lowe (1998) point out, it (and its predecessors) have been *a* department *of* the environment and not *the* department *for* the environment. The non-environmental aspects of DETR's work remain significant and the essentially anti-environmental contribution of the Ministry of Agriculture, Fisheries and Food (MAFF) needs to be addressed. Most environmentalists would like to see ever closer scrutiny of government policy by a department *for* the environment, much in the way that the Treasury holds a powerful financial brief.

There are also some significant and new interactions between the environment and other traditional policy areas. Most of the recent concern agriculture–environment interactions the negative impacts of intensive modern farming practices on landscape and nature conservation. To these must now be added two further concerns. The BSE crisis over the last decade has served to put questions of food safety on the political agenda. Labour has established a Food Standards Agency, but this has not been given high priority. What will become of MAFF if it is shorn of its food responsibilities is an interesting question and might make the creation of more environmentally coherent department more feasible. Concerns about genetically modified organisms (GMO) also link agriculture, environment, food and science policy areas. An EU Directive on GMOs has been issued, with further legislation currently under consideration; all member governments will come under pressure from mainly American multinational agro-chemical and food companies to allow such foodstuffs to enter the market in a lightly regulated way. Public opinion and more especially consumer groups are deeply sceptical about the benefits of GM foodstuffs and would prefer to see a complete ban. These issues are likely to become embroiled in wider discussions about world trade liberalisation.

Ultimately many environmental problems stem from the excessive consumption of the industrialised countries of the North. Environmentalists have called for policies to curb consumption. Taxation is frequently held to be the way forward. Consumption taxes by their nature are regressive and so ways have to be found to redirect spending to less environmentally damaging products and to combine any drive to green taxation with the maintenance of social justice.

This same challenge of matching environmental action and social justice is even more apparent at the global level. For the last decade or more, there has been much talk of threats to the environment at the global scale, especially of global climatic change, loss of biodiversity and of the need to move to sustainable development. Sustainable development is held to be a way of linking economic prosperity, social welfare and environmental conservation. Its very popularity has led it to becoming a portmanteau concept, and apparently opposite courses of action are frequently justified as sustainable development. A great challenge will be to deal with pressing environmental problems and to work out in practice just what sustainable development means.

Climatic change has probably been the most talked about global environmental issue. At the Rio Earth Summit in 1992, world leaders had the evidence and advice from the experts of the Intergovernmental Panel on Climatic Change that global warming was almost certainly occurring and that action could no longer be delayed. While some countries, most notably the USA, wanted further and definitive proof, the world started the process of trying to cut greenhouse gas emissions by negotiation. This process has been protracted and has predictably generated conflicts of interest, not just between North and South but within the G8 group of industrialised nations. The mechanisms to achieve cuts have proved controversial. The notions of trading in carbon dioxide emissions rights and of offset agreements, where developed countries in return for funding forest planting or renewable energy development in a Third World country can claim to have met their own targets, have been particularly contested. At such meetings, both John Prescott and John Gummer, his Conservative predecessor, have made strenuous efforts to achieve agreements and, particularly, tried to keep the Americans in the agreement. Further rounds of negotiations are likely to prove as difficult, again with American concerns tending to be the problem. The cuts presently agreed are relatively small, have yet to be fully implemented and will still leave atmospheric carbon dioxide levels well above their pre-industrial levels.

Many of the difficulties in securing international agreements on climatic change stem from the real and complex relationships with global social justice. The USA, with about 5 per cent of the world's population accounts for almost 25 per cent of the world's annual energy consumption. Global warming, as the South points out, has been triggered and is still largely sustained by the energy and resource use of the North. Furthermore, policies of structural adjustment and trade liberalisation so enthusiastically endorsed and frequently required by the World Bank and the World Trade Organisation have had a deleterious effect on the environment and the ability to achieve sustainable development in the developing countries. Much deforestation and consequent soil erosion and environmental degradation has occurred in this way. There has yet to be much sign of Robin Cook's ethical dimension to foreign policy here.

Sustainable development is at the heart of the longer-term environmental problem not just for the UK but for the world. It calls for a balance between environmental concerns, economic development needs and human welfare. Translating this into practical terms will not be easy. For the poor to enjoy social justice and to protect the environment, then the wealthy will have to make real sacrifices. At the moment, everyone can pay lip-service to the ideal of sustainable development. Whether the British government, or indeed any other, is prepared to explain what this will entail and to give a lead by ending unsustainable development is the real challenge. As with all such changes, not only is the ultimate goal remote and perceived as problematic, but the route to attain it is far from clear, other than in the sacrifices required and difficulties to be faced.

7

Law and Order under Blair: New Labour or Old Conservatism?

STEPHEN P. SAVAGE AND MIKE NASH

Introduction

It used to be said that the Conservative Party was the 'party of law and order'. There seemed to be little dispute that when it came to 'getting tough' on law and order the Conservatives enjoyed something of a clear run. Traditionally, Labour had not sought to challenge this near monopoly – either because to do so might have been seen as futile, in the light of the Conservatives' dominance of this territory, or because to engage in this enterprise would have been be too distasteful to Labour's liberal or even left leanings. How things have changed! Of all of the sea-changes heralded by the emergence of the New Labour agenda, the shift in Labour's strategy for law and order has perhaps been most explicit. In both rhetoric and in reality Labour's new approach to crime, policing and criminal justice stands a great distance away from that associated with previous Labour Party policies. The question is whether the distance thus travelled has been in the direction of a genuinely new Labour vision for tackling crime or whether it has been, on the contrary, in the direction of the old territory formerly the exclusive province of the Conservatives.

In this chapter we shall examine the agenda for crime and criminal justice which has emerged under New Labour and which sets the course for crime policy for the foreseeable future. This examination will have two primary aims: on the one hand to outline the defining characteristics of Labour's strategy for and policy on crime; on the other to assess

102

the extent to which this strategy constitutes a serious departure from that adopted by previous administrations. This is particularly appropriate in the light of criticisms made just prior to the 1997 general election that Labour had, in effect, allowed its agenda to be unduly shaped by that of the Conservatives, under the then Home Secretary, Michael Howard (Charman and Savage, 1999). As a prelude to this, therefore, it is necessary to review the destiny of crime policies under the Conservatives and the factors shaping those policies. There are good reasons to trace this back as far as the point at which the Thatcher government first took office in 1979.

Law and Order under the Conservatives: A Full Circle?

The Conservatives took office in 1979 with a major pledge on law and order. On the eve of the 1979 general election Margaret Thatcher exclaimed 'What the country needs is less tax and more law and order' (see Savage, 1990). That stance set the scene for the first stage of what can now be seen as the 'three phases' of Conservative policy on law and order stretching from 1979 to 1997. The policy agendas in each case were shaped by the political and economic configurations of that period; in the politics of the 1980s and 1990s, crime policy was very much a dependent variable.

The Tory agenda for crime which emerged during the early 1980s was in essence one which signalled a 'tough' approach. Commitments were made to increase the resources available to the police and increase police numbers; pledges were also made to increase police powers in the 'war against crime'. New sentences were made available to the courts, mainly targeted at young offenders which, when applied to the newly re-vamped detention centres, complied with the rhetoric of the 'Short Sharp Shock'. To complete the deterrent package, the government announced a massive prison-building programme – a shortage of prison cells was not to constrain sentencers in carrying out their duties. A strengthened police force, stiffer sentences and a more expansive penal regime were to spearhead the Conservatives early crime policy.

Despite the heavily authoritarian rhetoric of this era and the plethora of nakedly deterrent measures, it is important not to ignore the fact that the legislation largely responsible for the tougher approach, the Criminal Justice Act 1982, also heralded steps to divert some classes of offenders from custody and to stiffen the conditions under which custodial punishments could be metered out. Quietly, behind the more public assertion of deterrence through custody, 'bifurcation' or 'twin-tracking' was emerging. Bifurcation, as Hudson (1987) has argued, is an approach to crime policy which strengthens sentences for some groups of offenders/offences while reducing them, or orienting them in a non-custodial direction, for others. This approach was to be sustained through much of the 1980s and 1990s, until the arrival of Michael Howard as Home Secretary (as we shall see later).

From the mid-1980s onwards, the non-custodial model began to move from a secondary strand of Conservative crime policy to the centre stage. A quiet revolution was taking place: a definite shift in attitude towards the role of custody in criminal justice had emerged within the Home Office. In official papers criticisms of the effectiveness of imprisonment (for all but the most serious offenders) appeared. Preference was expressed for the more extensive application of tougher *non-custodial* forms of punishment, 'community penalties'. Community service and supervision orders were to take priority over prisons as weapons in the war against crime. Alongside this 'liberal' development, the government also began to place value on *crime prevention* as an effective strategy for crime reduction. Criminologists had long argued that crime policies that focused on reducing opportunities for crime, such as 'target hardening' (better security of premises, alarm systems, etc.) would reap more rewards in cost–benefit terms than offender-based measures. The Home Office began to take seriously the principles of 'situational crime prevention'; the launch of 'Crime Concern' in 1987, set up to mobilise partnerships between public and private agencies for crime prevention purposes, was at least a symbolic expression of this. It is not without significance that the Home Secretary for much of this period was Douglas Hurd, very much on the liberal ('wet') wing of the Party. Again, we should not ignore the process of bifurcation during this phase. The Criminal Justice Act 1988 actually toughened sentences for sex- and drugs-related offences. But in this case the pendulum had swung in the opposite direction: it was the non-custodial measures which were in the limelight. While this shift may have been disguised to an extent by the right-wing dressing of notions such as 'just deserts' (see Savage and Nash, 1994), it was difficult to deny that what was taking place was a definite move towards a more liberal criminal justice strategy – more 'tender' than 'tough'.

The legislation which embodied this phase above all – the Criminal Justice Act 1991 – was ironically also to be its swan song. The political upheavals of the early 1990s were to see to that. It was no accident that the cultural shift which took place from the mid-1980s, heralding a much more 'reasoned' policy approach – i.e. one less red in tooth and claw and more steeped in criminological research – took place during a period in which the Conservatives were politically secure. The opposition parties offered little threat and internal dissent within the Party was muted and ineffectual. That was certainly not to be the case by the early 1990s. Criminal justice policy was to bear the brunt of that.

It is difficult to envisage a policy reversal in any area of public policy on par with that which took place in criminal justice policy under Michael Howard. From a point somewhere in 1992, the whole edifice of the late-1980s agenda began to crumble. The factors underpinning this shift are discussed elsewhere (Savage, 1998a; Dunbar and Langdon, 1998; Wilson and Ashton, 1998:), but they include the traumas and public anxieties associated with the killing of James Bulger, a two-year-old murdered by two young boys, internal dissent within the Conservative Party over Europe, and the rapid decline in public support for the Conservatives relative to Labour post- the 1992 general election. Law and order policy was to become a key player as this crisis unfolded.

At the 1993 Conservative Party Annual Conference, Howard announced his notorious '27 measures' to combat crime. These covered virtually every aspect of the criminal justice process, from amendments to the right of silence – against the recommendations of the 1993 Royal Commission on Criminal Justice, suspects were to lose their unfettered right to remain silent (judges could now comment negatively on a suspect's decision to remain silent) – to a clamp-down on squatting, anti-hunt demonstrations and even 'rave' parties! But it was the declaration that 'prison works', discussed later, which attracted most attention. At a stroke it created clear blue water between the Howard regime and the Conservative criminal justice policy which immediately preceded it. The prison had returned as the key weapon against crime. We were back to getting 'tough' again.

Howard had dramatically raised the stakes of the law and order debate. Perhaps he was forced to. Whereas as late as April 1992 opinion polls were showing that 41 per cent of those polled thought that the Conservative Party had 'the best policies on crime', by March 1993 that figure had dropped to 19 per cent (*The Guardian*, 21 March 1994). The 'party of law and order' was losing ground fast. The potential electoral fall-out from this threatened to be disastrous. 'Regaining the high ground' on law and order had become a number one priority. Howard's pledges, however, set in motion a spiral of rhetoric which the Labour Party in opposition was soon to engage with, and with surprising (some would say distasteful) enthusiasm. Rather than seek to counter

Howard's new agenda with a critique of the effectiveness of custody as
a penal strategy, Labour chose a very different tack: it decided to take
the Conservatives on at their own game, although to a certain extent it
initially did this by a policy of quiet support, rather than the development of new policies.

Labour – the New Party of Law and Order?

Traditionally, law and order had never been particularly high on
Labour's policy agenda. Indeed, it has been argued that Labour's record
had been one more of a policy vacuum than a specific and positive set
of policies (Downes and Morgan, 1997). In so far as policies existed
they related more to concerns over civil liberties, prisoners' rights, or
police accountability than with particular policies on crime reduction as
such (Goddard, 1997). When it came to finding 'solutions' to crime,
emphasis was placed on unemployment, deprivation, and so on, an
explanation all too often cast as an 'excuse' by the Conservatives (Nash,
1994/5). While legitimate in itself, this approach failed to address the
scope for crime reduction which existed from *within* the criminal justice system itself.

Labour's stance was to change dramatically in the political discourse
that emerged between the 1992 and 1997 general elections. The slogan
which best expressed this shift was Blair's dictum 'Tough on crime,
tough on the causes of crime' (*The Independent*, 4 December 1993), one
launched while Blair was Shadow Home Secretary and one eventually
to figure in the Labour Manifesto (Labour Party, 1997b). It signalled
that Labour was concerned not only to tackle the (social) causes of
crime (whereby crime policy becomes in effect a sub-set of social policy), but it was to go a step further and enter into the less familiar territory of 'blame', 'condemnation' and 'personal responsibility'. This new
politics was made clear in Blair's subsequent statement, now as leader
of the Party:

> We should [not] seek to disavow personal responsibility for crime.
> That is, ultimately, to deny individuality. Those who commit crime
> should be brought to justice. Not to do so is unjust to their victims.
> (Blair, 1996)

This opened up a new agenda for 'action' against offenders and it was
Labour's way of avoiding the old accusation from the Right that in

focusing solely on the causes of crime they were in effect soft on crime or apologists for criminals. By setting up an agenda for tough action on crime Labour found itself able to claim, as it did in the Party Manifesto, 'Labour is the party of law and order in Britain today' (Labour Party, 1997b).

When Jack Straw took over as Shadow Home Secretary, the stakes were raised even higher in the game of rhetoric with Howard. To the bemusement of many on the Left, Straw proved to be no shrinking violet in the dark art of 'law 'n' order' speak. For example, he lambasted 'squeegee merchants' and 'winos' as part of his attack on 'anti-social behaviour':

> In conjunction with tackling the underlying causes of crime, the community has the right to expect more responsible and less anti-social behaviour from its citizens. That means less intimidation, bullying and loutish behaviour on the streets and in our towns and city centres. (Straw, 1995)

It is important, however, not to exaggerate the importance of Straw's pre-election posturings on crime and disorder, as some of his critics were prone to do. Much of what Straw had to say was about rhetorical horse-trading; behind that Labour had developed a fairly coherent set of policies which those critics were soon to find comfort in (see Charman and Savage, 1999). As rhetoric it seemed to have achieved its goal: to challenge the Tories' past monopoly as the party which could stake claim to be *the* party of law and order. At the very least, it helped neutralise the Conservatives' threat in this area of policy – in the months running up to the 1997 general election, public opinion polls had the two parties running neck-and-neck in terms of public support for their approach to law and order (*The Times*, 28 February 1997).

On winning the election, it was now a question of which policies were to follow. The Labour Party Manifesto had highlighted a number of priorities for future action. These included: fast-track punishment for persistent young offenders, a crackdown on petty crimes and 'neighbourhood disorder', reform of the Crown Prosecution Service, crime prevention and more police officers 'on the beat'. Many of the Conservatives' 'heavy end' measures in terms of sentencing and dealing with sex offenders would be pursued with vigour. Whatever the populist flavour of some of the measures proposed, what underpinned the new agenda was a serious and far-reaching programme to tackle crime, employing strategies far more radical than many liberal critics had, at that stage at least, realised. The way in which those strategies might be developed, the overall tenor of the policies, however, can be open to more than one interpretation. It is to those *policies* that we now turn, beginning with policing.

Policing Policy

It may appear as mundane for the Labour Party to declare in its 1997 Election Manifesto 'The police have our strong support'. However, what this sentiment symbolised was a cultural shift which marked New Labour out from Labour of old. Whilst it would have been an exaggeration to dub Labour 'anti-police', it is difficult to deny that Labour's relationship with the police, particularly through the 1980s, was less than warm. The clashes between Labour-dominated metropolitan authorities and certain chief constables in the early- to mid-1980s, over the question of 'who controls the police?' (Reiner, 1992), had fuelled the view that Labour was indeed 'anti-police'. At the very least, what emerged was an atmosphere of mutual suspicion surrounding the two parties (see Savage and Charman, 1996). The problem for New Labour was how to claim the title 'tough on crime' while being perceived as hostile to the police – the Conservatives could always accuse Labour of being more interested in controlling the police than controlling crime.

A turning point in this context came with the heated debate which surrounded the passage through Parliament of the Police and Magistrates' Courts Act 1994 (PMCA). This Act introduced radical changes to the relationship between central government, local police authorities and the police (see Leishman, Loveday and Savage, 1996). The Act reformed the local police authorities by reducing membership from the local authorities, introducing 'independent' members onto the police authorities, requiring police authorities to produce a 'local policing plan' and, most controversially, obliging all local police authorities to work towards 'national policing objectives' set out by the Home Secretary. For many, it was a step towards government control of policing and a significant loss of local accountability. What the legislation did was help form some unusual campaign alliances (Cope, Leishman and Starie, 1996), including one between senior police officers, in the shape of the Association of Chief Police Officers (ACPO), and Labour politicians, who together fought against central features of the Act, with some success (ibid). Tony Blair, as Shadow Home Secretary, made a keynote speech at the ACPO Conference in 1993, one apparently well received by the audience. A new understanding seemed to be emerging; Labour could begin to undermine its image as being 'anti-police'. From that point onwards, Labour, first in opposition and subsequently in government, has worked more closely than ever with organisations representing the police in developing a policy for policing, some on the left would say too closely (see Savage, Charman and Cope, 1997).

Labour's subsequent policies on policing have been both a continuation of and a departure from the policies of the Conservatives. Labour has accepted the constitutional reforms of the PMCA but has seen within the Act the potential, perhaps underestimated by its critics (see Savage, 1998b), for *increasing* local influence over policing. For example, the Home Office has encouraged local police authorities to engage in extensive local consultation in drawing up the 'local policing plan' for the area. More generally, the Home Secretary has made clear his view that local police authorities should move from being the 'Cinderella' of the tripartite system (in comparison with the Home Office and the chief constable) to a central player in the development of policing policy. There is no doubt that the 'best value' agenda, which introduces new powers for local authorities to scrutinise and challenge the performance of service providers (DETR, 1998), will further this process. The enhancement of the local police authorities is likely to be reinforced by the relatively greater assertiveness emerging from within by the new body representing all police authorities, the Association of Police Authorities (APA). This was apparent in the first Annual Report of APA, which stated that the establishment of the Association was 'the first time police authorities have been able to speak with one authoritative voice, *alongside our tripartite partners*, ACPO and the Home Office' (APA, 1998, p. 1; emphasis added). Ironically, Labour has, with the apparent support of the police, rekindled the agenda of extending the local accountability of the police which so damaged Labour's relationship with the police in the early 1980s (Reiner, 1992).

If Labour's strategy for police governance skews responsibilities and power more in favour of the local authorities (a process accentuated by the Crime and Disorder Act 1998, as we shall see below), another development promises to change the shape of the whole system of local governance. The commitment to the process of *regionalisation* (see Chapter 2) will have a profound impact on the geography of police governance (Savage, 1998b). Labour's commitment to the establishment of regional assemblies will, it could be argued, mean that in the not too distant future a dozen or so 'regional police forces' could replace the existing

43 separate forces in England and Wales. The Conservatives had caused consternation by including provisions for amalgamations of police forces in PMCA; regionalisation could dwarf that agenda. While the Conservatives' interest in amalgamation was largely driven by the concern for efficiency savings, the regionalisation of policing will be more concerned with the process of 'power sharing' through devolution and, arguably, involve the diminution of central controls over policing (ibid). Perhaps more radically, regionalisation could pose new challenges to the hallowed doctrine of 'constabulary independence', the principle that senior police officers can invoke, whereby no authority can direct a chief police officer on policing policy or police actions – that has been the exclusive province of the police themselves (Lustgarten, 1986). Individual chiefs will now be under increasing pressure to develop policies for their forces within frameworks imposed by the regional authorities, rather than enjoy what has been effectively local autonomy of decision-making.

Another emerging theme of Labour's approach to the police has been the more robust stance it has taken, in comparison to the Conservatives, on the issue of police *expenditure*. There is evidence that Labour is not prepared to 'bank roll' the service in the way the Conservatives had done. Throughout the 1980s and early 1990s, the police were made very much a 'special case' *vis-à-vis* the rest of the public sector and levels of spending were kept above the going rate for other public services. They were of course not exempt from the Financial Management Initiative, but they were not subjected to anything like the 'Value for Money' regimes of their colleagues in the other sectors. Although Labour have not fully reversed this trend, the fact that in the 1998 spending review the police were required to achieve efficiency savings of 2 per cent over the year sent out the message that they are to be brought more in line with the rest of the public sector; this will in many ways be a painful process for the police, particularly so in the light of the relative laxity of financial regimes of the past. To this is coupled the demand for 'best value' in policing, as noted earlier, in line with the other public services. In the policing context, where 'best value' parts ways with the old 'value for money' principle is in its insistence that service policy is constantly reviewed in terms of public, or 'consumer', satisfaction and that all policies be judged in terms of evidence of their successful 'outcomes' (Savage, Charman and Cope, 2000). This heralds an era of much greater attention, inside and outside of the service, to the effectiveness of police methods and strategies.

Another source of change within policing policy stems from Northern Ireland (see Chapter 13). As part of the peace process the government set up a Commission, under former Conservative Party Chairman Chris Patten, to examine the Royal Ulster Constabulary (RUC) and consider possible areas for reform. The Commission's deliberations and recommendations, whilst targeted primarily at the specific situation in Northern Ireland, will almost certainly help to shape the debate over the future of policing in the rest of the United Kingdom. The Commission's recommendations cover areas such as a fully independent system for the investigation of complaints, new powers for local authorities to determine policing policy and more robust forms of monitoring and accountability of police decisions and actions (Independent Commission on Policing for Northern Ireland,1999). These have resonance far beyond Northern Ireland; in many respects the work of Patten and his fellow Commissioners constititues the nearest thing to a 'Royal Commission on the Police' since the early 1960s. The messages are there for all who wish to see them.

On a final note in this respect, despite the development of a positive working relationship between the Labour government and the police, there is evidence that the Home Secretary has been less than satisfied with the quality of the service the police are delivering or of the senior police officers responsible for it. In the late 1990s Labour set up a series of working parties to review police recruitment and training, including the selection and training of chief officers. Anxieties within the government stemmed from a number of sources. The apparent growth of police corruption, most notably within the Metropolitan Police Service – accounting for one-fifth of the police service of England and Wales – set off alarm bells about the types of officers employed by the police and about the ability of police managers to adequately supervise and control them. The highly publicised case of Stephen Lawrence, a young black man brutally murdered by white racists, has raised even more concerns. The failure of the Metropolitan police to act professionally in the pursuit of his killers was associated with problems of racism and poor management, factors spelt out explicitly in Macpherson's Report on the incidents surrounding the Lawrence case. More generally the debate over the extent of police racism, 'institutionalised' or otherwise, had been placed back on the agenda with a vengeance. All of this points to more radical reform of the British police in the years ahead, as Labour seeks to address what seems to be some deep organisational deficiencies within the service.

Criminal Justice Legislation

It has been noted that the 1980s was a period of intense activity in terms of criminal justice legislation. Labour has shown no sign of being any less active. Crime policy was an early priority for the incoming government and it lost no time in putting into place a number of major legislative measures, some of which were effectively inherited from the Conservatives and adapted, and others which very much bore the hallmarks of the New Labour agenda.

The Crime and Disorder Act 1998

Undoubtedly the centre piece of the new policy framework for crime control was the Crime and Disorder Act 1998 (CDA). This single piece of legislation, above all, mapped out the very different approach to crime policy which Labour intended to inaugurate. Most certainly, it constituted a radical departure from the Conservatives' 'offender' and 'deterrent/punishment' oriented philosophy for crime reduction. It set in motion strategy much more targeted at *crime prevention and community safety* than deterring potential offenders through tough punishments.

The CDA is extremely far-reaching (Leng, Taylor and Wasik, 1999). However, its main features can be summarised under headings:

1. *Community Safety*: The Act introduced a range of measures designed to make communities 'safer'. This includes new 'anti-social behaviour orders' which, as mentioned earlier, are available to combat 'noisy neighbours' and rowdy behaviour, more generally to deal with 'petty incivilities and public nuisance'. Additionally, under this heading are new procedures for limiting the mobility of and increasing the monitoring of convicted sex offenders (this in response to public anxieties over child sex offenders living in close proximity to children – expanded below). More fundamentally, under the community safety umbrella comes a major initiative in crime prevention. An obligation is placed on local authorities, the police, police authorities, health authorities and probation committees to work *in partnership* to develop and implement a strategy for tackling crime and disorder in their area; they will have a joint and formally stated responsibility for protecting the public and for maintaining *community safety*. As part of the process of forming a strategy for tackling crime and disorder, the police and the local

authorities will be required to conduct a *crime audit* for their areas, which reviews patterns of crime and problems of disorder in those areas, which will form the basis of action against crime. This is consistent with the government's backing for 'evidence-based policy', as referred in other chapters in this collection.

2. *Youth Crime and Youth Justice:* A range of measures are introduced to target youth crime, in line with Labour's acceptance of the principle of *social crime prevention*, an approach which emphasises the effectiveness of early intervention with 'vulnerable' young people as a crime control strategy (Pease, 1997). Young offenders can now have passed on them a 'detention and training order' and, as part of their sentence, be required to follow an 'action plan', a package of interventions designed to rehabilitate the offender in a more structured and purposeful way than previously. New 'parenting orders' are established placing various requirements on parents to take formal responsibilities for their offending or disorderly children – including an obligation on 'problem parents' to undertake counselling in parenting skills. 'Child curfew' schemes and powers for the police to 'round up' truants support this package. More strategically, the Act seeks to establish an effective youth justice system and a more concerted local policy for dealing with young offenders. Local authorities will be required to establish *youth offending teams* and the statutory bodies will be required to formulate 'annual youth justice plans'; a range of measures will be taken to speed up the process of youth justice through the youth courts.

3. *Criminal Law and Sentencing:* The Act introduced a number of new offences relating to racial violence and racial harassment. Concern had been raised in ethnic minority communities that racial or racist motives behind harassment and violence had not been acknowledged in law. The brutal murder in 1993 of Stephen Lawrence, a young black man killed by a gang in London, brought this issue sharply into focus. The Act sought to address this by creating new categories of offences relating to 'racially aggravated' assault and 'racially aggravated' criminal damage. The courts would now be able to pass more severe sentences where a racial motivation was thought to be an element of the offence. Another significant innovation in the Act lies with the 'reparation order'. In addition to the new orders for young offenders referred to above, the courts can now require an offender to 'make good' the damage they have done by working in the community for specified periods of time on tasks relating to their offence, for example, by cleaning up graffiti or

making repairs to property. This seeks to go further than a 'compensation order' which is essentially a financial measure, and is designed to positively encourage the offender to accept the damage and hurt they have caused. This is broadly consistent with the principle of 'restorative justice', fast becoming established as a paradigm for criminal justice (Pease, 1997), which stresses the importance of encouraging offenders to understand the impact of their crimes by engaging them in a positive relationship with the victims of their behaviour.

On a final note regarding sentencing, the Act seeks to enhance consistency in sentencing by the courts by creating new mechanisms for the setting of sentences. The Lord Chancellor is responsible under the Act for setting up a panel to act as an advisory body which will be tasked with developing more definitive *sentencing guidelines* for the courts, thus, it is hoped, strengthening the framework within which sentencing can take place. However, this may be viewed as a watered-down measure compared with Labour's original support for a Sentencing Council.

The CDA will most probably act as the flagship of New Labour's agenda for criminal justice and to a great extent has the potential to become an essentially liberal and progressive piece of legislation, one accepting of the criminological research on the most effective strategies for crime control. However, the Act also contains the potential, as do other Labour policies, to be as tough, if not tougher than the Conservatives. The effect of Labour will now be considered in the light of other areas of criminal justice policy and emphasis will now be given to the potential down-side of the new agenda.

Probation to Correction?

The final phase of the Conservative government also appeared to be signalling the end of the line for the probation service 'as we know it'. There had of course already been significant shifts in the policy and working of that service under successive Conservative governments. It had responded to an ever more punitive climate in ways which, at least in the short term, appeared to guarantee its future. It had been placed at the centre stage of criminal justice policy delivery by the 1991 Criminal Justice Act (CJA), although in so doing began to shift significantly from its social work roots. Although it might be argued that this was inevitable, the rapidity and extent of the change, supported by a bullish managerialist culture, undoubtedly eased the path towards the fundamental shifts which will be described below (for views on this debate, see for example, Worrall, 1997; Brownlee, 1998; and McWilliams, 1985, 1986 and 1992).

We have already commented on the 'non' debate on criminal justice which emerged during the last Conservative government. However, it should be noted that by quietly accepting the Conservative agenda, the Labour Party effectively went about raising the stakes, with serious consequences for a variety of criminal justice agencies. Within this 'debate' on the future of criminal justice policy, the probation service was again to play a major role, although initially it appeared as if this role was to see a decline in its importance. The Home Secretary having declared that 'prison works' in 1993, the service was faced with the bleak prospect of falling resources, privatisation of key elements of its work, greater central control and a more punitive, correctional role. This for a service which had already transformed itself as a result of government initiatives (and at times in attempting to be one step ahead, e.g. ACOP, 1988). Discussion of rehabilitation was not really a feature of the political scene in the lead-up to the 1997 election; indeed agencies found themselves pushed into an ever tighter corner as a result of Howard's attempts to save the government from defeat (Nash, 1999a). The probation service looked particularly vulnerable, not least when the Home Secretary decided to end the requirement for probation officers to hold the professional qualification in social work in 1994. As public protection began to dominate the agenda, fuelled by the importation of various American populist measures (Dunbar and Langdon, 1998; Nash, 1999a), agencies such as the probation service were being re-cast in the mould of public protectors whose first duty was to protect the public. Unfortunately perhaps, the method of achieving this task was not to include much of the good work which the probation service had done in the past with serious and high risk offenders (Shaw, 1996; Coker and Martin, 1985), but was to follow a managerialist-friendly group-work-based agenda, which may already begin to be showing signs of not being as universally applicable as the government would have us believe.

The election of the Labour government in 1997 did not hold out any immediate hope for a quick reversal of the punitive climate in which the probation service had become enmeshed. Jack Straw, both in Opposition and as new Home Secretary, did not make any early changes to the law-and-order rhetoric; indeed it could be argued that he had become more punitive than his predecessor, not only implementing the Crime (Sentences) Act but going further in the measures against sex offenders (itself driving the wider agenda). There was to be no hoped-for reversal of the social work training decision, although Straw's delay in implementing the change did lead to a significant concession in allowing the new award of a Diploma in Probation Studies to be linked to a first degree awarded by universities. Tough talk has continued and the threat to the continued survival of the probation service has not disappeared. Indeed there were two significant events which certainly cast doubt upon that survival. The first ever appointment of a joint minister for prisons and probation (Joyce Quinn) gave an indication of perhaps yet another recasting of the probation service role. This was followed by a review of both organisations, established by Straw and reporting in July 1998. It considered, as one of its options, the amalgamation of these two services, ostensibly to create a seamless transition from custody to community penalties. The final report (Home Office, 1998b) recommended against merger but a much greater harmonisation of the objectives of each service.

Undoubtedly the move towards the probation service becoming a Next Steps agency, fewer probation areas, and greater central control over the probation officer training curriculum, will all lead to a considerable reshaping of role, responsibility and accountability. The reduction in the number of probation areas will introduce coterminosity with CPS and police areas, again a move towards harmonisation of goals. A change of name had remained a strong possibility, with the Home Secretary allegedly favouring the title of 'corrections officer', and the probation service, perhaps predictably, favouring 'community justice officers'. The government then announced that the new name would be Community Punishment and Rehabilitation Service. This was met with hostility and derision with critics quickly reforming the acronym to make CRAP and probation officers becoming CRAPOS. The resistance to the name, resurrecting much of the Parliamentary support for the probation service, eventually led to a government climb-down. In the Criminal Justice and Court Services Bill (CJCS) placed before Parliament in March 2000 the new name was announced as The National Probation Service for England and Wales. However the government renamed probation orders as community rehabilitation orders, and community service orders as community punishment orders – it was still pulling the strings. The forthcoming loss of the civil work functions of the probation service, moving to the Lord Chancellor's Department in April 2001 and renamed Children and Family Court

Advisory and Support Service (CAFCAS), is a further strong indication that public protection and punishment in the community will remain the immediate task for the probation service and anything which appears to be linked with a 'social work' ethos will disappear.

One of the most significant developments of criminal justice policy under Blair has been the rapid move to shared and common agendas, a growth in multi-agency working and a very strong steer from the centre. The prisons/probation review is one example of this, as is the tremendous development of shared working between police and probation services in the area of dangerous offenders (Nash, 1999a and 1999b). The provisions of the CDA have put this collaboration on a statutory footing and perhaps is nowhere better shown than in the new arrangements for dealing with youth offending, summarised above and now considered in greater detail.

'No More Excuses'

The very title of this important Home Office document (Home Office, 1997a) is reflective of the political climate which not only marked the end of the Conservative government, but also the early months of its Labour successor. The tone of non-acceptance, perhaps as much for public consumption as for any policy end, is not immediately encouraging of an approach which will be 'tough on the causes of crime', yet there is enough within the new proposals to suggest that this is possible with the right political will. The measures themselves can be seen as grouping around the notion of 'responsibility', much loved by the previous administration. Parental responsibility was a feature of many Conservative policies and this has been continued and extended by the Blair administration. Many of the ideas can be seen as American imports, such as the local child curfew orders and parenting orders mentioned above. These orders aim to curb the movement of children at certain times and in certain places and also reinforce parental skills, crime being seen as seated within the family. Underpinning much of the government's criminal justice strategy is a policy of 'confronting offending', making offenders face up to their responsibilities. Unfortunately this approach tends to negate what has gone before and, in the words of the Home Secretary concerning youth crime, 'This White Paper seeks to draw a line under the past and sets out a new approach to tackling youth crime.' As Jack Straw said, there was to be an end to the 'excuse culture', although perhaps here he fell into the same rhetoric of his predecessors which viewed explanation as excuse (Nash, 1994/5).

Undoubtedly the measures outlined for tackling youth crime constitute a fundamental shake-up of the previous system. As well as the measures mentioned above, a host of others have been established. These include reparation orders (up to 24 hours), a child safety order (to protect at risk children under 10 years of age, requiring them to be at home at certain times or keep away from certain places) and, under a general heading of 'restoring hope and opportunity', to support families by seeking to improve school achievement, the provision of nursery places, action on drugs and jobs/training as well as a determined assault on school exclusion under the personal direction of the Prime Minister. Such measures reveal a slightly hybrid character to the new legislation. Many of the measures aimed at limiting movement of children and resocialising parents could be viewed as draconian, the 'tough' part of Blair's slogan. Yet many of the other, more long-term measures, undoubtedly reflect the 'causes' approach. As ever with criminal justice policy it will be interesting to see if the long-term approach is given an opportunity to succeed. Certainly in the short term the measures are tough, and in proposing to abolish *doli incapax* (the principle that young children cannot be deemed liable for their 'criminal' actions) represent a massive break with the past. The opportunity to incarcerate younger children for longer has been given by the new detention and training order (10–17-year-olds), a considerable departure from the discussions which preceded the 1991 CJA concerning the abolition of custody for children.

Another key feature of the new agenda is a reduction in the time it takes for matters to be dealt with by the courts, with the government intending to reduce the average time that it inherited by one half. The reduction of delay within the criminal justice system is to be a major feature on the Blair government's agenda. Home Office Circular 24/1998 is concerned with reducing delay and proposes measures which impact upon many areas of the criminal justice process. The government intend to 'introduce clear and enforceable statutory time limits on the stages in criminal proceedings' by the autumn of 2000. The pursuance of greater speed in court proceedings will also challenge many established practices. The report produced by Narey (Home Office, 1997b) has led to what have become known as 'Narey pilots' in six areas around the country. These have the following features:

- CPS lawyers to provide out of hours service
- CPS lawyers and caseworkers to work in police stations
- CPS caseworkers reviewing and presenting uncomplicated cases in the Magistrates' Court

- early first hearings in Magistrates' Court
- a system of case management in Magistrates' Court
- indictable only cases sent direct to Crown Court after initial hearing to deal with bail

It could be seen that some of these measures represent a regression to previously abandoned practice. For example, the siting of CPS staff back into police stations takes the situation back to pre-1984 and calls into question the 'independence' of people working within that environment (although the Runciman Royal Commission (1993) had also proposed this measure). It remains to be seen if proposals aimed at ensuring a speedier delivery of justice to offender and victim alike, compromise principles of justice in pursuit of management efficiency.

Prisons on the Receiving End

Prisons have undoubtedly been the main 'beneficiaries' of the more punitive penal climate which emerged after 1993. 'Prison Works' managed to significantly raise the prison population even before the legislation was passed in Parliament, demonstrating the close link between public opinion and prison use (Bingham, 1997). Prison population growth was phenomenal during the 1990s, outstripping all official forecasts, and in 1999 just about holding steady at approximately 65,000. This sustained growth has meant that the Home Secretary has not been able to honour his own commitment to end prison privatisation, something which was regarded as 'morally repugnant' prior to the election. Indeed, privatisation is expected to continue apace and has even stretched to probation bail hostels. Such is the problem with prison overcrowding that on 28 January 1999, an experiment began of releasing prisoners early from their sentences provided that they agreed to electronic 'tagging'. This measure has been supported by the probation service. Up to 30,000 prisoners were expected to be released under 'home detention curfews' (sections 99–105 CDA 1998) in the first year. Prisoners will be released for the final two months of their sentence following internal prison service assessment.

The prison population explosion has not only been fuelled by tough talk, however; legislation has contributed significantly to the problem. Once elected, the Labour government moved quickly to implement the Crime (Sentences) Act, 1997. This Act, the brainchild of

Michael Howard, introduced a range of minimum, mandatory sentences for specific crimes, along the lines of America's 'three strikes and you're out' provision (Schichor and Sechrest, 1996). The Act makes provision for mandatory life sentences for certain second-time violent and sexual offences as well as mandatory minimum seven-year sentences for certain third-time drug dealers. A provision for a mandatory minimum three-year sentence for third-time burglars was not included in the Act by the Labour government. However, in January 2000 this provision was taken off the shelf, dusted down and enacted by Jack Straw. It is this ability to extend the use of sentences such as these to a variety of offenders that perhaps causes most consternation amongst rights activists (see, for example, Thomas, 1997). However, as long as the new sentencing arrangements were cast in the clothes of 'public protection' it was unlikely to receive much opposition (Nash, 1999a).

Public protection has indeed driven the criminal justice agenda in the past few years, with seemingly little difference in policy between Conservative and Labour administrations. The Sex Offenders Act, 1997 is another example of a Michael Howard measure upon which the Labour government has built. The Act, among other things, introduced the Sex Offenders Register, requiring a range of sex offenders to register their whereabouts with the police. The duration of the registration depends upon the original sentence, but for anyone who had served more than 30 months in custody, the period was indefinite. The register does not however offer much in the way of proactive protection, as chief police and probation officers have pointed out. To cover some of the loopholes in supervision, a sex offender order enables the police to apply to the courts for essentially injunction-type measures which may prohibit certain sex offenders from frequenting certain places at certain times. The measure is a civil one based on the balance of probability, but breaching it is a criminal offence carrying a maximum penalty of five years in custody. It is a measure which massively increases the responsibility of the police in dealing with sex offenders in the community and has been a major stimulus to the growth in its working with other agencies. Once again little opposition has been raised against these measures but it is increasingly likely that challenges will be made under the Human Rights Act, 1998. It must be of concern that a caution for one of the qualifying offences is sufficient to trigger the legislation and there will undoubtedly be implications for advice given to suspects in the police station in the future.

Tough Talk – Tough Action

Earlier in this chapter we described the u-turns in Conservative policy. However, the Labour Party in government, if not turning so sharply, have already shifted a long way. Jack Straw, for the first fifteen months of office, uttered not much that was different from Michael Howard. Despite the longer-term social crime prevention measures outlined earlier, the rhetoric was still tough and the prison population rose in line. However, in July 1998, prison works suddenly became 'prison doesn't work – official!', with the move to and endorsement of evidence-based practice. This way of working is to cover the whole range of criminal justice agencies, from police through to prison and probation officers. This undoubtedly reflects the bigger-picture approach of Labour and a sincere desire to establish common goals across a range of criminal justice agencies. However, in so doing it is likely that individual and agency discretion will be severely reduced and that central control will increase considerably. The Conservative tradition of 'funding following effectiveness' will continue under Labour but there is a chance that effectiveness becomes the achievement of managerial objectives rather than a real reduction in crime. At the present time the government is convinced that crime will be reduced by effective working but the real test of its resolve will come if crime rates do not fall but opinion poll ratings do. The populist measures persist however, with the CJCS Bill promising three months in custody if a probationer fails for the second time in 12 months and continuing discussions concerning the loss of benefits for non-compliance.

Conclusion

It can be seen that Labour's strategy for crime and disorder is very much a mixed package. On the one hand we have bold – many would argue, eminently sound – measures which draw upon the evidence that crime prevention is a more effective means of controlling crime than approaches which focus primarily on the penal system and deterrent methods for crime reduction. The general insistence on 'evidence-based' policy, with an emphasis on judging criminal justice agencies and their activities in terms of their impact on the community rather than simply their costs, is laudable and, in the wake of the Conservatives, refreshing. On the other hand, as we have seen, Labour remains committed to penal measures, particularly those relating to the extension of custodial punishments, which appear to be more politically driven than formed on the basis of 'evidence'. There is an inconsistency here which is difficult to reconcile. This is exacerbated by the apparent determination of the Home Secretary to push through measures to restrict the right to trial by jury – by ending the automatic right of defendents in 'triable either way' offences to elect for jury-trial. This is something even Michael Howard balked at, despite its appeal. Furthermore, what this reveals above all is the capacity for crime policy to be prey, periodically at least, to the forces of political expediency. Even a government so explicitly committed to 'joined up' and 'research-based' policy seems unable to resist that temptation.

However, perhaps the most enduring legacy of the Blair government for many will be the Human Rights Act, 1998. This Act will make the European Convention on Human Rights far more central to the law in Britain and will necessitate all past and future law passed in Parliament being compatible with the Convention. Whether or not this Act makes the criminal law less susceptible to the type of crude politicking charted in this chapter remains to be seen, but undoubtedly politicians may have to think twice in the future. This Act personifies the 'big picture' approach of the Blair government and offers hope that measures such as the Crime and Disorder Act will build on the positives rather than fall prey to the potential pitfalls of everyday politics.

8

Health Policy

NANCY NORTH

The NHS, over which Labour assumed control after eighteen years in opposition, had a changed structure, orientation and culture, but its allegiance to the founding principles remained. In May 1997 the fundamental commitment to provide an extensive range of health care to all the population on the basis of need rather than the ability to pay was still intact, although debates about what should be provided were now more resonant and acute. Claims that the NHS was underfunded, though undoubtedly reasonable when compared with health spending in European counterparts, were part of a continuing professional and occasionally public dissatisfaction with the adequacy of service provision. In general, levels of satisfaction with the NHS were more unstable and less positive (Bosanquet and Zarzecka, 1995) and the patient more prepared to go to litigation to secure redress. There were elements of the Conservative reforms which sat uncomfortably with even the revised doctrine of New Labour, but others were apparently worth preserving. This chapter will chart the major developments in health policy during the 18 years of Conservative governments: the legacy of May 1997. The Labour government's emerging policies, signalled in its first years of office, will be discussed, as will possible future developments.

The most obvious change to the NHS during the Conservatives' years in office was the creation of the internal market. The policy had been instigated by a small review group established and led by Margaret Thatcher in 1988 in response to mounting criticism about funding levels and NHS performance. Committing the state to increasing levels of health care expenditure was never on the agenda and brief consideration of alternative systems of funding confirmed the view that the control of expenditure, afforded by a centrally funded service, could not be improved on (Klein, 1995). Instead the review proposed a purchaser–provider split, described by Timmins as 'a core idea of the Thatcher era, applied not just to the welfare state, but to a large part of government' (1995, p. 458). This removed hospitals and community services from the managerial control of health authorities and allocated them, respectively, provider and purchaser roles. Providers could no longer depend upon year by year funding of their services but had to 'compete' for contracts, *ipso facto* they would become more efficient and responsive to purchasers' requirements. Health authorities were quite predictable as purchasers in any such division of responsibilities, but a far more radical element in the policy created another type of purchaser: GP fundholders.

In order to limit the risks of GP fundholding the Conservative government restricted first wave applications to practices with patient list sizes over 11,000 and limited the range of items that could be purchased to the predictable, quantifiable and less expensive items – certain elective procedures and outpatient sessions. A cap of £5,000 for hospital costs per patient per year was also introduced, and the calculation of funds, although somewhat variable, was generally thought to err on the side of generosity (Day and Klein, 1991), to the disadvantage of patients of non-fundholders (Pollock *et al.*, 1995). GP fundholders seemed to exert an influence over trusts far in excess of their purchasing capacity, dwarfed as it was by that of health authorities. The very size of health authorities was their problem. They could not readily exit from local health care markets without destabilising local providers. The undoubted entrepreneurial virtuosity of some GP fundholders was no doubt aided by the trusts' realisation that fundholders could more easily take their business elsewhere, though an Audit Commission (1996) report indicates that this was uncommon.

Research suggests that fundholding led to improvements in the organisation of secondary care for fundholders' patients (Glennerster *et al.*, 1994) and perhaps more generally (Harrison and Choudhry, 1996). The Audit Commission (1996) similarly identified improvements, such as improved communication with providers and better management of waiting lists, but was critical of the lack of coordination between health authority and fundholder purchasing plans and of the tendency of fundholders to ignore evidence about clinical effectiveness in their purchasing arrangements. Additionally the initiative has been criticised for more generously resourcing fundholders' patients than non-fundholders (Whitehead, 1993; Dixon and Glennerster, 1995). As a result of this and the leverage fundholders could exert on providers, a 'two tier' system was created (Mohan, 1991; Baggott, 1994). The Conservative government acted quickly to prevent the most obvious injustice, the 'queue-jumping' of fundholding patients on hospital waiting lists, but did not require health authorities to reclaim any proportion of fund under-spends. The savings of some earlier fundholders and the use to which they were sometimes put were also controversial (Butler, 1994) but to disallow savings would have discouraged existing and potential fund-holders. With successive fundholding 'waves' the proportion of patients covered by fundholding practices gradually increased, from 7 per cent in 1991/2 to a politically significant 51 per cent in 1996/7 (source for figures: NHS Executive, personal communication,1997). The 1996/7 total included two further categories of fundholders (community fund-holding and total fundholding) and practices whose list size was 5,000 or more. These measures represented an attempt to trawl the small, lure the reluctant and extend the enthusiastic. Thus by May 1997 the new Labour government was presented with a significant core of GPs who, having opted to become fundholders and invested the additional effort it required, were loath to surrender the privileges and power associated with the scheme.

The internal or quasi-market aroused a great deal of criticism. More accustomed to treating each other with suspicion, the Labour opposition and the BMA were as one in their belief that any semblance of a mar-ket in British health care should be forcefully resisted on principle (Klein, 1995). Others raised more pragmatic concerns, such as the potential transaction and administration costs of an internal market (Bartlett, 1991), the threat of privatisation and the risk of destabilising 'Britain's best loved institution' (Labour Party, 1996, p. 269). However, the 'steady state' imposed on health authorities in the first year was not followed by widespread purchaser promiscuity. Despite uncertainties in the new arrangements, which occasionally translated into purchaser heroics (Rea, 1995; North, 1997, 1998), more realistic relationships developed. These reflected local provider monopolies of services and, perhaps more critically, of information on services' costs and volumes and treatment effectiveness. The rhetoric about 'markets' and 'purchas-ing' was softened to 'managed care' and 'commissioning' which never-theless captured the tilt in the balance of power away from secondary care providers and clinicians to health authorities and primary care medical practitioners. Not opposed to this change in internal NHS pol-itics, Labour's opposition gravitated towards the particular – transaction costs, the yearly contracting round and fundholding – rather than the general principle of a separation of responsibilities for commissioners and providers (Labour Party, 1996).

In what might be considered an attempt to appease the patient, who could in no way be considered to be a true consumer in the internal maket, the Conservatives launched The Patient's Charter in 1991. This set out several undemanding service standards as well as a number of pre-existing rights. Providers, including GPs, were exhorted to develop their own local charters, against which they could be held accountable. Additionally, in what was possibly a well-meaning attempt to inform the public as well as applying further competitive pressure, the Department of Health published tables comparing the performance of trusts based on such measures as treatment waiting times and the percentage of treatments undertaken as day cases. The preoccupation with outputs rather than outcomes remained, but the shortcomings of both The Patient's Charter and the performance tables were overtaken by their symbolic importance. Such ratcheting of patient expectations presents something of a *fait accompli* for any government bent on controlling expenditure; an electorate protective of the NHS as an institution and made up of increasingly sophisticated consumers is likely to create pressure for more resources.

Quasi-markets and consumerist initiatives were therefore important strategies in the Conservatives' bid to improve efficiency and effectiveness in the NHS whilst controlling costs, a process which had begun with the introduction of general management. The recommendations of the NHS Management Inquiry (DHSS, 1983) ended consensus management, with its generous arrangements for representing the professions' views, and introduced a cadre of general managers sensitised to the requirements of central government by line management and personal performance reviews. However, progress was slow since medical enthusiasm for the proposals was predictably muted. Research by Harrison *et al.* (1992) found that the success managers enjoyed in exerting control over nursing and paramedical activities was not duplicated in medical practice. If anything, managers tended not to raise difficult issues in order to avoid confrontation with consultants. Nevertheless the Griffiths management reforms began a process of cultural reform in the NHS which challenged assumptions about the inviolability of medical decisions.

The ever-obvious gap between health care funding and the clinically possible was an important reason why the process of resource allocation had to be more pluralistic and informed, but of equal concern were apparent differences in medical practice, which might translate into unacceptable variations in clinical outcomes. Media coverage of tragic service failures has exposed the inadequacy of clinical review systems and the deficiencies of medicine's self-regulation. The much criticised performance indicators (see Radical Statistics Health Group, 1995; Powell, 1997), first introduced in the 1983/4 financial year, were not designed to review clinical practice. In June 1999 the Labour government produced tables ranking trust performance, based on such indicators as operative mortality and readmission rates; the tables were criticised for their methodological crudity but the initiative should be applauded as an initial attempt at exposing the unpalatable.

Whilst more refined versions of the league tables may signal the need to change professional practice, clinical audit pinpoints where and what form of remedial action is required. *Working for Patients* (Secretary of State for Health, 1989) made the hitherto voluntary system of medical audit mandatory for both hospital doctors and GPs but subsequent lobbying by the profession secured the principle of audit by peer review. A greater opportunity for the reform of hospital-based medical practice will come from a continued separation of commissioning and providing functions as the bank of information on best medical practice is developed and informs commissioning decisions. There is recognition that the clock cannot be turned back (Berwick *et al.*, 1992), a perception heightened by events at Bristol and elsewhere (see Treasure, 1998; Smith, 1998). Eighteen years of Conservative government had encouraged the realisation that the concept of clinical autonomy was relative not absolute, and, showing signs of some exasperation with professional self-regulation (driven no doubt as well by a series of high-profile medical 'scandals'), the Labour government has taken further, definitive measures.

Nor did the Conservatives leave GPs to their own devices. As part of a general strategy to contain health care costs, primary care, and in particular the prescribing and referral practices of GPs, needed managing. The Family Health Services' (FHS) proportion of NHS costs had risen sharply, both at the beginning of the 1980s and the 1990s (the latter partly due to the resourcing of fundholding), and within FHS costs the General Medical Services' bill increased steadily (source: Office of Health Economics Compendium of Health Statistics, 1997). The Conservative governments' strategies centred on controlling firstly prescribing behaviour and later, via an imposed new terms of service in 1990 (the GP Contract), a broader range of activities. The contract was designed to increase productivity in some areas (e.g. the uptake of immunisations and cervical smears), sensitise GPs to patients' requirements (by increasing the proportion of GP income derived from capitation payments) and improve health promotion. Although the initial, vitriolic hostilities over the contract's introduction subsided, conditions of service remained a source of rumbling discontent amongst GPs, feeding the perception of a growing workload in primary health care (Chambers and Belcher,1993; Leese and Bosanquet,1996). On the one hand, flattered by the attention and influence afforded by the Conservatives' vision of a primary care-led NHS (see, NHS Executive, 1994), by 1997 GPs were actively seeking a reinterpretation of their core functions as providers of primary medical care. The Labour government therefore inherited a medical workforce more responsive to the direction of NHS policy-makers but not particularly eager for new responsibilities.

The GP contract, though much criticised by the profession (*The Lancet*, 1989) reflected a reawakened, though narrowly defined, interest in public health. Like other European states, the UK formally adopted the European Regional Strategy in 1980. Based on the WHO's Declaration of Alma Ata, the Strategy offered a characteristically broad interpretation of states' responsibilities for the health of their populations. The Conservative government was slow in developing a national strategy, leaving it to local government and health authorities to coordinate a local response (Baggott, 1994). However, the Acheson Report (DoH, 1988) and, over a period, the influence of its author, Sir Donald Acheson, Chief Medical Officer, encouraged a more consistent approach. The publication of *The Health of the Nation* (Secretary of State for Health, 1992) marked a shift in policy which recognised a broader constituency responsible for the improvement of the nation's health than the NHS alone (Klein, 1995), but the White Paper has been criticised for setting overly modest targets (Mooney and Healey, 1991) and for its refusal to acknowledge the role of socio-economic factors in ill health. In contrast, the individual's responsibility for his/her own health was firmly delineated. Thus the Conservatives' approach to public health could be characterised as piecemeal. The government's refusal to tackle tobacco advertising contrasts with the zealousness of health authorities who, guided by directors of public health, incorporated Health of the Nation targets in their commissioning plans.

The Conservative governments' master plan for the NHS had been to squeeze more 'value for money' from the Service whilst keeping a tight reign on funding and an eye on the public sector borrowing requirement. There are inherent difficulties in determining whether the levels of NHS funding have been adequate (Ham, 1992; Powell, 1997; Ranade, 1997). Whilst expenditure on health care rose in real terms in the 1980s, even taking into account health inflation there was evidence of cuts in services (Powell, 1997). Ranade suggests that an annual budget increase of 2 per cent per annum is needed to cope with rising demands within the NHS, and despite efficiency savings required from health authorities the NHS experienced cumulative underfunding in the 1980s, which resulted in the funding crisis of 1997. In contrast, the introduction of the internal market was oiled by generous infusions of cash (Timmins, 1995) and primary health care in particular appears to have benefited, with allocations to the Family Health Services increasing from £7,847m in 1990 to £10,243m in 1996 (Office of Health Economics, 1997). Despite the Treasury's magnanimity, successive winters raised the spectre of a failing service as hospitals ceased elective surgery in order to cope with increasing numbers of emergency admissions. This is not so much an indication of a sicker population as perhaps a combination of a higher readmissions rate, failing community care arrangements leading to bed-blocking (Audit Commission, 1997), and of GPs more predisposed to seek admission for patients they might previously have managed in the community (Hensher and Edwards, 1996). The Labour government came into office with the pressing concern of how hospitals – or more accurately, patients – would survive the winter of 1997/8. More than three years on, there are still extreme difficulties.

New Labour – New Health Policies

Whatever other criticisms may be lodged against the new Labour government in their first term of office, lethargy was not one of them. In opposition Labour had criticised the internal market for its high transaction costs and for engendering a two-tier system whereby fundholders' patients gained preferential access to services. The demise of fundholding had been signalled by the abolition of the eighth wave of fundholding a few weeks after entering office, an action which the government declared would also release some £20m for patient services (Brindle, 1997). Subsequently the White Paper *The New NHS* (Secretary of State for Health, 1997) set out the broader strategy for dismantling the more competitive aspects of the internal market in England, although some sort of purchaser–provider divide was to remain. Similar measures were to be introduced in Wales (Secretary of State for Wales, 1998). *The New NHS* declared an intention to tread a path between the competitiveness of the previous arrangements and the 'command and control' planning systems of the 1970s. There was to be an emphasis on cooperation between commissioners and providers of health care services, as well as greater collaboration with social services and other agencies that might contribute to the health of communities.

In England and Wales, GPs have remained as the 'movers and shakers' of the new system. Primary Care Groups (PCGs) or Local Health Groups in Wales, covering localities of about 100,000, now commission community and hospital services from a budget covering these services, plus prescribing and general practice infrastructure costs. For those with little previous experience of locality commissioning there was to be a gentle introduction, but PCGs have been encouraged to progress towards independent Primary Care Trust (PCTs) status. The first of these was operational from April 2000. *The New NHS* may have signalled a more decentralised and pluralistic decision-making process, in that not only GPs but also community nurses, health authority members and executive officers and social services personnel now sit on PCG boards, but in reality GPs have dominated the political process. In the hard lobbying that followed publication of the White Paper, GPs gained numerical supremacy on, as well as the chairpersonship of, boards. In effect, they constitute a high-status, articulate and usually well-coordinated local interest group. PCT boards, comprising 11 members with a lay chairperson and four non-executive members, will wipe out this numerical advantage, since they will include only three professional representatives on the board. However, they will be selected from what probably will be the real source of decision-making in PCTs, an executive committee.

PCTs would appear to do away with the purchaser–provider divide, at least between primary and community health care services. Scotland's health service has already had some experience of this. Since fundholding never really took hold, the Health Boards have continued to be responsible for service development. They are expected to maintain a close relationship with Scottish Primary Care Trusts (SPCTs) in which GPs are expected to play a central management role (Secretary of State for Scotland, 1997). In that they provide a forum for both community health trusts and primary care, though without direct control of commissioning budgets, SPCTs might be considered as interesting but partial precursors of English PCTs

Although the apparent rejection of market culture was evident in both the rhetoric and the organisational reshuffling of Labour's early reforms, nevertheless a form of 'commissioner'–provider divide remains. Elsewhere the market was embraced more obviously and with greater enthusiasm. In opposition the Labour Party had been critical of the private finance initiative (PFI), introduced by the Conservatives in 1992 to encourage the private financing of capital projects in the NHS (Labour Party, 1996). In government Labour appears to have adopted a less radical approach, as befits a party that has moved from a socialist to a quasi-social democratic platform. Early criticisms of the scheme were that the servicing of the associated debt might force trusts to provide more profitable as opposed to needed services, or to extend operations in the private health care market (Mohan, 1997). Recent research on fourteen PFI schemes by Gaffney and Pollock (cited by Price, 1997) suggests that some changes in service provision were driven by the pressure placed on hospitals to service the debt rather than the desire to deliver improved health care outcomes. In addition the authors found that monies were transferred from other sectors of the health service. An early Labour government review and cull of some major acute sector schemes in the application process did indicate a more discriminating approach, but the scheme survives. Price suggests that there is broad support amongst health service managers because the restructuring of services away from large acute hospital provision requires investment in a new health infrastructure. However, the problems associated with servicing the debt remain regardless of what new economies emerge. PFI is not likely to be a blessing in the long term but it has the advantage of delivering new health service buildings for relatively little initial outlay – surely every politician's dream.

A much publicised objective of the new Labour government was to remain within Conservatives' spending plans for the first two years. Early displays of ministerial machismo by Dobson may indeed have been intended to dampen expectations of government magnanimity, but fear of an impending crisis over winter hospital admissions extracted an extra £269m from the Treasury for the 1997/8 period. The policy on NHS spending again proved vulnerable when the announcement of the 1998/9 health authority allocations revealed a £1bn cash increase amounting to 4.7 per cent real-terms growth. Within this global amount the Family Health Services budget (for general practice, dentistry, ophthalmic and pharmaceutical services) would increase by 4 per cent to nearly £600m (Crail, 1997), reflecting a continuation of the previous government's development of the primary care sector. A degree of political pragmatism was again apparent in the announcement, in the July 1998 Comprehensive Spending Review, of £21b extra for the NHS over the following three years. Further announcements of government beneficence were to follow.

Disclosures about the inadequacy of some services in the NHS, which had been further exposed by a winter flu epidemic, the rationing of care through waiting lists, and obvious inequities in the funding of some treatments, contributed to a growing public disquiet over the NHS. Just as the Conservatives before them, Labour reacted decisively, but somewhat differently. In the budget speech in March 2000, the Chancellor Gordon Brown announced a dramatic increase of £2bn in April 2000/01, which will contribute to an average 6 per cent increase over the rate of inflation during the four years from April 2000. This announcement came a few weeks after Blair's pledge to raise public (and presumably private) spending on healthcare to the level of the EU average. This promised level of spending goes beyond that which is required to soften up the British electorate in the run-up to the next election, or to patch up the more obvious shortcomings of the NHS. In tacitly recognising the past inadequacies of funding and, in effect, consigning future governments to a new baseline of expenditure – since retreat from this would be deemed perverse by the electorate – New Labour have adopted a new policy stance on NHS funding and have temporarily confounded their critics on the Left. There was, however, a *quid pro quo* for this generosity. Blair followed up with a challenge to NHS staff that indicated a programme of reforms based on performance-related bonuses and tighter standards and the threat of management takeovers for failing hospitals. There is to be a veritable cat's-cradle of strings attached to the new monies.

Any government or third-party payer concerned with extracting greater efficiencies from health providers cannot afford to ignore medical practice, variations in which would suggest unfortuitous treatment choices by some doctors. The cost-inefficiencies (of less than effective treatments) implied in such patterns is reason enough for action, but the political mission to harmonise medical practice has been endowed with additional urgency and rectitude in the wake of a series of very public failures of medical performance. Two initiatives signalled in *The New NHS*, The National Institute for Clinical Excellence (NICE) and the Commission for Health Improvement (CHI), have linked but differing tasks in this regard. NICE assesses the effectiveness of new technologies and can be expected to influence increasingly the prescribing and treatment choices of both hospital and primary care doctors. CHI is responsible for monitoring the Trusts' quality control systems. This is based on an ambitious new performance framework, which replaced the Purchaser Efficiency Index in April 1999. In addition to the by now established goals of efficiency and effectiveness and improvement in public health goals, it places a new emphasis on access, patient and user experiences and health outcomes as opposed to outputs (NHS Executive, 1998).

Further direction on quality comes in the form of National Service Frameworks (NSFs), service blue-prints, the first of which for Mental Health was issued in September 1999. The Health Improvement Programmes (specifying local priorities for health) produced by health authorities will be informed by the NSFs, and one stage on PCGs/PCTs will be required to incorporate standards ensuring cost effectiveness, a trait not particularly evident in fundholding (Audit Commission, 1996). Thus over time there is likely to be more conformity of standards in the NHS, reflecting a return to the goal of universalising the best – a reaffirmation of the principle of equitable access to care of similar quality.

In the early months of office, the Labour government's approach to the professions seemed more emollient than its predecessor's. Unlike the small and secretive review process that preceded *Working for Patients*, the Labour government consulted professional groups over the contents of *The New NHS*. As well as promoting a new *entente cordiale* with key professional groups, the government endorsed cooperation as the *modus operandi* of the future NHS. However, the apparent inability of the medical profession to police the performance of members and a lack of robustness in dealing with those who operate below acceptable standards have created obvious tensions. Against a background of manifest government dissatisfaction, the General Medical Council and the Royal Colleges are, with some urgency, introducing measures which will reassure both government and the public (Beecham, 2000; General Medical Council, 1999)

The wherewithal to improve patient care is also to be achieved by improvements in the overall allocation of resources in the NHS as well as measures to improve the effectiveness of care. The Department of Health is presently undertaking a wide-ranging review of the formula for resource allocations, with the intention of introducing a fairer method of resource allocation between, firstly, health authorities and, subsequently, PCGs. Alongside this, a new formula for establishing target prescribing allocations for general practice based on deprivation rather than historic prescribing costs, was recommended to be incorporated in the 1999/2000 allocations for general practice prescribing. Inevitably, since there is a unified budget for prescribing, hospital and community services and practice infrastructure costs, overspends in prescribing are likely to affect services elsewhere.

Access to care, patient/carer experiences and health outcomes form criteria for the assessment of NHS performance that, with others, will replace the much criticised Purchaser Efficiency Index. There is also an annual survey of patient experience carried out at health authority level, but with results published both nationally and locally. It remains to be seen to what extent the views of users are to influence service development. In a further move away from the narrow consumerist model of the internal market, the Labour government announced a new NHS Charter, a draft of which was subsequently produced in December 1998 and is currently undergoing a period of consultation. This, it was promised, will focus on outcomes of treatments and care, 'things that really matter' (Secretary of State for Health, 1997, p. 66). It will also explain patients' responsibilities. Whatever the final version, clearly rights are to be balanced with duties for the New Labour citizen.

First impressions were of a government committed to shouldering the broader responsibilities associated with improving public health. Unlike its predecessor, the Labour government has readily acknowledged links between ill health and social inequalities and therefore the necessity of a broad definition of public health responsibilities at national and local level. The centrality of public health matters within health policy was underlined by the appointment of a Minister for Public Health, Tessa Jowell. In June 1998 Dobson declared that 'the whole machinery of Government' had to be used 'to tackle the things that make people ill' (DoH Press Release, 25 June 1998). However, the emerging policy on public health was one of the first casualties of idealism. A high-profile anti-smoking conference targeted tobacco advertising and sports sponsorship but the government's willpower was later to dissolve in the face of intensive lobbying by the motor-sports industry. The affair demonstrated considerable political maladroitness, perhaps to be anticipated in a government unused to governing. Elsewhere the evolution of public health policy looked more promising. A Green Paper, *Our Healthier Nation*, was produced, and as a result, health authorities have a new statutory duty to improve the health of their population. In discharging this duty they are expected to act in concert with local authorities and other bodies. A small number of projects, Health Action Zones (HAZ), which were to focus on public health issues, service reconfiguration or localities, were selected to test the principle. Bids for HAZ status were apparently assessed for their potential to overcome local organisational barriers and there is some indication that preference was given to HAZs in deprivation areas, thus creating an elegant association of objectives.

In line with their policy on more open and transparent governance, the Labour government have declared their intention to create a NHS which is 'accountable to patients, open to the public and shaped by their views' (Secretary of State for Health, 1997, section 2.4, p. 11). Prior to the publication of the White Paper, Trusts were instructed to hold their board meetings in public and encouraged to take steps to ensure a more representative membership of the local community than had previously obtained. In addition to the local survey of patient and user experience, consultation of the general public over the development of Health Improvement Programmes is obligatory for health authorities, which are also to ensure that PCGs and PCTs have effective arrangements for public involvement. It remains to be seen whether this will mean consultation on or participation in service development. However, there is to be a more pluralistic membership of planning fora. Local Authority chief executives are to participate in health authority meetings and PCG steering committees and PCT boards will include representatives of local organisations. Membership does not necessarily equate with influence; how much lay members will defer to GP representatives remains to be seen. Thus broader participation in service planning may be one outcome of the proposals, but perhaps a more significant trend will be towards a more open service producing *informative* information for the public as well as for the constituent parts of the NHS.

Review and Preview

The Labour government's record in relation to health in the first years of office has been impressive, if only in terms of its productivity. Their pre-election promise to dismantle the internal market in health care was fleshed out in the new government's first major White Paper on the health service, but perhaps the changes are of style rather than substance. Fundholding has been abolished, and with the exception of Northern Ireland the last vestiges disappeared in April 1999. There is to be an extension of what were annual contractual agreements and more emphasis on collaboration. However, the purchaser–provider divide will remain, and performance – of commissioners as well as providers – will be monitored according to ability to secure or achieve externally imposed priorities and standards of clinical effectiveness and quality, rather than driven by the threat of competition.

Nevertheless there is a considerable amount of work to be done, not least in the development of new responsibilities and relationships.

Predictably PCGs were not welcomed by fundholders who saw a dissipation of influence and no doubt material benefits which formerly accrued to some practices. Despite early ambivalence, most PCGs got under way and there has been progression towards stage-4 PCTs in most areas, though sometimes with the prodding of health authorities. The next crucial test will be the emergence of PCTs and the determination of control, not only within these new structures, but between them and the health authorities, which must also adjust to a dramatically changed role.

PCT boards will not have a majority of professional representatives but they will need to engage the support of local GPs in particular. Their legitimacy would otherwise be seriously compromised and with it the significant reform agenda that they face. As suggested above, it is likely that key discussions will happen away from PCT boards and that GP interests will be well represented. Trade-offs will, however, take place against a centrally authored framework of directives and standards. Whatever sectional interests pervade PCG/ PCT politics, progress on the central agenda of delivering more effective and equitable local services, including primary care, will be expected.

In addition to managing the changes in the organisation and culture of the NHS, there are several areas which are likely to require more specific intervention and action. If the Labour government is to address unequal access to services it need look no further than NHS dental services which, following the introduction of a new contract for dentists in 1990, have in some areas been decimated. Increasing numbers of dentists transferred to private practice, refusing to continue to treat defaulters or new residents under NHS terms. The recent announcement of additional funding for dental services should be seen as a partial attempt to correct matters rather than a fundamental solution. Other areas which are to be reviewed, but which are not readily resolved, are long-term care and mental health care. These sit on the margins between health's and social services' responsibilities and, more importantly, given the contrasting funding arrangements of NHS and local authorities, the boundary between statutory and private subsidy of care. The Report of the Royal Commission on Long Term Care (1999) which proposed that nursing care in residential care be funded by the state, has presented the government with some difficult choices. Whatever their decision, it seems likely that the government will see new efficiencies, delivered by better collaboration, as one way of finding the necessary resources. A recent announcement of work to facilitate common health and social care budgets is intended to promote more effective service arrangements, but these are not likely to release much in the way of new resources. Given the Labour government's intention to overhaul the welfare state, including benefits payments, the principle of means- as well as needs-testing is likely to be enforced with equal rigour in community care and may be extended to cover jointly commissioned health/social care in the community, thus further privatising health care.

Greater collaboration both within the NHS and with other agencies appears to be the means, if not the end, of a number of related health policy objectives. Having formally acknowledged the impact of social and economic disadvantage on health, an integrative approach to local as well as national health care initiatives is inescapable. In addition to a gradual redistribution of resources, taking more account of the impact of deprivation, both *The New NHS* and the Health Action Zones initiative identify the need for remedial action for disadvantaged communities requiring the cooperation of several authorities and agencies. We can expect to see a continuing emphasis on the reduction of social inequality as well as greater inter-agency collaboration. This reflects not so much a desire to reify improved collaboration to the level of policy, as a recognition of the difficulties of achieving a functional level of collaboration. Health authority managers and public health doctors have been accustomed to the sharing of information and perhaps have adopted more pluralistic approaches in the development of joint purchasing strategies, but what is called for is much more extensive, requiring GPs and community nurses within PCGs/PCTs to work with local authority representatives and possibly voluntary sector organisations in planning local services. This is likely to be a novel experience for many GPs who are more used to operating autonomously or as employers, team leaders or members of peer professional groups.

If these cynicisms can be put aside, there is the potential for WHO-style health care at the local level, with corrective resourcing of socially deprived areas and an opportunity for local communities to work with health professionals to improve health, as opposed to simply health care. At the other end of the political spectrum and equally difficult, the Labour government also appears to be prepared to take on a more active role in the global and European communities. The UK's presidency of the EC has not seen much headway with the campaign against tobacco advertising but it should at least secure a place on the agenda. Perhaps the sphere of activity where the government might succeed most with an integrative approach to health policy is at national level between ministries, as they create and implement policy. The creation of the Food Standards Agency, independent of MAFF, which will fundamentally be concerned to safeguard health, is an indication of a wider interpretation of the state's responsibilities for public health.

In its introduction to *The New NHS* the Labour government described the changes as evolutionary rather than revolutionary. This relates to the proposed pace of change as well as a determination to retain elements of the Conservatives' reforms, although if a culture of cooperation in pursuit of effectiveness is achievable it will have been a radical change indeed. A more accurate description of the Labour government's health agenda in its entirety is that it is ambitious, perhaps unrealistically so, and signifies a rethink of the state's role. This is certainly a 'rolling forward' rather than 'rolling back' of the state, but it is an engagement which is predicated on the citizen's involvement as opposed to simply the assumption of responsibilities, and which encompasses new partnerships between communities, professional groups and the state. Thus the 'New Public Health' approach adopted by New Labour calls for a more active state at national, local and increasingly international levels of government. There will undoubtedly be problems of coordination and motivation between levels and laterally, between different policy sectors and agencies. However the task of driving forward the changed approach to public health pales into insignificance beside the related objective of reducing social deprivation. Recognition of the links between it and ill health do not so much obviate the responsibilities of the NHS – they require if anything greater precision and success in the targeting of resources – as call for extensive engineering of social and economic policy. Carrying out this task against a background of robust financial parameters is likely to be the most severe test of New Labour's resolve.

9

Housing Policy

PAUL DURDEN

This chapter examines two broad aspects of housing policy: firstly, developments in the years of Conservative government, 1979–97, and, secondly, problems arising therefrom and the policy options addressing those problems open to the 1997 Labour government. Because of lack of space, certain topics have been excluded – for example, the gender and ethnic dimensions of housing policy (for an excellent introductory approach to these issues, see Gilroy and Woods, 1994), and homelessness (see Burrows *et al.*, 1997).

The Background

The issues to be examined here are Conservative policies intended to encourage owner occupation, reshape the housing responsibilities of local authorities, and to revitalise the private rented sector (for a more detailed account, see Balchin, 1996).

The 1977 Green Paper, *Housing Policy: A Consultation Document* (DoE, 1977), indicated that in England (though not necessarily in other parts of the United Kingdom) there was an approximate balance between the current number of households and that of dwellings, though many dwellings were of an unsatisfactory standard. In the years 1977–9 there was a significant fall in demand for local authority housing (Holmans, 1991) and so the Conservatives could claim with some justification that there was no longer a need for the large-scale construction of 'social housing' (defined as dwellings provided by non-profit-making agencies in receipt of public subsidies, thus including both local authority and housing association properties).

139

The Conservatives had set themselves the task of reducing the role of the state and were particularly anxious to contain public spending, this being required by their commitment to monetarist economic policies. They saw encouragement of owner occupation as the most cost-effective way of meeting most of the foreseeable demand for housing, leaving local authorities with a residual role in that regard. To that end the Thatcher government pursued two major policy initiatives: firstly, the sale of council housing (and some housing association dwellings) to sitting tenants under the 'Right to Buy' provisions of the Housing Act 1980, and, secondly, deregulation of the building societies under the Building Societies Act 1986.

The first of these policies reduced both the scale of local authority involvement in housing, and public indebtedness; local authorities were allowed to retain for housing purposes only 25 per cent of their capital receipts from the sale of council housing, the remainder being used largely to repay existing local authority debts. A significant additional saving was that the maintenance costs of those dwellings sold were shifted to their new owners. The substantial discounts offered enabled many more council tenants to become owner-occupiers than would otherwise have been the case and this was to the political advantage of the Conservatives. In the years 1979–99, 1.6 million local authority dwellings were sold mainly under the 'Right to Buy' scheme, reducing social housing from 31 per cent to 21 per cent of the housing stock of Great Britain (DETR, 2000a). A substantially proportion of the growth of owner-occupation in the years 1980–95 can be accounted for by council tenants exercising their 'Right to Buy'. Little attention was paid to the possible social costs of this policy.

Public aspirations to owner-occupation were a justification for the deregulation of the building societies. Once relieved of strict government controls the building societies were free to give higher percentage (of price) mortgages and mortgages which were a higher multiple of the applicants' earnings, thus mortgages could be more readily obtained by people of modest means.

The Thatcher years saw much growth in the incidence of owner-occupation, despite a substantial rise in house prices in the late 1980s. The 'feel good' factor arising from higher house prices was of electoral advantage to the Conservatives, though of harm to the economy, for many owner-occupiers, feeling richer, borrowed against the value of their dwellings (known as 'equity release') and used the money so raised for additional consumption, thus pumping inflation. It was difficult for the Conservatives to deal with this problem, given their commitment to 'freeing up' the housing market. In the early 1990s a downward turn in the economy and the consequent loss of earnings experienced by many of the new lower-income mortgagors led to a sharp increase in the incidence of mortgage default. This was exacerbated by falling house prices and so an increase in the number of households with a mortgage debt greater than the market value of their dwelling (known as 'negative equity'). Negative equity impairs labour mobility and so for some people may prolong unemployment. These developments were a salutary reminder of how vulnerable many new mortgagors were (and are) to loss of income, especially if they have taken on a mortgage in later working life.

However, Conservative support for owner-occupation was not unequivocal, for the tax revenue forgone through Mortgage Interest Tax Relief (MITR) was of concern to the Treasury, and so the Finance Act 1983, and subsequent legislation, eroded the tax privileges of those with mortgages. The Labour government has maintained this stance and in 2000 abolished MITR. The medium and longer-term effects of this are hard to assess. Given low interest rates, high employment, and 'consumer confidence' it is likely that the ending of MITR will have at most a marginal impact on the willingness of people to take on mortgages; if those conditions do not pertain then a slump in the demand for mortgages might well occur (in 1998 the initial mortgage interest payment of a first-time buyer was about 18 per cent of their income, compared with 33 per cent in 1990 (DETR, 1999).

The Housing Act 1988, and the Housing and Local Government Act 1989, imposed further restrictions on local authorities' expenditure and borrowing so that they were obliged to cut back their Housing Investment Programmes (HIPs), bringing a sharp decline in the construction of council housing. This legislation also changed the system of subsidies for council housing, obliging many local authorities to increase their rents more rapidly than the rate of inflation. The burden on low-income households of higher council rents was, of course, alleviated by housing benefit, but growing dependence on housing benefit has proved problematic in that it constitutes a poverty trap (hence a disincentive to work), is inflationary, and has proved to be very costly. Higher rents had the effect of further encouraging the better-off council tenants to become owner-occupiers; where they did so by exercising their Right to Buy this could lead to the regeneration of council estates, but in poorer areas only served to accelerate the process of residential polarisation whereby many council housing estates came to have a substantial population of unwaged and other low-income households (Burrows and Joseph, 1997). In 1977–8 21 per cent of social housing tenants were 'economically inactive' (but not retired), compared with 32 per cent in 1998–9 (DETR, 1999a).

Conservative housing legislation from 1980 onwards was intended to privatise council housing not only by sale to tenants, but also by shifting the ownership of council housing to other agencies. The Conservatives believed that local authorities made poor landlords (when compared with housing associations), supposedly being unresponsive to the needs of their tenants, especially in regard to the maintenance and renovation of run-down council housing. Whether this Conservative view of local authority housing activity was justified is a matter of debate, but they were anxious to mobilise private capital for renovation and believed that could be done only if the dwellings were in the private sector. This can be seen as part of the Conservative strategy to expose local authority services to market forces, exemplified by introduction of 'compulsory competitive tending' under the Local Government, Planning and Land Act 1980. The Housing Act 1985, and subsequent legislation, gave local authorities permission to dispose of their housing stock to private sector landlords, and the Housing Act 1988, established 'Tenants' Choice', enabling individual tenants of council houses (and tenants of council flats collectively, though with provision for dissenters) to choose their own 'approved landlord'. To be 'approved' landlords have to meet criteria laid down by the Housing Corporation; in practice, this means transfer to housing associations. The 1988 Act also provided for the designation of Housing Action Trusts (by the central government) empowered to take responsibility for the renovation of run-down council estates even against the wishes of the parent local authority. These measures achieved little initial success (Karn, 1993). However, Large Scale Voluntary Transfers (LSVTs) authorised by the 1985 Act, gained momentum in the later 1990s. Under the latter Act, authorities may transfer much of their housing stock to what are now termed 'Registered Social Landlords' (RSLs), mostly housing associations. In the years 1988–99 some 400,000 dwellings were transferred from 100 local authorities to registered social landlords, and from 2001–2 transfers are to occur at a rate of up to 200,000 per annum (DETR, 2000a) Registered social landlords are in the private sector and hence largely obliged to raise finance from the money market (though they may continue to receive what is now termed 'Social Housing Grant').

It is true that many housing associations do have a good reputation for managing relatively small housing stocks, but whether they can scale up their operations successfully is questionable. Concerned with the latter issue, the Blair government has indicated that it hopes for competition between registered social landlords seeking to take over local authority housing, and that normally no one landlord will be allowed to take over more than 12,000 dwellings in a given area (DETR, 2000a). Since 1988 the role of local authorities in housing has changed from direct provision of low-rental housing to 'enabling' provision of a wider range of housing to meet the needs of different groups within the community (Balchin *et al.*, 1998) Local authorities did, however, retain responsibility for meeting the needs of the homeless, though their ability to do so was diminished by their loss of control over much of their former housing stock and consequently greater pressure on that remaining.

The Housing Acts 1980 and 1988 took major steps towards deregulation of the privately rented sector. These Acts authorised two new forms of tenancy: 'shorthold' tenancies, under which for new lettings landlords and prospective tenants could negotiate fixed-term agreements, with determination of the rent by the rent assessment committee in certain circumstances; and 'assured' tenancies, under which for new lettings by approved landlords rents would be set by the market, but tenants would have more security of tenure than would be the case with 'shortholds'. Under the 1988 Act, 'assured tenancies' were also given to new tenants of 'approved landlords'. These measures gave landlords greater effective control over their properties and a better rate of return, but Balchin (1996) has questioned their success.

A further measure intended to help revive the sector was extension of the Business Expansion Scheme (in the 1988 Budget) to provision of new dwellings to be let privately; within certain constraints this provided generous tax relief for investors willing to invest in such dwellings (withdrawn in 1993), but in four years only 16,000 additional private rental dwellings were provided (Balchin *et al.*, 98). The long decline of private letting did abate in the early 1990s (from 10 per cent of all dwellings in 1991, private letting is expected to reach 12 per cent in 2001), and, according to Holmans, Morrison and Whitehead (1998), in the period 1991–6 the private rented sector absorbed about about 35,000–40,000 per year of the need for 'assisted' housing. However, this revival was largely due to recession and the slump in the housing market at that time, leaving many owners preferring to let rather than sell at a lower price than they considered acceptable; whether this revival proves sustainable remains to be seen, although the greater availability of 'buy to let' mortgages and the increasing number of estate agents specialising in the rented sector may help to sustain it further.

The Conservatives claim that their housing policies in the years 1979–97 were largely successful and, if one measures 'success' by public acceptance, that claim is justified. Most people were better housed in 1997 than they had been in 1979, but there were increasing numbers of low-income households in poor-quality housing in both the public and private sectors. The obvious costs of Conservative housing policy were borne largely by the poorer members of the community, but there were other costs of wider if less obvious impact, such as the economic and social consequences of higher house prices (Muellbauer, 1990), higher rents which soon fed through to the Cost of Living Index and so necessitated payment of higher social security benefits (as well as higher housing benefits), and in some places increasing 'ghettoisation' of the poor.

The Future

The concluding section of this chapter examines ways in which the present government could address, with a reasonable chance of success, the pressing problems they have inherited from their predecessors. Development of an adequate and sustainable housing strategy requires that certain tasks be addressed, these being (1) finding out what people really need; (2) finding the money to do the job; (3) finding better ways of helping people with their housing costs; (4) giving people choice and quality in housing; and (5) building better communities.

Housing Need

From the Labour government's Housing Policy Review in 1977 until the White Paper *Our Future Homes* (DoE, 1995a) there was little attempt by the government to estimate current unmet housing need or to estimate need in the near future (though for land use planning purposes the then DoE prepared estimates of the demand for sites for dwellings). This was because the Conservatives thought in terms of 'demand' revealed by the functioning of the market and were influenced by the existence of numerous vacant local authority dwellings in some areas (Bramley, 1998). Their critics were more concerned with 'unmet social need' identified by sustained research. A problem with the latter ('needs' focused) approach is the lack of consensus over what constitutes an acceptable methodology for such investigations; thus estimates of need for social housing differ considerably, from the 22,000–72,000 dwellings per annum of the report produced by the Department of Applied Economics at Cambridge in 1997 (DETR, 1997) to the 115,000 dwellings per annum recommended by Kleinman *et al.* (1999). Probably the most useful starting point is the projected increase in households over the period 1996–2021 (DoE, 1995b). Government figures suggest that about 3.8 million additional households will form in that period, approximately 150,000 per annum (DETR, 2000a), though it must be remembered that it is difficult to predict with any real accuracy household formation rates over a twenty-year period. Furthermore, the probable distribution of these additional households between the tenure categories is not easy to determine. To this additional need must be added current unmet social need, which Holmans *et al.* (1998) estimated to be in the range of 650,000 to 700,000. Unmet social need is unevenly distributed throughout the country, most being in the three southern regions (including London), which is why we have at one and the same time a net surplus of dwellings (770,000 vacant dwellings in 1998–9 according to the DETR (2000a), a high incidence of vacant social housing in some areas, and yet a serious shortage of low-rental dwellings in other areas.

Holmans *et al.* (1998) agree that some of the current unmet need for social housing could be met by redeployment of existing dwellings. However, they go on to suggest that when one adds to the estimated growth in households and current unmet social need an allowance for homes lost through demolition (at current rates), provision of 4.9 million new dwellings (including conversions) in the period 1991–2011 appears necessary, of which approximately 2 million would need to be social rented housing. This would require the construction of at least 100,000 low-rental dwellings per annum over two decades, and more probably the 115,000 per annum recommended by Kleinman *et al.* (1999), given the low level of such construction in the early years of the Blair government; output of social rented housing in 1997–8 was only 24,000.

Although much informed opinion supports Holmans's estimates (Bramley, 1998), the DETR response to the 1998 Comprehensive Spending Review indicates that the estimates produced by the 1997 Cambridge report (DETR, 1997) have prevailed and that the Blair government hopes to minimise future public sector provision of new low-rental housing. It is significant that neither the government paper

Housing in the South East (DETR, 1999b) nor the 2000 Housing Green Paper *Quality and Choice: A Decent Home for All* (DETR, 2000a) sets targets for the construction of social housing. This is in part because of the government's awareness of the poor condition of much of the existing social housing stock, the cost of bringing English council housing alone up to a satisfactory standard being estimated at £19 billion (DETR, 2000a).

The private sector should be able to accommodate most of the currently projected additional effective demand for housing, but the number of households unable to afford to purchase a decent dwelling gives much cause for concern. The DETR has published figures suggesting that in the counties constituting the South East planning region approximately 50 per cent of new indigenous households could not afford to purchase a suitable dwelling (DETR, 1999b). It is clear that, whether one takes the higher Cambridge figure (77,000 dwellings per annum) or that of Kleinman *et al.* (115,000 per annum), much additional low-rental housing must be provided if the needs of low-income families are to be met. As the 1995 White Paper said, 'the most cost-effective way of ensuring that people with permanently low incomes have a decent home is to give direct subsidy to landlords to provide social housing at rents below market levels' (DoE, 1995a; Malpass, 1996).

Only non-profit making housing agencies, such as local authorities, housing associations, and (perhaps) 'local housing companies' authorised by the Housing Act, 1996 (Wilcox *et al.*, 1993), receiving supply-side ('bricks and mortar') subsidies, are likely to provide the number of low-rent dwellings required to meet mainstream estimates of housing need. Most of that provision would have to come from new construction (as opposed to the redeployment, conversion and/or renovation of the existing housing stock). However, the present government, although claiming that it will allow local authorities to determine their own housing priorities, appears inclined to penalise local authorities that favour new construction at the expense of renovation (Armstrong and Blake, 1998).

Finance

It is not too difficult to determine what needs to be done to ensure that everyone in the UK is decently housed, and many people expected the Labour government on gaining office to introduce a major housing bill. This did not happen, probably because, like its Conservative predecessor, the Blair government is primarily concerned with retaining economic credibility, and, to do that, public spending must be contained. In other words, housing policy is constrained by broader economic and political considerations – not, of course, for the first time. There are a number of reasons for this. Firstly, any sustained commitment to resolution of the housing problems mentioned heretofore would be very costly. The traditional Treasury view is that investment in social housing is, in effect, a form of social consumption, not strictly comparable to 'productive' investment, though both social and market-provided housing generate a revenue flow and are in that limited sense 'productive'. Secondly, control of aggregate expenditure on housing (especially that of the building industry) is at times useful as an economic regulator, as was the case in the 1990s, that regulator being used to contain inflation. Thirdly, save when the public is aware of a housing crisis or a general election near, housing has tended in recent years to be have been a marginal political issue, although, of course, it was more at the centre-stage of adversarial politics during the Thatcher years.

A long-established Treasury accountancy convention dictates that all borrowing by public agencies must count as part of the Public Sector Borrowing Requirement (PSBR), even when intended for investment purposes, hence be 'in play' in shaping economic policy. The Blair government has said that it intends to differentiate between borrowing to meet current expenditure and borrowing for capital investment, but as yet there is little evidence of that being applied to housing. Furthermore, although professing sympathy for the idea of 'arm's length management of social housing', exemplified by the proposed 'local housing companies', the government is hesitant about excluding borrowing by such 'companies' from the PSBR. However, the Housing Green Paper (DETR, 2000a) does indicate that in the future and under some circumstances the government might be more flexible on this matter.

To date (early 2000) little additional public funding for social housing appears to be available other than release of a further £3.9 billion of local authorities' capital receipts (from the sale of council housing) over the lifetime of the present Parliament, thus fulfilling the government's manifesto commitment to release £5 billion 'set aside' capital receipts. Some £3.6 billion is to be available to local authorities, primarily for the renovation of social housing over the years 1999–2002, though (as stated earlier) the total repair bill for English council housing alone is estimated at £19 billion (DETR, 2000a). Some £300 million is to be available to the Housing Corporation for their Approved Development Programmes. Furthermore, much of the £800 million allocated to the

New Deal for Communities Initiative is likely to be spent on housing, as will some of the £2.3 billion Single Regeneration Budget. Even so, there are reasonable fears that the present Parliament will spend less on new social housing than its predecessor (Roof, 1998; Wilcox, 1999).

Given that, it can be argued that there is a case for greater reliance on private finance (perhaps through the Private Finance Initiative) and on the private rented sector. There remains the problem of how to raise capital for investment in private rental dwellings; individual investors have shown little enthusiasm for investment in rental dwellings, save when offered generous tax concessions, and even then their enthusiasm has proved short-lasting, as illustrated by the questionable success of the Business Expansion Scheme when applied to housing. There is, perhaps, more hope of institutional investment; indeed, some mortgage lenders have experimented with investment in residential rental property. It is possible that property investment trusts (possibly held within Individual Savings Accounts) will generate capital for rental dwellings, but most of their investment is likely to be in up-market dwellings or go into commercial and industrial properties. Sustained revival of the private rented sector is likely only if landlords can be assured of a reasonable rate of return on their investment, and that would require either substantial tax concessions of some kind, for example, a depreciation allowance (as in the United States and some of our European neighbours), or substantially higher rents (and housing benefits), and both courses of action would have a significant impact on the public purse. Evidently, this government (like its predecessor) remains concerned about the possible effects on inflation and interest rates of a substantially higher level of public spending on low-rental dwellings.

As indicated above, rent levels are also of considerable economic significance. The 2000 Housing Green Paper suggests that social housing rents should bear a closer relationship to cost rents and should reflect, if only in part, the notional capital value of the dwellings (DETR, 2000a); in practice this is likely to mean higher rents. Extensive deregulation of private sector tenancies has inevitably led to substantial increases in rents and hence to the cost of housing benefit , expenditure on which in 1998 exceeded central government subsidies for new housing, though the housing benefit caseload by that year was slightly lower than in the mid-1980s (Kemp, 1998).

To constrain growth in the cost of housing benefit, 'local reference rents' for some private sector tenancies (set by rent officers) were applied in 1997. Kemp (1998) refers to two major problems with housing benefit (other than that of cost), these being work disincentives and the lack of a 'shopping incentive'. As most housing benefit recipients are not significantly affected by changes in their rent there is no incentive for them to seek cheaper accommodation. Some 41 per cent of housing benefit recipients are aged 60 or over (DETR, 2000a), but for those of working age the loss of housing benefit as other income rises means that for those whose earning capacity is low, going to work (or seeking higher wages) incurs a very high marginal rate of tax (currently 65p of housing benefit is lost for every £1 of extra income), thus housing benefit is a major component of the poverty trap. The Blair government does intend to review the working of the housing benefit scheme, to make it easier to understand, to remove anomalies, to increase the efficiency of the administration, and to minimise fraud. Proposed reforms include introduction of a flat rate system with 80 per cent of the rent met through housing benefit or its successor, the rest being paid by tenants who would have an incentive to shop around for cheaper housing. It would be necessary to increase income support by 20–25 per cent of average local housing costs to ensure that claimants would suffer no loss. These messages might be integrated (as a 'housing tax credit') with the employment tax credit proposed in the 2000 budget (DETR, 2000a; Roof, 2000).

However, there is a strong case for bolder reform, for the creation of a system paying housing benefit irrespective of tenure (as found elsewhere in Europe), so that owner-occupiers, with or without a mortgage, and households in all categories of rental accommodation would be eligible to apply for an income-related housing benefit. If this were to reflect not only income and household composition, but also housing costs, it would go some way to address the problem of low-wage 'priority workers' in high housing cost areas (the 2000 Housing Green Paper suggests mortgage interest rate subsidies for low-income 'priority workers'). This 'European' approach would work effectively only if the problems of interaction between housing benefit or tax credit and other transfer payments (for example, Working Families' Tax Credit) were resolved in such a way as to minimise the poverty trap.

However, there is reason to believe that the introduction (from April 2000) of the 'Best Value' procedures for assessing local government activities will serve to make their housing policies and practices more transparent (see DETR, 2000b).

Housing finance is a complex business and for that reason only a brief summary is presented above; for a good general introduction to the issues see Balchin and Rhoden (1998), and for the current situation see Wilcox (1999), the DETR Annual Reports for 1999 and 2000

(DETR, 1999c; DETR, 2000c) and the 2000 Green Paper (DETR, 2000a).

The Social Dimension

Under the 'Right to Buy' provisions of the Housing Act 1980, a substantial proportion of the better-quality council housing stock was sold to sitting tenants; as these have not been replaced (though some have been bought back) there are fewer dwellings available to accommodate households on the local authority housing waiting lists. As the dwellings that are available are often relatively undesirable, commonly because of poor maintenance and their location, many local authorities find that only the most vulnerable and/or desperate applicants on their waiting lists are willing to take such dwellings; these applicants are often unwaged, not infrequently lone parents, and commonly housed under legislation addressed to the needs of the homeless (Burrows, 1997). In some areas this has led to a situation approaching the ghettoisation of the poor, perhaps not to the same degree as in parts of the US, but sufficiently so to give much cause for concern.

By the mid-1990s the social and economic circumstances of those allocated council housing under the homelessness legislation were not markedly different from those who reached the top of their local authority's waiting list (Lee and Murie, 1997), and considerations of equity require that the two groups should not be treated differently. It can be argued that most homelessness is no more than a special case of the broader problems of housing need and dependency on transfer payments. This view appears to have been shared by the Major government which in the Housing Act, 1996, removed the right of registered homeless households to priority in the allocation of permanent social housing. The 1996 Act required the government to issue a code of guidance on the responsibilities and powers of local authorities in regard to the homeless; a draft code of guidance was published in 1996 and issued to local authorities (revised in 1999), but both versions were and are drafts and so their status is debatable. In practice, the Blair government has instructed local authorities to restore priority for homeless.

However, this government seems to share the preoccupation of its predecessor with 'street homelessness'. The Social Exclusion Unit set up in 1997 was given responsibility for production of a report on 'rough sleeping' in London and was guided in that task by the Ministerial Committee on Rough Sleeping (the latter being intended to show the government's commitment to the issue). The outcome of that report was the establishment of a DETR-based London 'rough sleepers' unit, with a budget of £145 million (subsequently increased) and the goal of reducing the number of 'rough sleepers' in London by two-thirds by 2002. The London unit is paralleled by a Homelessness Action Programme for outside of London, in operation from April 1999, with a budget of £34 million over three years; this is intended to build on the success of the Conservatives' Rough Sleepers Initiative. It is clear that a major objective of the present government is a marked reduction in the number of people becoming 'street homeless'; the retreat from 'care in the community' and the £375 million programme for children and young people are indicative of this (the latter extending from the age of 16 to 18 the duty placed on local authorities to support young people leaving care). Commendable as this concern with 'rough sleepers' may be, some see it as little more than a means of distracting public attention from the deeper problem of the housing shortage in some areas.

Land Use Issues

The late conversion of the Major government to a needs-focused approach (indicated by the 1995 White Paper) arose largely because of the political impact of public anxiety over the use of 'greenfield' sites for new housing, which led that government to set a target of 50 per cent of new residential construction on 'brownfield' sites (Prescott, 2000), that is, sites made available by the demolition and clearance of existing buildings. Whatever the reason for this acceptance of a needs-focused approach, the change in policy was a marked departure from that of his predecessor.

It is clear that a high proportion of the demand for new homes is in the southern regions (including London) where there is well-organised opposition to 'greenfield' developments which are likely to diminish the amenity value (and hence market value) of existing dwellings. Many residents of these regions argue that if new dwellings must be constructed, 'brownfield' sites should be given higher priority. This opinion is shared by the Blair government which has set a new target of 60 per cent of new dwellings on 'recycled land or buildings' (Prescott, 2000) Although in principle the use of 'brownfield' sites makes much sense it does present serious problems. Firstly, such sites are often costly to clear (especially when they have been used for industrial purposes) and so the aggregate cost of new dwellings built upon them may well be higher than that of those built on 'greenfield' sites. Secondly, the provision of dwellings affordable to households of modest income (whether to rent or buy) on relatively high-cost sites would probably require high population density and/or heavy subsidisation. In practice, a cost-effective high population density might prove difficult to achieve, especially in the South East. Although a high proportion of those needing housing are likely to be in single person households, very many are likely to be older persons who expect something better than a single-bedroom starter home, and so it would be difficult to achieve a high population density without resort to multi-storey dwellings which might prove hard to sell or let. A third problem that intensive use of 'brownfield' sites is likely to present arises from the existence of a strong 'car culture'; many households would expect to run a car even when living in an inner-city area and so would require a garage and/or parking space, thus further reducing the space available for dwellings, and adding to traffic congestion. Land use planning and transport planning need to go hand in hand; both may raise the politically sensitive issue of the economic and social costs of motoring.

These problems indicate the need to consider 'opportunity costs' (alternative uses of a site to ascertain which might be more cost-effective in terms of burden on, or yield to, the public purse). There is some reason to believe that the complexities of land use planning do affect the affordability of housing in the UK (Barlow and Duncan, 1994) and hence should not be separated from debates about housing need and demand.

The issue of where to build the 3.8 million new dwellings thought necessary (4.4 million if one accepts Holmans's figures) remains moot; indeed, is one of the most difficult problems confronting the Blair government. Much of these new dwellings will have to be provided in just one region, the South East. The government paper *Housing in the South East* (DETR, 1999b) suggests that in the South East region (excluding London) there will be an increase of 1.1 million households in the years 1991–2016, of which 825,000 will come from natural increase and 278,000 from migration inward, but it is precisely there that resistance to new construction is strongest. The 1.1 million figure has not been accepted by the government as a guideline for construction, in part because of evidence suggesting that provision of an additional 900,000 dwellings in the South East would have adverse consequences and might require a fundamental change in the planning process (DETR, 1999b). Instead, a target of 43,000 new dwellings over a twenty-year period was announced in the House of Commons by the Secretary of State; for London a construction rate of 23,000 dwellings per annum for twenty years was proposed, the majority being on 'brownfield' sites

(Hansard, 2000). This leaves the South East with a possible shortfall in excess of 10,000 dwellings per annum. The proposed targets for construction in the South East and London cannot be met from 'greenfield' and 'brownfield' sites alone, some use of sites being currently allocated for industrial or commercial use. Use of this 'employment land' might well impede economic growth and so the provision of new jobs in those areas affected.

It is the intention of the Secretary of State to concentrate the use of 'greenfield' sites by building extensions to existing towns (rather than by expanding rural communities), and, as far as possible to minimise growth in the south-western part of the South East, the two towns chosen for expansion being Milton Keynes and Ashford (Hansard, 2000). For an introduction to basic planning issues, see O'Leary (1998); for greater detail see the Inquiry into Planning for Housing (Rowntree, 1994).

Conclusion

Traditionally public policy in the UK has been in practice essentially pragmatic, driven by economic circumstances and considerations of political expediency; this is ce rtainly true of housing policy which is usually little more than an aggregation of tenure specific policies (see Malpass, 1996; Williams, 1997). UK housing policy has never had the pursuit of equity as a major objective.

The Blair government may seek to establish a 'joined up' housing policy (to use a term favoured by the present government), but it is extremely difficult for any government of the UK (and elsewhere) to establish a comprehensive, coherent and sustainable housing policy, for that requires fortunate circumstances, time, skill, money, and determination, which UK governments have lacked.

10

Education Policy

IAN KENDALL AND DAVID HOLLOWAY

Introduction

Central to the New Labour project is education; it is seen as pivotal to reform in a number of key economic and social policy areas. Underpinning New Labour policies are the beliefs that education enables individuals to obtain employment and stable income sources in a competitive global market, that education is crucial to overcoming the low-skill equilibrium of the British economy – low productivity and supply-side constraints to sustained growth. Education is also seen as a way to break the cycle of dependency that confronts British welfare provision by addressing issues of social exclusion. The unsurprising outcome was a general election manifesto in which education policy was a predominant feature. 'Education, education and education' were identified as the 'three major priorities' (*sic*) for the new government.

This is not to imply that the preceding (1979–97) Conservative governments had neglected education policy – indeed their radical changes provoked the conclusion that 'the educational system in England and Wales has been transformed since 1980' (McVicar and Robins, 1994, p. 203). We shall review the nature of that transformation below, and the extent to which it has been continued by New Labour. However it is important to observe that alongside some very significant changes in the organisational context in which state-funded education is provided, certain basic parameters of the relationship between the state, education and the community have remained largely unchanged for some time.

Following the raising of the school-leaving age to 16 (1972), the obligation placed on parents to provide an education for children and young people between the ages of five and sixteen years old has continued to be matched by the continuing right of all such children and young people to receive that education at an educational provider supported primarily from public expenditure. At the same time, successive governments headed by Heath, Wilson, Callaghan, Thatcher, Major and Blair have continued to voice support for an increased utilisation of post-compulsory education opportunities and to acquiesce to increasing levels of public expenditure in support of such opportunities – indeed the goal of 30 per cent of the age group going on to higher education (HE) by 2000 set by Major's government (DES, 1991) was achieved before it lost the 1997 election. Major also endorsed the goal of providing nursery education *for all*, partly in response to the National Commission on Education (1993). Whilst he made no related commitments in terms of target dates and public expenditure, it did indicate a further extension of state responsibility for educational provision beyond the free state nursery education *for all who wanted it* which had been included in a White Paper published when Margaret Thatcher was Secretary of State for Education (DES, 1972). This White Paper commitment was associated with a growing proportion of 3- and 4-year-olds in maintained state schools – a trend that has continued under successive governments, including New Labour.

Setting the significantly increasing utilisation of state-funded non-compulsory educational opportunities (for under-fives and over-sixteens) against a modest rise in the proportion of all pupils in private schools (from 5.8 per cent in 1979/80 to 6.3 per cent in 1994/95) it is difficult to avoid the conclusion that successive Conservative governments, although often associated with anti-statist rhetoric, presided over a continuation of state domination of the nation's educational provision. This is despite legislation in 1980 which established the Assisted Places Scheme, providing a system of means-tested benefits to allow parents, who otherwise could not afford to do so, to exercise a choice to 'opt out' of the state system entirely and send their children to private schools. However the funding regime for the Assisted Places scheme resulted in a very modest scheme relative to the number of children in the state system. Indeed the proportion of pupils in private schools was falling for all age groups between 1990 and 1995 at a time when there was the most dramatic increase in participation in predominantly state-funded HE.

Over a similar time period, issues relating to school standards have been on the political agenda at least from 1974, when the new Labour government set up two units – one to produce up-to-date national measures of school performance and the other to study ways of improving standards achieved by children from deprived backgrounds (see Glennerster, 1998, p. 30). It was a Labour Prime Minister (James Callaghan) who sought to instigate a 'Great Debate' on education in a speech (1976) in which he expressed concerns about both standards (e.g. literacy and numeracy attainments in primary schools) and equality of educational opportunities and outcomes (e.g. was our system of education still focusing on the needs of the academically able – remaining essentially elitist even if somewhat more meritocratic). Before he became the next Labour Prime Minister, Blair returned to the same location (Ruskin College) to deliver a rather similar message (Glennerster, 1998, p. 30), indicating both a considerable continuity in the educational concerns dominating the political agenda, and presumably some reservations about the achievements of the intervening Conservative administrations.

What the 1979–97 Conservative governments did undertake was a radical recasting of relationships *within* state education, such that the 'so-called "secret garden" of education decision-making ... was wrecked in the 1980s' (McVicar and Robins, 1994, p. 204); and in particular the role of local education authorities (LEAs) was dramatically diminished. Between 1944 and 1979 the LEAs had been a major influence on, and the dominant service provider of, all but HE – although they had also become the major provider (measured in student numbers) in the latter sector by 1979. Only the direct-grant secondary schools, the (old) universities, and a relatively modest private sector operated outside the ambit of LEAs. However by 1997 their role had been much diminished. One of our aims in this chapter is to identify the extent to which the Blair government has felt constrained or content to work within the new organisational framework created by its Conservative predecessors. We shall consider this question using the unchanged parameters of compulsory and post-compulsory education.

Compulsory Education

Since 1979 the diminishing role of LEAs can be identified in relation to five interrelated roles. These are:

- as service providers;
- as managers of educational services;

- in relation to curriculum content;
- in relation to regulating standards; and
- as service planners.

These are examined in turn, identifying the nature and extent of the changes introduced by the 1979–97 Conservative governments and the extent to which the changes have been abandoned, maintained or extended by New Labour.

There were two major attempts to supplant the LEA role as a *service provider*. The Education Act 1986 allowed for the development of City Technology Colleges (CTCs). These new secondary schools would offer free education, but could be selective in recruiting pupils. As well as gaining part of their foundation costs from industry or other sponsors, their running costs would be met by the Department of Education and Science (DES) and they would operate quite independently of LEAs. A subsequent Act (Education Reform Act (ERA) 1988) empowered the DES to enter into arrangements with non-state bodies to set up City Colleges for Technology or the Arts. It was this same piece of legislation (ERA 1988) which introduced another measure to reduce the significance of LEAs as providers of compulsory education. This allowed LEA schools to 'opt out' of LEA control altogether by creating a new category of 'grant maintained schools' which, like CTCs, would be directly financed by the DES. All secondary and primary/middle schools with over 300 parents were to be eligible for this status. The location and number of 'opted out' schools was to be driven by parental choice rather than educational planners, the starting point being expressions of parental interest, followed by a ballot of all parents – a model that New Labour has adopted for the future of the remaining grammar schools (see below).

The outcomes of these changes were less significant than some hoped and others feared. There was little support and interest from industry in CTCs and only a small number were established. Meanwhile only 315 out of a possible total of 25,000 schools decided to opt out by 1993. It was partly in response to this that the 1992 White Paper (DES, 1992) streamlined the opting-out process and created the Public Funding Agency for Schools, with powers to create new grant-maintained, centrally-funded schools free of local authority control, and set a target of 1,500 'opted out' schools by April 1994. This target had not been achieved by the 1997 general election and paradoxically the majority of those that had done so were located in the traditionally Conservative rural counties (Barber, 1997). Following that election the policy of 'opting out' has been abandoned, with a new framework locating all state-funded schools into one of three categories: community, aided and foundation schools. Only the community schools are subject to LEA-determined admissions policies. Those schools choosing foundation status are allowed by the Schools Standards and Framework Act (1998) to select 10 per cent of their intake on the basis of aptitude in a particular specialism.

One of the reasons why 'opting out' of LEA control proved to be of limited attraction to most schools, was that the relative balance between themselves and LEAs as *managers of education services* was changed by Local Management of Schools (LMS). LMS involved strengthening 'institutional (school-based) management' particularly by clarifying the status and enhancing the powers of Boards of Governors of schools relative to LEAs (and also changing the balance between elected parent governors and LEA-appointed governors on those Boards). The essential elements of LMS were far from innovatory since arrangements of this sort had been operational in some LEAs since the 1950s – but they were no longer to be a matter of local (LEA) discretion. The Education Act 1986 extended the responsibilities of governors for the general conduct of the school and some oversight of the curriculum. From April 1990 (following ERA 1988) headteachers and governing bodies of all schools with over 200 pupils became responsible for all non-capital expenditure and certain collective services. This trend has been continued by New Labour with proposals (in September 1998) for a further delegation of budgets to schools by 2000, including school meals and building maintenance; and also for capping LEAs deemed to be spending too much on 'bureaucracy'. In June 1999 the first league tables were published showing how LEAs divide their funding between schools and administration, with the government suggesting that some LEAs were failing to pass on appropriate levels of funding to their schools.

Whilst there was a long-standing tradition of devolving responsibility for *curriculum content* to LEAs and head teachers, the establishment of a national curriculum was another almost as long-standing aspiration of central government (in the Ministry of Education and later the DES). The national curriculum introduced by the ERA 1988 was intended to cover schooling up to the age of 18 and to constitute no less than 70 per cent of the total curriculum for 14–16-year-olds made up of a core curriculum (English, mathematics and science – and Welsh for Welsh-speaking schools) and seven other foundation subjects. Once established it was unlikely that any subsequent central government – Conservative or Labour – would relinquish this long-sought-after control over the school curriculum and this has proved to be the case. The national curriculum has been retained by New Labour – although revised in May 1999. The only exemption is that subjects can be dropped from the national curriculum in primary schools to accommodate the Daily Literacy Hour (introduced September 1998) and the Daily Maths Lesson (introduced September 1999) – both of which were in the new government's first White Paper (DfEE, 1997). The retention of the national curriculum, the literacy and numeracy initiatives and new pre-school targets for LEAs, indicate that central government control over the school curriculum is here to stay.

An obvious corollary of establishing a national curriculum is putting in place the means of monitoring its implementation by *regulating standards*. There was already a well-established tradition of externally set and assessed examinations, but these had been focused predominantly on the end of the child's schooling and the more able academically. The ERA 1988 established four key stages at 7, 11, 14 and 16 years of age – at each of which pupils were to be assessed. Attainment targets set out national standards in each subject area at each key stage, so that pupils, parents and teachers could assess individual, class and school progress. The 1992 Education (Schools) Act required schools to publish the exam results achieved by their pupils in both the long-established external examinations and the new National Curriculum tests. From this point onwards schools have been the subject of league tables. The 1992 legislation also contained proposals for the identification and treatment of 'failing' schools – poorly performing schools would be taken over by education 'hit squads' who would attempt to identify and remedy problems. Responsibility for the school would then transfer to a new governing body, where the majority of governors would be appointed by the DES. A key element in the new regulatory regime was OFSTED, which from 1992 introduced a new approach requiring all schools to be inspected on a four-year cycle using standardised procedures to explicit, published national criteria. The inspection covers all aspects of a school resulting in the publication of a report. The OFSTED regime has come in for considerable criticism from teachers and researchers. The criticisms range from the bureaucratic nature of the inspection process that distracts teachers from the business of teaching pupils, the costs of preparing for the inspection visit, to highly technical issues regarding the reliability and validity of the inspectors and the inspection instruments.

Despite these criticisms, Blair's government has enhanced and extended the inspection regime. Within a month of its election a new

Standards and Effectiveness Unit – to advise on improvements – was announced. The new government's first White Paper (DfEE, 1997) set targets for improvements in schools' performance, amended existing performance indicators to compare present with past results, and introduced new targets for performance in literacy and numeracy. Under the School Standards and Framework Act, 1998 schools that fail an OFSTED inspection are expected to improve within two years. Those considered to be making insufficient progress can be closed and reopened as 'Fresh Start' schools. The intention is to halt the decline of Britain's worst-performing schools. In March 2000 David Blunkett (Secretary of State for Education) urged LEAs to consider Fresh Start procedures in schools where less than 15 per cent of GCSE candidates achieve 5 grade-C passes within three years. One hundred schools were below Blunkett's threshold, although at the time there were only eight Fresh Start secondary schools – and two months later it was announced that one of these was scheduled for closure (*The Independent*, 9 May 2000, p. 9). Meanwhile 'coasting schools' have been identified as another target – that is, schools which attain a reasonable position in the league tables but should be doing better considering the nature of their intake.

Traditional notions of LEA *service planning* were challenged by one of the major themes of the Conservative Party's election manifestos in 1979 and 1983 – enhancing parental choice. A major concern of educational planners had been to ensure reasonable recruitment (via enrolment targets) for all schools, moderated in some instances by concerns for 'balanced intakes'. The outcomes could be a resource allocation sensitive to key efficiency criteria (e.g. few unused places) but insensitive to standards. If, on the other hand, parents could be given a greater influence over the selection of the schools to which their children could go, then enrolments would drop at the 'poor' schools and the staff at these schools would 'make strenuous efforts to improve their performance or, in the last analysis, face closure' (McVicar, 1990, p. 135).

The Education Act 1980 required LEAs to 'make arrangements for parents to prioritise the schools they wanted their children to attend and had a duty to comply with these preferences unless it would prejudice the provision of efficient education' (McVicar, 1990, p. 136). In addition, the legislation provided for local appeals committee to hear grievances over school allocations and limited the capacity for LEAs to limit parental choice by fixing enrolment targets. The latter was restricted further by the ERA 1988 and LEAs could no longer use the excuse of efficient service delivery as a way of moderating parent demand.

Governing bodies and LEAs had also to set out the criteria of selection they will use if demand exceeds the number of places available. Since its election the Labour government has retained the degree of parental choice introduced by its predecessors, but has recognised the continuing significance of a planning role for LEAs by their new obligation to provide Education Development Plans. It has also sought to complement parental rights by revisiting the concept of parental responsibility, introducing parent/school contracts and emphasising the legal responsibility of parents for ensuring that their children attend school.

The Future of LEAs

Successive Conservative governments seemed to have a general distrust of all local government, and hence all LEAs (and by implication probably a significant proportion of all LEA schools). This view is not shared by the New Labour government. On the other hand, the approach of the new government does owe as much to the ERA 1988 as the Education Act 1944. In particular they do not presume that all LEAs will make an equally good job of providing education in their area – a view for which the Audit Commission has provided evidence by finding significant differences between LEA performances in similar social and economic circumstances (Audit Commission, 1998a) and that LEA services vary widely in cost and quality (Audit Commission, 1999). The Commission also suggested that LEAs might be abolished if they do not reform (Audit Commission, 1998b). In January 1999 it was announced that all LEAs would be subject to their own OFSTED inspections by 2001 and subsequently at least once every five years. LEAs may be judged to be 'failing' on the basis of these inspections and their own Education Development Plans. In such cases private companies and non-profit organisations may be considered – along with other LEAs – to take on the education services in these 'failing LEAs'.

If New Labour has adopted or adapted much of the organisational framework inherited from the 1979–97 Conservative governments, it did introduce at least one major new organisational initiative which also appeared to pose a threat to the future of LEAs. These were the Education Action Zones (EAZs) proposed in *Excellence in Schools* (DfEE, 1997) and introduced by the School Standards and Framework Act 1998. In some respects they parallel the Health Action Zones (HAZs) (see Chapter 8). They were intended to be located in 'deprived areas' and to involve partnerships between LEAs and others. In particular it was indicated that businesses and parents should play a leading role in planning and developing the projects – business involvement being the subject of criticisms by LEAs and teaching unions (see *The Times*, 7 January 1998). Every EAZ had to raise £250,000 from outside the education system. They would have considerable discretion to vary the curriculum, the school day, the school year and teachers' contracts; and to merge or open schools. Twelve EAZs were to start in September 1998 and a further thirteen in January 1999. In the event, EAZs have been, like much else, less radical than the hopes of their supporters and the fears of their detractors. Teachers contracts, the national curriculum, the traditional academic year and, perhaps most significantly, the role of LEAs remain much as before. On the other hand it is a popular initiative. By March 2000 there were 73 EAZs with a further 12 'mini-EAZs' in inner-city areas. There will be a further 30 EAZs by September 2000 by which time 1 in 10 of Britain's schools will be involved in the initiative. Like HAZs, some of the hoped-for benefits of EAZs may take some time to appear, and there will anyway be the difficult task of disentangling the impact of EAZs from the other initiatives intended to raise educational standards. However after 18 months of operation some test results for EAZs were showing improvements above the national average.

That New Labour should seem to inherit a degree of suspicion of the attributes of LEAs should really come as no surprise. This is not, after all, an exclusively Conservative inheritance for New Labour. Throughout the twentieth century UK governments with radical social policy aspirations have been suspicious of the capacity of existing organisations to deliver much more than the status quo. In particular, the more radical reforms of the post-war Labour government diminished very dramatically the welfare role of local government (in health and social security). It is therefore unsurprising that the significance attached to education by successive governments, especially since James Callaghan instituted 'The Great Debate', has been accompanied by a significant enhancement of central control and regulation of many aspects of education policy and practice; and by the same token a steady diminution (and in some areas marginalisation) of the role of LEAs in the planning, regulating, resourcing and day-to-day provision of educational services. On the other hand, the future threat to LEAs seems to lie less in an ideological mistrust allied to the vagaries of local expressions of parental preferences, than in the evidence generated by the regulatory regimes which are now in place (OFSTED, league tables and the work of the Audit Commission). The significant LEA role in the EAZ initiative indicates that the future role of LEAs is now more in their own hands – at least with regard to compulsory education. By way of contrast there seems no way back for LEAs in the post-compulsory sector, as the following sections illustrate.

Further Education (FE)

During their eighteen years in power successive Conservative governments had been particularly active in changing the structure, governance and curriculum of the post-compulsory sector; and in particular to have created a new sector of education with the passing of the Further and Higher Education Act (FHEA) 1992 (Smithers and Robinson, 2000). Underpinning the changes were a set of political and ideological beliefs that FE institutions were inflexible, 'producer dominated' and unresponsive to the needs of employers, their local economies and communities. Critical reports identified inefficient resource utilisation (Audit Commission, 1985) and unacceptably high rates of student wastage and non-completion of courses (Audit Commission/OFSTED, 1993). In addition there was concern dating back to the 1970s (OECD, 1975) regarding the low national participation rate in post-16 education and what was perceived to be poor performance in the sector in terms of basic skills and examination achievements. The approach of the Blair government to the FE sector has been characterised by a range of policy initiatives and legislation culminating in the Learning and Skills Bill currently passing through the Parliamentary process. Taken together they suggest that New Labour has a stronger commitment to the sector than its Conservative predecessor, although profoundly influenced by the legacy of marketisation, privatisation and, crucially, the funding methodology.

FHEA 1992 completed the process started by the ERA 1988, of removing post-16 education institutions from LEA control. A new sector of 465 institutions was created on the 1st April 1993 comprising 224 colleges of further education, 63 tertiary colleges, 116 sixth-form colleges, 35 agricultural colleges, 13 art and design colleges and 14 other institutions including the WEA and two nautical colleges. These further education colleges (FECs) acquired their own legal identity and became independent self-governing institutions responsible for their own staffing, estate and finances. College governing bodies were reconstituted allowing members drawn from business backgrounds to become dominant. LEAs were no longer necessarily represented on governing bodies.

The Act also established the Further Education Funding Council (FEFC), accountable to the DfEE, to allocate and monitor funds, advise on reorganisation, institutional mergers and closures and take over the LEA responsibility for inspection and quality. In fulfilling its duties under the Act, the FEFC is required to strike a balance between securing maximum access to the widest possible range of FE opportunities and avoiding a disproportionate charge on public funds. The FEFC receives guidance from the Secretary of State for Education and Employment on its functions, and on government policies and particular matters relevant to the exercise of those functions; it is entirely dependent upon the Secretary of State for its funding. FEFC was not intended to be a planning organisation, but to have an 'arm's length' relationship with FECs, operating in a regulatory rather than a managerial role. FECs were in a market environment responsible for their own strategic planning and day-to-day management within a financial and quality framework determined by FEFC.

FECs have expanded substantially since incorporation in April 1993 in response to the policy of the Conservative government both to increase and widen participation. Enrolment has increased from 2.9 million in 1993 to 4 million students of all ages and abilities with particularly strong growth in part-time numbers masking a decline in full-time students since 1995–6. Driving the expansion has been a funding methodology explicitly designed to reward efficient successful colleges and improve participation and retention of students (see McClure, in Smithers and Robinson, 2000). Failure to achieve agreed targets results in the FEFC 'reclaiming' the excess funding in the next financial year. FECs were forced to compete with each other and establish relationships with other organisations. While much of this collaboration has been advantageous for both provider and learner, Gravatt and Silver (in Smithers and Robinson, 2000) direct attention to a specific form of collaborative provision known as 'franchising' whereby colleges subcontract to employers for training provision. This arrangement enabled some employers to receive considerable subsidies from public funds to meet their training provision and led to the investigation of the financial probity of a number of institutions in 1998 and 1999.

The design of the funding methodology was undoubtedly influenced by critical Audit Commission reports (Audit Commission, 1985, 1993) which may also be seen as underpinning the move, in the 1990s, from a public service to more market orientated model characterised by a strong managerialist thrust (Holloway 1999). The funding regime has affected virtually every area of FEC activity: there has been expansion in the use of sophisticated management information systems throughout the sector, and aspects of good marketing practice have been developed including attempts to establish stronger linkages between marketing, strategic management, the management of the curriculum and the management of resources including personnel. FECs have made a concerted effort to transform their image, 'sloughing off their technical school past and evolving towards a broader community-wide comprehensive future' (Scott, 1996) in order to enter new markets, respond to employer training demands and since 1998 address the New Labour 'Lifelong Learning' agenda.

The real costs of the funding regime have often been borne, however, by the sector labour force. With corporate status, college principals became chief executive officers with responsibilities for financial control, educational planning and student discipline. Well-publicised salary increases accompanied the new roles but many principals found the pressures hard to cope with – it has been reported that only one-third of principals who were in post on the 1st April 1993 are still in office. Driven by the need to make 'substantial efficiency gains' and reduce costs, college managements embarked on reorganisations and 'restructuring' involving 'delayering', 'flexibility', redundancies and changes to staff roles and functions. The national agreement that codified conditions of service and remuneration was scrapped and a 'new model contract' imposed as staff took industrial action. The sector has long made extensive use of part-time staff but by 1997 casualisation had resulted in a situation where 45 per cent of college staff were on non-permanent employment contracts (NATFHE, 1998, cited in Smithers and Robinson, 2000). Whether such developments are indicative of deprofessionalisation remains unknown; the cynicism, suspicion and low morale found amongst teaching staff cannot be doubted.

While in Opposition, New Labour supported reform of the sector's funding methodology. However, despite two reviews carried out by the National Audit Office (NAO, 1997a, 1997b), an internal review chaired by Helena Kennedy QC (FEFC, 1997), and scrutiny by the Education Sub-Committee of the Parliamentary Education and Employment Committee, the arrangements have survived and are likely to remain in place. The Parliamentary Sub-Committee recognised, as did the New Labour government, that the roots of the problem rested not in the allocation system but in the long-term underfunding of the sector. This is well illustrated by evidence of reductions in total FEFC funding for the sector which revealed a decline from £3,168 million in 1993/4 to £3,039 million in 1997/8, a period during which student numbers had increased by approximately 30 per cent (Education and Employment Sub-Committee, 1998, cited in Smithers and Robinson, 2000).

In February 1998, *The Learning Age: A Renaissance for A New Britain* Green Paper (DfEE, 1998a) was published setting out the government's 'lifelong learning' agenda. Arguably the key proposal was for the introduction of Individual Learning Accounts (ILAs) intended to encourage individuals to invest in their own education and training with financial support from the government. Echoing the concerns of the previous government is the signal that ILAs could be used 'to make providers more responsive to learners' needs' (DfEE, 1988a). While the Green Paper did not provide detail on the working of the scheme, it did allocate £150 million to support pilot projects in conjunction with 34 Training and Enterprise Councils (TECs).

The Green Paper also gave substance to an idea for extending and developing work-based learning that had been in Labour Party documents since the mid-1990s. It proposed a supply-side policy solution, the establishment of the University for Industry (UfI) to 'offer access to a learning network to help people deepen their knowledge, update their skills and gain new ones' (DfEE, 1998a). Inspired by the success of the Open University in widening access to HE, the UfI is intended to act as a broker between learners and learning opportunities by providing advice and guidance through a telecommunications service, Learning Direct, coordinating a national network of learning centres, identifying gaps in existing provision, commissioning and quality assuring products and services.

After extensive consultation the government published a White Paper, *Learning to Succeed* (DfEE, 1999), and the Learning and Skills Bill that is currently passing through Parliament. The Bill proposes the replacement of the FEFC and the TECs from April 2001 with a new Learning and Skills Council (LSC) – a Non-Departmental Public Body with a budget of approximately £6 billion and responsibilities for FE, work-based training for young people and workforce development. It will take over the funding responsibilities of the FEFC; advise the government on National Learning Targets; fund the Modern Apprenticeship scheme and other workforce development initiatives currently supported through the TECs; develop in conjunction with the LEAs arrangements for adult and community learning; provide information, advice and guidance to adults; and seek to establish coherence across 14–19 education work.

It is proposed that the LSC should operate through 47 local LSCs which will have responsibility for co-ordinating local area plans and building on the work of Local Learning Partnerships. Addressing the quality agenda, the Bill also introduces a new inspection regime replacing the current arrangements whereby FE is inspected by the FEFC and TEC funded training schemes audited against quality standards established by the former Employment Department. Yet despite the criticism of the current inspection arrangements that they are excessively bureaucratic, complex and fragmented, the Bill separates inspection processes for young people up to the age of 19 years from those for adults, with OFSTED assuming responsibility for the former and a new Adult Learning Inspectorate (ALI) being created for post-19 learners.

The passage of the Bill through Parliament has not been smooth. Challenges to the government strategy followed the release of FEFC data in April 2000 revealing a decline in student numbers for the second year running after twenty years of growth. The data shows a 0.3 per cent decline from November 1998 to November 1999 following an earlier 1 per cent decline. The biggest fall was amongst full-time adult students (*Times Higher Education Supplement*, 21 April 2000) and this has led to a questioning of the government's optimistic forecasts for student numbers. It has also led to questions again being asked about the way in which the funding system is driving the FECs to recruit students on to low-cost courses while neglecting areas that require a high level of tutor support in the information technologies (*Education Guardian*, 2 May 2000).

Higher Education (HE)

The period from the early 1960s has seen an almost continuous growth in the number of students attending higher education institutions (HEIs), a shift from an elite model towards a mass model of HE. In 1961/2 there were 203,000 full and part-time students in the sector; by 1970/1 that number had risen to 621,000 followed by slower growth during the 1970s. The 1980s saw a rapid expansion to almost one million students at the end of the decade followed by further expansion to 1.6 million when Labour came into office in 1997. Over 30 per cent of school-leavers now attend HEIs, leading some commentators to claim that the expansion has been 'more of the same'. But this would ignore the proportion of women in the total student population rising from approximately 30 per cent to 50 per cent during the period, although the proportion of entrants from working-class families has remained the same and participation rates for some minority ethnic groups and people with disabilities remains low.

McVicar and Robins (1994) claimed that HE policy in the United Kingdom since the early 1980s had been 'a curious mix of few long term policy objectives together with a large number of contradictory short term policies'. During the period of Conservative governments a combination of pragmatic incrementalism and long-term ideologically driven strategic planning created a major policy shift. Underlying the policy shift it is possible to discern similar themes to those which could be identified in both the schools and FE sectors: a reduction in the scale of public expenditure as a percentage of the total expenditure on HE; the removal of HEIs from LEA control; major changes in the governance and regulation of HEIs; and the introduction of the 'new managerialism' accompanied by the centralisation of power and authority.

Before the passing of the FHEA 1992, HE consisted of two distinct sectors: a university sector and a public sector. The former comprised 43 independent, chartered institutions financed directly by government quangos – the Universities Grants Committee until it was replaced in 1989 by the University Funding Council (UFC). The public sector comprised 30 polytechnics and approximately sixty colleges and institutes of HE, owned and controlled by the LEAs but from 1979 financed directly by national funding bodies thereby allowing greater central government control. The FHEA 1992 brought the universities and the public sector HEIs together to form a unified sector by removing the latter from LEAs. Three national funding councils (FCs) for England, Wales and Scotland replaced previous arrangements and provide the largest proportion of HEI funding. The Higher Education Funding Council for England (HEFCE) currently states its mission as working 'in partnership, we promote and fund high quality, cost-effective teaching and research meeting the diverse needs of students, the economy and society'. The three FCs advise the government on the funding needs of the sector and are responsible for allocating funds to HEIs and to those FECs that provide HE programmes. It has been argued that in the absence of strategic planning responsibilities the FCs have difficulties in developing coherent policies across a range of issues and in particular that the methodologies for funding teaching (to encourage participation) and funding research (to encourage selectivity) were pulling in opposite directions. The FCs' function is to implement the government's predetermined objectives through second order policies, with individual HEIs retaining responsibility for their own strategic planning and development.

The lack of a clear strategic direction for the sector combined with a financial crisis created by the effects of rapid underfunded expansion in the mid-1990s, led the Conservative government to establish a National Committee of Inquiry into Higher Education under the Chairmanship of Sir Ron Dearing. The Committee was required to make recommendations on how 'the purpose, shape, structure, size and funding of HE, including support for students, should develop to meet the needs of the UK over the next twenty years, recognising that higher education embraces teaching, learning, scholarship and research' (NCIHE, 1997). The terms of reference and committee membership were agreed by the major political parties arguably indicating the need for a national consensus on the reform of HW, but perhaps also to keep the contentious issue of student contribution to tuition fees off the agenda for the 1997 general election.

The Dearing Committee reported after the election of the New Labour government, making 93 recommendations. The report addressed key debates taking place in the sector: the balance between research and teaching, institutional missions, funding issues, the curriculum and its delivery and improving the quality of teaching, learning and research in the sector. In response the government published *Higher Education for the 21st Century* (DfEE, 1998b) in which it gave support to many of the Dearing recommendations. The key policy proposal in the document addressed New Labour's social inclusion agenda by advocating widening participation in HE. This would be achieved by targeting social groups under-represented in HE, introducing sub-degree programmes, encouraging teaching and learning strategies required for the new groups of learners entering the sector and using the funding mechanisms to provide financial inducements. While this can be seen as a departure from the approach of the previous Conservative government which until the mid-1990s did not encourage the HEFCE to fund special initiatives to steer the system, there is little evidence of any shift in the overall approach to funding HE.

This is clearly shown by the continuation of Conservative government policies reforming the student funding arrangements where New Labour is completing the transition from state-financed maintenance grants to a loan-repayments model. Despite its commitment to additional spending on post-compulsory education, a key funding initiative introduced by New Labour has been highly controversial with consequences extending way beyond education debates into areas of constitutional reform and the elections to the Scottish Parliament. New Labour implemented a recommendation of the Dearing Committee to introduce annual tuition fees of £1,000 for all undergraduate courses. The policy had not featured in the general election manifesto or campaign but it can be argued that it is congruent with underpinning New Labour philosophies that those who benefit from education should make a greater financial contribution towards it and that individuals should take more responsibility for their own learning. This latter belief is also underpinning the ILAs proposed in *The Learning Age* Green Paper. The tuition fees have been introduced at a time when the number of applicants for entry to HE has been declining. This decline is particularly marked for the applicants aged over 25. The government has drawn attention to the measures designed to encourage students from disadvantaged backgrounds and is actively promoting expansion of part-time HE provision through targeted initiatives. Whether or not these measures are sufficient to persuade adult learners back into education as part of the lifelong learning agenda remains to be seen. It can be argued that New Labour is addressing the problems confronting HE guided by the recommendation of the Dearing Report. However, this leaves New Labour open to the criticism that its initiatives, rather like the Dearing Report proposals, lack coherence and a clear long-term vision.

Conclusion

The stated intentions of the 1974–79 Labour and 1979–97 Conservative governments were broadly similar, and expressed in much the same language (see Glennerster, 1998, p. 29). In many respects the post-1997 Labour government has maintained this continuity. The key aim is to raise the standard of educational attainment, and the chosen means still include organisational change (from FEFC and TECs to LSCs), organisational innovation (EAZs), funding methodologies (FE/HE) and a close scrutiny of LEAs – whose future, even in their diminished role, remains uncertain. Meanwhile the new government has enthusiastically embraced a number of initiatives which it is actively promoting, including UfI, ILAs, out-of-school child care and learning activities, literacy schools during the holidays for primary school leavers, family literacy centres, early excellence centres, homework clubs, and mentoring. In addition 75 'beacon schools' are being identified to share their best practice. The number and range of these initiatives raises the inevitable question of their strategic coherence and understandable concerns about 'initiative overload'.

Whilst pursuing a plethora of new initiatives, New Labour has sought to minimise conflict in two areas which have at times been associated with fiercely partisan positions. Both the existence of a small private sector in education and a number of grammar schools, appear to be of limited concern to New Labour. The Assisted Places scheme was abandoned (in the Education (Schools) Act 1997) and the public expenditure re-directed towards reducing class sizes in primary schools. Meanwhile they have established a modest Independent School State School Partnership (ISSP) which by April 2000 involved 127 partnerships, 390 schools and 35,000 children. The fate of the remaining grammar schools is seen as something which should not concern central government, but return to being a matter of local discretion; the regulations to allow local communities to decide on the future of grammar schools were approved in January 1999.

The area where many people were hoping for fewest signs of continuity with previous governments was in relation to public expenditure on education. It was a characteristic of the 1979–97 Conservative governments, especially those led by Margaret Thatcher, that they were rarely prepared to concede that deficiencies in the quality of public services might be attributable to insufficient expenditure relative to stated policy goals, preferring to blame the failings of public sector bureaucracies and professionals. There is certainly not a simple relationship between expenditure and standards, as indicated by the American evidence, where significant increases in spending per pupil between 1970 and 1990 had no discernible impact on standards of achievement (see Glennerster, 1998, p. 42). More parochially it has been a constant feature of Audit Commission reports that the achievements of LEAs and FECs vary even where expenditures and circumstances are broadly similar. Nonetheless, the UK education system had been subject to a lengthy period of constrained expenditure originating with the 1974–9 Labour government. In 1960 the UK was spending a higher proportion of its GDP on education than most comparable nations, but by 1988 an OECD 24-nation study showed that the UK spent less of its GDP on education than any other member (see McVicar and Robins, 1994, p. 204). This was the result of the

> public spending strategies of successive Governments which reduced the share of the GDP allocated to publicly funded education from 6.5% in 1975/6 to 4.7% in 1998/99. The significance of this change should not be under-estimated. No such previous reduction

in education's share of the nation's resources had occurred this century ... (it) is not to be found in the experience of any other leading nation. (Glennerster, 1998, p. 36)

As a result there has been a further area of continuity between the governments led by Major and Blair: how to deal with the consequences of a decade and half of major constraints on education expenditure instituted by Callaghan's Labour government and continued by Thatcher's Conservative governments. Major's governments set out to address the backlog of underspending by increases in real spending between 1991/92 and 1994/95 (including 4.7 per cent in 1992/3), but this tailed off rapidly to no real increase in 1995/96 and a real decrease in 1996/97! In its first two years the new Labour government was restrained by an election commitment to live within the previous government's public expenditure, although its first (1997) budget did include an additional £1 billion for schools (not post-compulsory education) from the contingency reserve. There is little doubt that the 'public expenditure inheritance' of the new government is significant and problematic – and there seems little doubt that the sort of real increases in education spending currently planned (5 per cent for 1999–2002; see HM Treasury, 1998c) may well need to be sustained for several years to redress the impact of that inheritance.

Equally, and many would argue directly related, there is little doubt that New Labour has also inherited some major problems in relation to educational standards in the UK despite the attention they have attracted from successive governments. Various research findings have continued to identify Britain's relatively poor achievements in schooling and vocational training, and the associated 'back-log' of underachievement represented by 7 million adults with serious problems with maths and reading (see Prais, 1995; ONS, 1997; and Working Group on Post-School Basic Skills, 1999). The resulting under-achievement and the absence of basic skills being linked to both economic and social consequences.

There is evidence that some of the new initiatives are having an impact, with dramatic improvements in English and Maths, including some better than average improvements recorded in EAZs. GCSE and A-level pass rates continue to improve and the inspectors say primary school standards are rising; meanwhile schools are coming out of 'special measures' faster than they are going in (*The Independent*, 9 March 2000). Also, by January 1999, there was evidence that the government was starting to fulfil one of its election pledges by decreasing primary school class sizes – these had been increasing significantly throughout the 1990s. On the other hand this same evidence indicates the continuation of wide gaps between 'good' and 'bad' schools.

The government has also recorded some success in relation to pupils being permanently excluded from maintained primary, secondary and special schools. These numbers were increasing rapidly under the previous government (up 13 per cent between 1994/95 and 1996/97) but showed an immediate reduction by 1997/98 (of 3 per cent). The School Exclusion Unit has proposed cutting such exclusions by one-third by 2002 (School Exclusion Unit, 1997). This ambitious target may be achievable but not without conflict, with many teachers and parents concerned at the impact of non-excluded 'disruptive' pupils on the educational standards of their classmates. The government responded to some of these concerns by a pledge to provide 'sin-bins' in schools. This does lead to the inevitable cautionary note that it may take some time to judge the effectiveness of the education policies associated with New Labour – whether they represent genuinely new departures, or amendments and adaptations of the policy initiatives of their predecessors. In particular, of the many changes introduced since 1997 at least some (LSCs, the new curriculum for 16–19-year-olds, sin bins) are, as we write, not yet or only just operational.

New Labour's strategy for education combines a continuing (and in certain respects greater) control of classroom activities (e.g. national curriculum, literacy hour, daily maths lesson), continuing public access to outcomes (e.g. improved league tables) and continuing (and in certain respects extended) regulatory regimes (OFSTED, Audit Commission); this is allied to a strategy of sustained and real increases in public expenditure on education with the intended outcomes of both overall improvements and less disparities in UK educational standards. None of these approaches are by themselves especially new or distinctive. On the other hand what we do have is a particular combination of approaches which no previous post-war government has attempted. If this combination can be sustained over a sufficient time period it is possible that it will address some of the concerns about relative educational performance by and within the UK, but it may also be some time before we can make definitive judgments on their degree of success.

11

The Personal Social Services*

Norman Johnson

Introduction

The personal social services are probably the least understood of the major areas of public policy reviewed in this book. Everyone has some idea, even if not wholly accurate and somewhat vague, of the functions of education, health, housing and social security services, but what the personal social services do, and who provides them, are far from clear. Baldock (1998, p. 306) sums up the position:

> There is a residual quality to the personal social services. Their responsibilities can sometimes appear to be a ragbag of disparate social rescue activities that are left over by the other parts of the welfare system. They have been called the 'fifth social service': seen as last not only in terms of size but also in terms of resort; the service people turn to when all else has failed.

This lack of prominence is confirmed by a comparison of the expenditure figures for 1998: expenditure on the personal social services amounted to £10 billion as compared with £133 billion on social security, £46 billion on health services and £38 billion on education. Personal social services consumed about 3 per cent of total public expenditure.

Given the restricted size of their resources, it might be tempting to dismiss the personal social services as an unimportant area of public policy. A quite different conclusion, however, results from a consideration of the services they provide and their significance in the lives of vulnerable groups in the population.

The personal social services consist of social care (as distinct from health care) provided by local authority social services departments and a variety of related agencies for:

- children and families
- older people
- people with physical disabilities
- people with learning disabilities
- people with mental illness
- people with drug or alcohol abuse problems
- ex-offenders

Services may be provided to individuals, groups or whole communities: they may be delivered in clients' own homes, in residential establishments or in day care facilities. The settings, the perceived needs of particular client groups and the types of workers involved are closely interrelated, but the distinguishing characteristic of the tasks carried out by social services departments is their diversity. For example, social work is usually thought to be the key activity of the personal social services, but social work itself is ill-defined and may take many forms, and the great majority of the people employed by social services departments (86 per cent) are not professionally qualified social workers: administrative and clerical staff; workers in residential homes and in day centres; those employed as home care workers or in the meals-on-wheels service.

A number of highly publicised child abuse cases, some of them allegedly mishandled by social workers, the police and local councillors, has meant that this aspect of their work is more readily recognised than the services they provide for other groups. It is therefore paradoxical that services for children in terms of the resources consumed and the numbers served are dwarfed by services for older people. In 1997/98 just under half of total expenditure was devoted to services for older people as compared with 23 per cent spent on children's services. These two groups together accounted for almost three-quarters of total expenditure. A long way behind came services for people with learning disability (13 per cent), adults (9 per cent) and mental illness (5 per cent).

The number of children being looked after by local authorities in England, Wales and Northern Ireland at the end of March 1999 was

59,000, of whom 66 per cent lived with foster parents. It should be noted that this figure relates to a particular day in the year: the number looked after in the course of a year (some for a relatively short time) is very much greater. Furthermore, the number of children looked after does not give a wholly accurate indication of the work done with children, since the work of the social services departments is not limited to children formally being looked after; there are, for example, 35,500 children on Child Protection Registers. At the end of March 1998 local authorities in England were supporting over 261,000 people in residential homes; about 80 per cent of supported residents were older people. In a survey conducted in a week in September 1998 over 630,000 meals were provided for 160,000 people in their own homes by or on behalf of English local authorities. A further 340,000 meals were provided by local authorities in luncheon clubs or day centres. In the same week local authorities provided or paid for 2.6 million hours of home care for 446,000 households. Elderly people are the chief beneficiaries of the meals and home care services. The majority of day centre attendances are accounted for by people with learning disabilities. In the survey week in 1998 local authority social services departments in England provided or paid for 643,000 day centre places for about 250,000 people (many of whom attended more than once a week). Although these figures are impressive and give an indication of the scale of the operations of the personal social services, three qualifications need to be borne in mind: (i) social services departments provide help for only a small minority of each client group; families always have been, and remain, the main providers of social care services; (ii) many people will never have the need to use the personal social services throughout their lives, and this presents a sharp contrast to health services and education; (iii) increasingly, social services departments are becoming enablers rather than direct providers of services.

The Conservative Legacy

When the Labour government took office in 1997, the National Health Service and Community Care Act had been in operation for almost four years. The Act implemented the proposals of the Griffiths Report (1988), making local authorities the lead agencies in community care, but requiring them to work in collaboration with health authorities, other statutory agencies and independent providers.

Principally, the role of local authorities was to assess the community needs within their localities, to take steps to ensure that these were met and to monitor performance. The main change was a purchaser/provider split in which local authorities ceased to be the main direct providers of services: they were expected to make the maximum use of commercial and voluntary sector providers. This led to the creation of internal or quasi-markets. The role of social services departments was to act 'as the designers, organisers and purchasers of non-health care services, and not primarily as direct providers, making the maximum possible use of voluntary and private sector bodies' (Griffiths, 1988, p. 1). Local authorities would remain the chief source of finance and regulation.

Clearly, the community care reforms are an aspect of privatisation, although the growth of privatisation began well before the implementation of the NHS and Community Care Act in 1993. Privatisation began to expand significantly in the 1980s, and this trend was strengthened by the community care changes. The most rapid extension of provision by independent providers occurred in residential care. In March 1998 the independent sector (commercial and voluntary sector combined) provided 88 per cent of the places in residential and nursing homes. This compares with 82 per cent in 1994 and less than 40 per cent in 1980. The vast majority of the places in 1998 were in commercially operated homes; indeed the proportion of places provided by the voluntary sector has actually declined since 1980. Close to 80 per cent of local authority supported residents were accommodated in independent establishments in 1999, as compared with 63 per cent in 1995 and 20 per cent in 1993.

A Statistical Bulletin (Department of Health, 1999a) gives details of three community services provided or paid for by social services departments: home help and home care; meals; day centres. The figures permit some estimation of the impact of the NHS and Community Care Act. The independent sector provided 45 per cent of the home help/care contact hours in 1998 compared with only 2 per cent in 1992. The non-statutory sector delivered 41 per cent of the meals going to people's homes and 39 per cent of meals served at luncheon clubs. Day centre provision remains predominantly in the hands of local authorities but the proportion provided by the independent sector has risen steadily since 1992 from 10 per cent in that year to 22 per cent in 1998. The independent sector has made greater inroads into services for adults than it has into services for children and families.

The Blair Government and the Personal Social Services

In the manifesto and the election campaign, the Labour Party identified education as its number one priority closely followed by health. Welfare to work and law and order were also highlighted. The personal social services were given much less prominence.

In its first year of office, the government's promises relating to education, health care and welfare to work occupied the centre ground of political debate and were the main focus of the media. Much less attention was paid to the personal social services. Since 1998 however, this has changed. There have been innumerable ministerial statements, sets of guidelines, a White Paper and legislation. The remainder of this chapter will attempt to summarise and evaluate the developments.

Resources

There has been some disagreement between the Department of Health and representatives of local authorities about the level of resources being made available to the personal social services. On the one hand, the Department of Health Statistics Division indicates that the total budgets for 1997/98 were 94 per cent higher in real terms than in 1986/87 (Department of Health, 1998a). On the other hand, a survey by the Local Government Association (LGA) and the Association of Directors of Social Services (ADSS), published in June 1998, reported that social services departments faced an average shortfall of 3.4 per cent against their spending plans despite an increase in government funding of 1.2 per cent in real terms. Cuts in services were planned by 54 per cent of local authorities and 60 per cent were either increasing charges, imposing them for the first time or increasing exemption thresholds. Other cost-cutting strategies included restricting access to services and increasing the fees paid to independent providers by less than inflation. Pressures were particularly acute, LGA/ADSS claim, because of the effects of accumulated reductions of central government funding in previous years – from 1992/93 to 1997/98 a fall of 6.1 per cent in real terms taking inflation and demographic trends into account. The dispute about resources rumbles on, but extra resources have been allocated to personal social services since the LGA/ADSS report referred to above. The three-year comprehensive spending review of July 1998 gave councils an extra £2.2 billion: in addition, £3.6 million was released from the sale of council houses and councils were expected to raise £2.75 billion from the sale of assets. An interesting aspect of the financial settlement was £800 million for what was termed 'a new deal for communities' to tackle unemployment, crime and low educational standards in about twenty of the country's poorest housing estates. But the Chancellor's calculations were based on the presumption of a 5 per cent increase in council tax, and local authorities claimed that there would still be a shortfall in 1999/2000 of £1 billion. The White Paper, *Modernising Social Services*, published at the end of November 1998, promised an extra £3 billion over three years and the establishment of a social services modernisation fund into which would be paid £1.3 billion (Department of Health, 1998b). The extra resources have now been made available and the modernisation fund has been established. The fund consists of five elements: two grants – the Partnership Grant and the Prevention Grant – are intended to promote independence; there is also a Children's Services Grant, a Mental Health Grant and additional money for the Training Support Programme. Extra resources have also been associated with particular policy initiatives, but these may be more conveniently considered in the next section when some of the policy initiatives are examined.

Priorities

The government's priorities stem from their identification of the shortcomings of current personal social services. The introduction to *Modernising Social Services* identifies a wide range of failings:

- Inadequate protection for children and vulnerable adults
- Lack of coordination
- Inflexibility
- Lack of clarity about roles, objectives and standards
- Inconsistency
- Inefficiency

The White Paper emphasises the government's determination to address these failings and sets down the priorities for both children's services and adult services. In the case of children, the priorities are protection, quality of care and improving life chances. For adults the priorities are independence, improving consistency and providing convenient, user-centred services. There has been considerable concern about the quality of care provided for children. and the government has launched a major child care strategy to improve the management of family and children's services, to improve the quality of services and to give considerably more protection. The first indication of this came in the 1998 report of the Chief Inspector of the Social Services Inspectorate which, like several before it, was highly critical of the inconsistent quality of the work done for children and families, and the complete absence of a coherent strategy in many authorities. In September 1998, the government announced a drive to deliver a new deal for children looked after by local authorities and set on foot the Quality Protects programme. The programme, accompanied by a document setting out the government's objectives for children's services in considerable detail, required local authorities to evaluate their provision, identify shortcomings and take action to remedy them (Department of Health, 1998c). Local authorities were required to submit to the Secretary of State a Quality Protects Management Action Plan by the end of January 1999. Growing public dismay about the number of children abused while being looked after by local authorities – especially those in residential care – has resulted in much tighter regulation. The Protection of Children Act 1999 transformed the vetting and registration of people deemed unsuitable for work with children. Access to the records of the Criminal Records Bureau and the Consultancy Index will create a one-stop shop for those about to employ someone for work with children. The Criminal Justice and Court Services Bill, presented to the House of Commons in March 2000, will complete the system.

The Care Standards Act 2000 will revolutionise the system of regulation. It provides for the establishment of a new independent regulatory body for social care and voluntary and private health care to be known as the National Care Standards Commission. It will be responsible for regulating, setting standards and arranging for the inspection of the whole range of residential and domiciliary services, and eventually a network of eight independent regional inspectorates will be formed. This new system will replace all the present regulatory functions of local and health authorities. The Commission will be required to appoint a children's rights director, a high-ranking official with the task of ensuring that the work for children is not swamped by the greater volume of work for adults.

It is interesting to note that local authority and voluntary adoption and fostering agencies will also be subject to inspection. The government has been critical of the operation of the adoption system. In April 2000 the government published a report showing that 2,400 children were ready for adoption and awaiting a match with a family. The time taken to make the necessary arrangements was unacceptably long and one suggestion made in the report is for the creation of a national computerised register.

Another major change in children's services will come about with the enactment of the Children (Leaving Care) Bill, introduced in November 1999. The Act will lay much stronger duties on councils to support care leavers up to at least 18. The Bill implements the proposals of a report published in July 1999 (Department of Health, 1999b).

The Blair administration has accepted the recommendations of an inquiry set on foot by the previous Conservative government into the organisation of training for social work. Training functions of the Central Council for Education and Training in Social Work have been taken over by an employer-led National Training Organisation. The new organisation, to be called the Training Organisation for the Personal Social Services, will be one of many such structures and, as its title suggests, its remit will go well beyond social work training to cover the training needs of all personal social services employees. The Care Standards Act takes this a stage further with the establishment of a General Social Care Council to regulate both the conduct and training of all social care staff. The Council will be responsible for setting up and maintaining a register of all social care personnel.

In July 2000, the Health Minister announced the establishment of a Social Care Institute for Excellence to give authoritative guidance on good practice and to reduce unacceptable variations in levels of service. He also promised a consultation paper in raising the quality of social services.

In describing the new and proposed legislation and changes in practice the emphasis so far has been on children. But clearly, many of the new arrangements apply to all categories of users. The provisions of the Care Standards Act, for example, are not restricted to children. The Protection of Children Act gives the Secretary of State the power to extend its provisions to vulnerable adults suffering from mental impairment. There are now plans to extend similar provision to older people, the impetus coming from cases of physical and sexual abuse or just sheer neglect of older people in both residential and domiciliary settings. The Department of Health (2000a) issued guidelines at the end of March 2000. Multi-agency codes of practice are to be developed, but social services directors are being given the responsibility for coordinating the development of the codes and ensuring that they are fully implemented by the end of October 2001.

One of the features of most of the new approaches is the use of measures to assess performance or standards of provision. This is the explicit intention of the Care Standards Act and the Quality Protects programme. Joint reviews of social services departments by the Social Services Inspectorate and the Audit Commission have been in operation since 1997. A full-scale review of the performance of each authority across the whole range of its social services responsibilities is carried out and a written report is published. Increasingly, extra government funding is made conditional upon the attainment of particular targets. Nowhere is this more explicit than in the community mental health services. New money totalling £46.4 million will be made available to local authorities against signed undertakings to use the additional funding to achieve specified policy objectives. These include the provision of social care staff to work on multi-disciplinary outreach teams; social care support for people in medium-secure units and units with 24-hour staffed beds; additional residential, day and respite care and the appointment of a senior manager with sole or predominant responsibility for mental health.

In 1998 the Department of Health commissioned the Centre for Policy on Ageing to devise national required standards for residential and nursing homes for older people. On the basis of the Centre's recommendations, the Department of Health (2000b) has produced a Charter for Long Term Care. A closely related issue is the responsibility for financing long-term care. In March 1999 the report of a Royal Commission on long-term care (Sutherland, 1999) recommended that the costs of long-term care should be split between living costs, housing costs and personal care. Living and housing costs should be the subject of a co-payment according to means, but personal care should be paid for from general taxation. The government's response was delayed until the end of July 2000 when *The NHS Plan* was published (Department of Health, 2000c). As had been widely predicted they agreed to pay only for nursing care – a much cheaper option than paying for all personal care which includes bathing, feeding and dressing.

In the election campaign, the Labour Party promised to look at ways of ensuring more effective support for carers. The role and needs of carers received more attention during the 1980s, and in 1995 the Carers (Recognition and Services) Act, promoted by a Labour MP, was passed. In 1998 the government set up a working party to look again at the issue. As an interim measure an extra £750 million was made available. The working party's report appeared in February 1999. A further £140 million was allocated specifically for respite care. In addition: more 'carer-friendly' employment practices would be encouraged with the government taking the lead; local authorities would be required to take carers' needs into account; the New Deal (welfare to work) would be extended to carers; more support for young carers would be provided; there would be special help for those caring for disabled children. The Chief Executive of the Carers National Association, Francine Bates, described the changes as 'a momentous leap forward'. Since then, the government has announced a national strategy for carers which includes improved access to support and information. The policies are given legislative form in the Carers and Disabled Children Act 2000. Formerly, carers could have an assessment of their needs only when the person they were caring for was being assessed. The Act allows carers to have an assessment in their own right. There will be a new power for local authorities to provide prescribed carers' services – including home helps, travel fares and mobile telephones – directly to the carer. The most widely welcomed change is an extension of the system of direct payments so that carers can purchase services directly related to their needs. Although the Carers National Association has welcomed these developments as a considerable advance, they are concerned about the level of resources available and they have argued strongly that carers should not be charged for the services they receive.

During the election the Labour Party represented itself as the party of the family. Since community care is mainly family care the changes made in family policy are relevant to the personal social services. The 1998 Green Paper on welfare reform talked of the need to support children and families, and Harriet Harman, the Secretary of State for Social Security (until the July 1998 Cabinet re-shuffle) pointed out that 'no fewer than seven Cabinet Ministers have a major interest in childcare' (1998, p. 3). Unlike the previous Conservative administration, however, there is no Minster for the Family. A Green Paper unveiled in November 1998 (Home Office, 1998c) states the government's views that marriage provides the best basis for rearing children and that the family should be 'at the heart of our society and the basis of our future as a country'. Among the proposals is the establishment of a National Family and Parenting Institute.

Labour's efforts in this direction are closely tied in with the aims of its 'welfare to work' initiative, the central philosophy of which is that whenever possible everyone (including single parents) should work. If parents are to work, however, affordable child care of an acceptable quality has to be made available. Labour has promised to ensure that day care will be available for all children aged four with extensions for younger children when resources allow. Another development is the allocation of £300 million to provide an extra million places over the next five years in after-school clubs which fill the gap between the end of the school day and the end of the parents' working day. Another attempt to encourage mothers back into the labour force is the proposed tax credit for child care. Under this scheme, low-income families will have up to 70 per cent of their child care expenses paid: the amount will vary according to the number of children and the level of income.

Since assuming the leadership of the Labour Party, Blair has constantly emphasised the importance of community which he claimed was the true basis of socialism. An influential work by Selbourne (1997) lends weight to the argument that civic duty should be given more prominence in theories of socialism. Etzioni (1995), certainly no socialist, has been promoting communitarianism with an almost religious zeal since 1990, and Labour politicians, more particularly Blair, Field and Straw, have been influenced by communitarian ideology. The emphasis in communitarianism is on duties and responsibilities rather than rights. Communitarianism is at its strongest in exposing the shortcomings of stark individualism, but communitarianism has enabled the Labour Party to abandon notions of social class, and Driver and Martell (1997, p. 43) argue that the various strands of communitarianism in the Labour Party can be seen 'as part of a wider shift from social democracy to "liberal conservatism" in Labour ideas'. There is strong prescriptive and ethical or moral element in Labour's communitarianism. Communities are distinguished by shared moral values which are seen as a means of restoring social cohesion. It is clear that communitarianism goes well beyond the long-standing commitment of governments of all political persuasions to community care in social and health care. From the 1960s onwards, the claim that community care was superior, in most circumstances, to institutional care was heard with increasing frequency in several policy areas – most notably in mental health services and services for children. A shift in the meaning of community care began to emerge in the 1970s, however: a shift from care in the community to care by the community. The significance of this change of meaning is that care by the community is principally care by family, friends and neighbours.

Communitarianism has implications for policy which go well beyond the personal social services and community care, but it has a particular significance in this area. Most simply, the explicit recognition of communities as vital units of social organisation is bound to add to the significance of community care. Second, communitarianism implies decentralisation and an enhanced role for local agencies. Third, greater use will be made of independent organisations, both voluntary and commercial. The Labour government sees the voluntary sector as an essential element of a civil society encouraging active citizenship. The voluntary sector has already taken on a bigger and more formal role in the provision of social care services, but a communitarian philosophy emphasising duties, responsibility and civic obligation will push the voluntary sector even further to centre stage as the mixed economy of care develops. Mikosz (1998, p. 13), in a discussion of Labour's Third Way, writes of: 'the rediscovery of the "civic sphere", that is, of voluntary and mutual organisations which are neither state nor private and whose existence strengthens the fabric of society (the idea of social capital)'. In November 1998, the government, after extensive consultation with all of the interested parties, published a document which described a Compact on relations between government and the voluntary and community sector (Home Office, 1998d). Many local authorities have designed similar compacts, and many more have re-thought their relationships with the voluntary sector. The larger voluntary organisations employ paid staff, but implicit in communitarianism is strong support for volunteering because it gives people the opportunity to serve others, and indirectly to benefit the whole community.

But the community also benefits if people help themselves rather than relying on state support. This has several strands. The first is a very general point about self-reliance, and taking responsibility for one's own welfare. There is a clear relationship here to Labour's notion of a stakeholder society. A second strand is the role of the family in providing care for its members. The family has been a conspicuous feature of American communitarian analysis, but the family has also been given prominence by the Blair government.

A third strand within the self-reliance theme of communitarianism is mutual aid or self-help. Frank Field, one of the architects of Labour's new approach to welfare and a staunch advocate of stakeholder welfare, made the following comment in 1996: 'Any new settlement will be dominated by the emerging values which prize ownership and control. What I have called the growing social autonomy of voters – wishing to do "their own thing" determined on a basis of free association – will be the touchstone of the new welfare' (1996, p. 11). Within the voluntary sector, self-help groups are probably the most innovative, and certainly the fastest growing, segment. Numerous among these are consumers' groups – including users of personal social services – which may campaign for a strengthening and extension of social rights. This accords with the Labour Party's emphasis, during the 1990s, on the empowerment of users and carers. The Labour Party pushed this message home throughout the election and after taking office. One of Field's arguments for stakeholder welfare is that it gives consumers more control over their own welfare.

In emphasising the importance of community, voluntary organisations, self-help and families the Blair government is firmly committed to a mixed economy of welfare. A fully pluralist system, however, requires markets, and the Labour Party under Blair has embraced markets with some enthusiasm, not only in commerce and industry but also in welfare. Blair's government seems to have no problems with welfare for profit. Associated with this is Labour's support for competition (albeit in a modified form) in public services. This commitment to competition is clear from the government's guidelines for the replacement of compulsory competitive tendering (CCT) in local services with a duty of achieving Best Value: a duty that 'local authorities will owe to local people, both as taxpayers and customers of local authority services' (Department of the Environment, Transport and the Regions/Welsh Office, 1997). The guidelines state that 'in most service areas, there will be a clear presumption in favour of open competition' (1997).

Best Value requires local authorities to set authority-wide objectives and performance measures and to carry out fundamental performance reviews of all their services on a five-year cycle. The government will establish Best Value performance indicators and Modernising Social Services sets out in some detail how these will apply to social services departments and form part of the joint reviews. Although thirty projects have been set up to demonstrate what could be accomplished, and most local authorities took steps towards Best Value ahead of legislation, Best Value did not become fully operative until April 2000 and it is too early to assess its impact.

The documents relating to the Best Value initiative emphasise the need for partnership. The benefits of partnership has been a central feature of social policy discussion for at least a decade, and the related concepts of coordination and cooperation have a much longer history, but the Labour government has made partnership a central part of its approach to welfare provision. Nearly every document it produces in relation to the personal social services mentions partnership, and Modernising Social Services devotes a chapter to the notion: among the partnerships identified are those involving the National Health Service, housing, education, criminal justice agencies, the employment service, the voluntary sector and users and carers (Department of Health, 1998b). The partnership that has received most attention is that between health authorities and social services. Section 27 of the Health Act of 1999 imposes a duty to cooperate and a Health and Social Care Joint Unit has been established to oversee the whole process. Many of the emergent or proposed partnerships are multi-agency. For example, the Youth Offending Teams will involve partnerships between social services, education, health authorities, the police and the probation service.

Conclusion

Some of the themes that have become the hallmark of public policy towards the personal social services under Blair had their first expression (although somewhat tentative) in the Policy Review of 1989. Five overarching themes can be identified:

- The role of markets, especially internal or quasi-markets
- The encouragement of Local communities and voluntary action
- The need for partnerships
- The empowerment of users and carers
- The importance of families

These themes are now well-established and are likely to remain the basis for policy in the immediate future and for the rest of this Parliament and beyond. A brief consideration of each of them will occupy the remainder of this chapter.

The Role of Markets. The Policy Review of 1989 showed a greater willingness than earlier policy documents to address the issue of markets. It accepted that markets were the most appropriate means of efficiently distributing many goods and services and that competition was one means of securing consumer choice. However, the review went to some length to point to the drawbacks of markets in education, health care and social care. In relation to the personal social services, the Review categorically rejected policies aimed at reducing the role of local authorities as direct providers.

The Labour Party under Blair, with some dissenting voices, is much more prepared to accept internal markets in social care; markets, competition and contracting will continue, although competitive tendering will give way to Best Value. The unequivocal acceptance of markets is illustrated in a Fabian pamphlet, written by Tony Blair and published in September 1998, in which the Prime Minister states that 'with the right policies, market mechanisms are critical to meeting social objectives, entrepreneurial zeal can promote social justice, and new technology represents an opportunity, not a threat' (1998c, p. 4). Thus, in the personal social services, the Blair government has adopted some of the major principles of Conservative policy. The main differences are those of emphasis and tone. For example, while markets and competition are accepted, it is recognised that these are insufficient on their own to guarantee equity, efficiency, effective high-quality services and user empowerment. Whereas the Conservatives saw markets and competition almost as the sole policy vehicle, Labour takes the view that they are part of a broader strategy which includes efforts to ensure that as many people as possible have a stake in society and that those who are unable to participate in the market economy are given the necessary support. The neo-liberal elements within the Conservative Party, particularly in the 1980s, based their support of markets on a crude form of individualism, in which the relentless pursuit of self-interest was seen as acceptable behaviour. According to communitarians, however, economic success depends upon social cohesion which, in turn, implies the moderation of competitive individualism by principles of mutualism, cooperation, fellowship and social responsibility, all of which have important implications for the personal social services.

Local Communities and Voluntary Action. Labour's commitment to developing and supporting local communities and voluntary organisations is plainly stated in Blair's Fabian pamphlet:

> A key challenge of progressive politics is to use the state as an enabling force, protecting effective communities and voluntary organisations and encouraging their growth to tackle new needs, in partnership as appropriate. (1998c, p. 4)

These clearly communitarian sentiments are closely intertwined with Labour's policies of decentralisation and vigorous but responsive local government. The Labour Party's centralist tradition began to be eroded during the party's years in opposition, and decentralisation and the devolution of power were firmly endorsed in the 1997 election manifesto. There are, however, some very clear pointers in the opposite direction in the personal social services which almost certainly will be subjected to greater central government surveillance and control than they were under the Conservatives. The Secretary of State has been highly critical of the standards achieved and has made clear his readiness to intervene. Performance indicators and targets are to be set centrally. Whitehall will monitor standards and ensure that performance targets are met. Blair's Fabian pamphlet (1998c) states that 'in all areas, monitoring and inspection are playing a key role, as an incentive to higher standards and as a means of determining appropriate levels of intervention' (p. 16). The requirements of Best Value, the National Care Standards Commission and its regional equivalents, and the General Social Care Council, together with the continuing work of the Audit Commission and the Social Services Inspectorate (including joint reviews), indicate less rather than more autonomy.

Partnership. The mixed economy of welfare necessarily involves a wider variety of providers. There is an obvious danger of fragmentation and lack of coherence. Forging partnerships among a variety of statutory providers and outside agencies, both commercial and voluntary, is one way to avoid these pitfalls. Partnership, as Modernising Social Services makes clear, is seen by the government as a quality issue. Although the White Paper recognises the necessity of partnerships between social services departments and a variety of other statutory agencies, the government attaches prime importance to partnerships with health authorities. Collaboration in this area has now been given statutory force. Given the increased role of voluntary agencies in the delivery of social care services, partnerships between social services departments and the voluntary sector are important. The compact between government and the voluntary and community sector, and the emerging local compacts, represent a move in the right direction, but evidence from urban regeneration suggests that partnerships are far from equal. The agendas and decision-making are dominated by the industrial and government interests. Local communities and voluntary agencies find it difficult to make their presence felt. This very clearly is an issue of empowerment.

The Empowerment of Users and Carers. In the 1970s there was much talk of more participatory social services in Labour circles, and this became a much more significant aspect of policy in the Policy Review (Labour Party, 1989). The changes introduced under the Conservatives in 1993 were intended to result in a needs-led service, but in practice there are always limited resources in relation to demand, and what emerges is a resources-led service with the consumer making the best of what is available. The Labour government has reiterated the theme of user and carer empowerment and added to it the need to consider duties and responsibilities as well as rights. There has without doubt been an extension and strengthening of user and carer rights during Labour's term of office: the rights of children and older people, for example, are much more clearly stated than they were, and one of the aims of inspection and regulation is to ensure that these rights are protected. One problem is that in the personal social services duties and responsibilities are far from clearly defined, and there is a lack of clarity about what rights are, and certainly a lack of knowledge on the part of consumers and potential consumers. Vulnerable people may not be willing or able to insist upon their rights (e.g. not wishing to complain) and the enforcement of rights may prove difficult. Empowerment may prove no less elusive than it has in the past.

The Importance of Families. Another central theme in public policy under Blair is the prime importance of the family which will remain an important element in a mixed economy of care. Blair and Straw constantly refer to the central importance of families (and indeed of marriage) in providing a stable environment for the rearing of children. The Green Paper, *Supporting Families*, opens with the following statement:

> Families are at the heart of our society. Most of us live in families and we value them because they provide love, support, and care. They educate us, and they teach right from wrong. Our future depends on their success in bringing up children. That is why we are committed to strengthening family life. (Home Office, 1998d, p. 4)

This paper is mainly concerned with the rearing of children, but combined with the communitarian emphasis on duties and responsibility it obviously has implications for other aspects of community care: the reliance on families for the care of elderly and disabled people has long been recognised and this is likely to be a prominent characteristic of future patterns of social care. Paradoxically, Labour's welfare to work policies may diminish the capacity of families to provide care.

Labour came into power with a firm list of priorities. The personal social services were not initially high on that list, coming behind education, health, welfare to work and law and order. However, as this chapter attempts to demonstrate, the government has raised the profile of the personal social services and from 1998 onwards there has been an avalanche of papers, guidelines and legislation: it is certainly difficult to complain of lack of attention. In the first twelve months of the Blair government's term of office, policy in the personal social services seemed to lack a coherent strategy. What appeared was a series of ministerial statements, mainly in the field of child care. The White Paper, and the implementation of large parts of it, has changed all that. As always, however, the outcome of the policies described in this chapter will depend heavily on resources. It is not without significance that the government refused to back a private House of Lords Bill which would have prevented local authorities from withdrawing care services on the grounds of inadequate resources.

Note
* Although the focus is substantially different, parts of this chapter bear some resemblance to an earlier version which appeared in M. Powell, (ed.) *New Labour, New Welfare State? The 'Third Way' in British Social Policy* (Bristol: Policy Press, 1999) pp. 77–100. The opportunity has been taken to update some of the material.

12

Social Security: Welfare Reform or Piecemeal Adjustment?

MICHAEL HILL

Introduction

In the 1997 election manifesto Labour declared:

> We will be the party of welfare reform. In consultation and partnership with the people, we will design a modern welfare state based on rights and duties going together, fit for the modern world.

That was not simply a pledge about social security policy, but clearly the party leadership saw social security change to be fundamental to welfare reform. The government made that particularly evident in their spring 1998 Green Paper on welfare reform.

Given that Britain is a low spender on social security, spending only about half as much per person as those of its European Union partners with which it likes to be compared, with only Spain, Portugal, Ireland and Greece spending less (Eurostat, 1997), it might be expected that a pledge to reform welfare would involve a commitment to spend more. But in fact that pledge has to be read alongside the election pledge to keep down taxation and public expenditure, a point that Tony Blair has re-emphasised in various ways. The crucial point here is that, despite the most strenuous efforts, the Conservatives had failed to curb the growth of social security expenditure. Thatcher's 'failure' in that respect has already been well charted by John Hills and others (Hills, 1990). The basic fact about the Major governments is that whilst there was about an 11.5 per cent rise in retail prices between 1992 and 1996 there had been a 23 per cent increase in social security expenditure (see Table 12.1). Hence, there were grounds for suspicion that 'welfare reform' would mean at best a set of incremental changes and at worst a new programme of social security cuts. This chapter will suggest that it has been the case that the changes to policy which have been adopted have been in practice quite slight. Hence the grandiose rhetoric of 'welfare reform' has done little more than to stir up anxieties amongst the many Labour Party supporters who had hoped to see the emergence of more progressive social security policies after a long period of Conservative attack upon benefit entitlements.

What Options for Welfare Reform?

A social security system like Britain's, which has a long history, involving the gradual accretion of elements and a variety of political compromises as efforts have been made both to respond to demands and to contain costs, is bound to contain a not altogether logical mix of policies. But the British system is in many ways exceptionally illogical. It may be described as a largely collapsed insurance system in which means-tested benefits, expected by Beveridge to play a merely safety net role, have come to dominate the system. There is therefore a good reason to seek to reconstruct British social security. What then are the options for 'welfare reform?' The one which would probably find most favour with the Labour rank and file is what may be described as a 'back to Castle'

Table 12.1: Social security expenditure growth before 1997

Expenditure on:	*(£ million)* 1992–3	*(£ million)* 1996–7	*1996–7 as % of 1992–3*
Benefits for the elderly	34,154	40,799	119.5
Benefits for the sick/disabled	16,125	23,500	145.7
Benefits for the unemployed	9,357	8,271	88.4
Total social security expenditure	75,337	92,846	123.2

Source: Department of Social Security (1997) p. 3.

option. The crucial reference point here is the period when Barbara Castle was Secretary of State in the Wilson government of 1974–6. In this period family allowance was replaced by child benefit, the state earnings-related pension (SERPS) was introduced and the main benefit-uprating principle was made indexing to prices or earnings according to which rose faster. Then the Thatcher governments, later, seriously undermined SERPS and changed the uprating principle to a link only with prices. The 'back to Castle' option in respect of pensions policy was advocated powerfully by Barbara Castle herself in a speech to the Labour Party conference in 1996 and in a pamphlet with the emotive title 'We CAN afford the welfare state' (Castle and Townsend, undated).

The 'back to Castle' option itself can be seen as a development of what has been called 'the back to Beveridge' or 'new Beveridge' approach to social security policy, which sees the ideal way forward to be a combination of the restoration of those parts of the original Beveridge social insurance edifice undermined by the Conservatives, the restoration of the earnings-related additions Labour put in during the 1960s (together with the restoration of SERPS to its original form) and with development of new ways to put into the social insurance framework protection for those who have difficulties in building insurance entitlements (carers, part-time workers, etc.). The comparative ideal here is the strong, and largely inclusive, Swedish social insurance system with its good minimum provisions for those unable to contribute.

A variant on this approach to the reform of social security is an even more radical option – the advocacy of a 'citizens income' or 'basic income' for all (Parker, 1989). There is also a version of this perspective which involves arguing for a 'participation income' for specific contingent groups such as the elderly or the sick (Atkinson, 1994). What is important about this approach is that it sees both means-tests with their deterrent effects and social insurance with its contribution tests as irrelevant and difficult to administer in a world in which much work is temporary, part-time and insecure.

The ideas mentioned so far would constitute a satisfactory basis for a 'radical' reform of social security. It does not take much imagination to see why they are tending to be rejected – because of their costs. A good idea of the cost implications of these options can be gained from looking at one of the most modest proposals from the 'back to Castle' perspective. If the link between basic insurance pensions and wages were to be restored to parity with the ratio between pensions and earnings established by 1979 it would mean an increase for every pensioner of at least £20 per week (Lynes, 1997a). That would mean an addition to the social security budget of over ten billion pounds a year.

What other options are there for radical social security reform? One is to increase the privatised element in the social security system. Already Britain is a long way down that road. Private pension schemes have always been salient elements in the British system. By 1963 about 48 per cent of employees were enrolled in occupational pension schemes. The percentage has remained much the same ever since (Lynes, 1997b, p. 323). Indeed, Beveridge's argument for a subsistence-level flat-rate pension was that individuals should be encouraged to make their own additional private provisions. More recently the Conservatives largely privatised the protection available for short-term sick people. The privatisation theme was particularly picked up by Frank Field, during his brief period in office. Field argued, in a public lecture:

> Part of our reform strategy is to restore the link between welfare and self-improvement. This may not prove as difficult as some think: people are increasingly providing for themselves and their families. Occupational pension funds are the unsung heroes of the post-war welfare system...We want to see a mixed economy of welfare provision, and we recognise the desire of people for more control over their own provision. (Field, 1998)

A stance on private provision could involve saying that the state will stand back and only protect those unable to protect themselves. That, in many ways, was the stance of the last Conservative government. The Field perspective (1997) goes further than that. Field has long been a critic of means tests. Inasmuch as he is now an advocate of private provision he sees the future as involving a public/private partnership. The state must be the regulator of the private sector and the guarantor of last resort. These may imply a role for some future government, which is not anticipated by the planners of today – if capitalism falls down on its long-term promises. But, more important for the politics of today, what this partnership involves is a state role to buy into private and funded provisions on behalf of those who cannot do so for themselves.

But this option was also bound to be viewed with suspicion because of the key role it gives to the private sector. Amongst the government's most immediate commitments was the recovery of benefits for people who were misled or robbed by the over-selling of private 'money purchase' pensions in the wake of the Conservatives' attack upon SERPS in 1986.

Field's approach is, as suggested above, very influenced by his opposition to means-testing. In the curious – part-private part-public – debate which went on within the government, Harriet Harman, who was Secretary of State during the first year of Blair government, indicated interest in the means-testing alternative. Of course, in some respects that was merely to endorse what is already there, the support through means-tests of those without private resources or significant social insurance entitlements. But it was not voiced quite like that; rather, it was to suggest that there could be new and better ways of means-testing than what exists already. The Labour Party has been here before. Both the shift from National Assistance to Supplementary Benefit in 1966 and the debate about the reform of Supplementary Benefit just before the fall of Labour in the late 1970s involved a similar search for better ways of means-testing. Nevertheless two new jargon expressions have emerged. One is 'affluence testing', involving capping universal benefits so that the relatively well-off are not able to get them. Or, as was apparent in the pledge to increase pensioners' incomes made just before Harriet Harman left office and in remarks by the Chancellor, Gordon Brown, on benefits for disabled people, the talk is, rather more evasively, of a 'guaranteed minimum income'. The Chancellor has also clearly taken a very strong interest in an idea, much debated in the 1970s (particularly on the Right), of integrating and simplifying means-testing in the form of 'negative income tax'. I will come back to this.

How Does the Government Seem to be Working Through These Contradictions?

First Moves

The Blair government started work on its welfare reform pledge by setting up a number of separate investigations – varied in form both in terms of their participants and in the extent to which the government has been prepared to make them public activities.

The only specific early measures increased the suspicions of the 'poverty lobby' about cuts to come. Amongst the carrying forward of administrative changes planned by the previous Conservative Secretary of State was a measure that led to the first significant backbench revolt against the new government, the elimination of lone parent benefits. Nevertheless, soon after, a speech by Tony Blair to his constituents was reported under an *Independent on Sunday* headline, 'Blair wants benefit cuts' (21 November 1997). In that speech Blair stressed that in his view the facts about social security expenditure 'are alarming'. He went on to quote data on social security fraud, and argued: 'This is not simply about trying to rein in the growth of welfare bills. It is about a fundamental change in the culture, attitude and practice of the welfare state to create a fairer and more efficient society'. The impression that when Blair talked of 'social security reform' he meant 'benefit cuts' was reinforced by his introduction to the Green Paper on welfare reform, published in March 1998:

> The question is often put: are these changes going to be 'cuts-driven' or 'reform driven'? The answer is clear: they are driven by the need for reform: but of course, in reforming, we want to spend the money in the fairest and most effective way. And in some cases, for example, for those severely disabled people with the greatest needs, or in our schools and hospitals, we will want to spend more. But in other cases, such as those who are socially excluded, we want to cut the cost of economic failure; not by lowering their standard of living but by raising their life chances. So we must have a system we can afford, but above all, we want a system that aids those who need it and helps people to help themselves. (Department of Social Security, 1998a, p. iv.)

The Green Paper of spring 1998 is the main source of government thinking on social security. Clearly what is envisaged is, if not exactly nil cost welfare reform, at least a minimal cost reform. Apart from savings arising from the more efficient prevention of fraud which are likely to have a fairly minimal impact on the steadily rising social security budget, the inference throughout the Green Paper is that savings will come through greater and more effective labour market participation. On the theme of fraud the Conservative administrative agenda has been carried forward quite cheerfully. Of course any government will want to be vigilant against this, but critics had argued that the Conservatives' efforts in this respect had already been excessive, confusing minor mistakes in claimants' reporting with deliberate fraud and giving much more attention to this than to the prevention of under-payment and the encouragement of take-up (Sainsbury, 1996).

Social Security, the Family and Labour Market Participation

It is, however, the issues about labour market participation which merit more detailed discussion here. Any social security reform strategy can be made easier if it is possible to reduce benefit dependency in general. The problem is that the only move in that direction, which can satisfy both the 'poverty lobby' and those concerned to cut public expenditure, is to reduce unemployment. After over twenty years of high unemployment and in a Europe where the problem is endemic, that is not an easy target for public policy. Nevertheless the Blair government has chosen to make it a high priority, setting out to achieve it through its 'welfare to work programme'. A fall in unemployment, approaching half a million between 1997 and 1999 suggests some success in this respect, but it is of course hard to judge the extent to which this is directly attributable to programmes for unemployed people.

Related measures involve changes to benefits for the working poor. In his budget speech in March 1998 the Chancellor announced that a 'working families tax credit' would be introduced in October 1999. This offers income enhancement for lower-paid workers with children, normally through their pay, rather than by way of Family Credit. A related measure to accompany this is a 'child care credit', meeting up to 70 per cent of childcare costs of low-income workers (up to a specified limit). The Chancellor also gave attention to the threshold for social insurance payments, taking steps to remove the anomaly under which those who cross the threshold at which payments start had to pay contributions on income below the threshold as well as above it.

Taken together these measures help to reduce the 'poverty trap' effect under which pay increases for many low-paid workers are all but obliterated by the combination of losses of benefit and increases in tax and contributions. However, while the 'working families' tax credit' taper is only 55 per cent instead of the 70 per cent for Family Credit, the absence of changes to the taper for housing benefit means that the overall impact of the changes only reduces the combined maximum tax and benefit taper effect from 97 per cent to 95 per cent. Ironically, it also has to be borne in mind that any reduction of the taper extends the range of incomes to which it applies.

Further progress towards reducing the poverty trap requires attention to the impact of housing benefit rules. The problem here is that any lowering of the housing benefit taper rate would extend entitlement up the income scale, substantially increasing the cost of the scheme. A solution to that problem is to reduce the availability of housing benefit, capping it at less than actual rent levels. Notwithstanding the hardship such a move would imply for many rent payers it seems to be the preferred option. But at the time of writing the position being adopted by the government on this is far from clear.

There is another Labour manifesto commitment which should be mentioned here – to introduce a minimum wage. In summer 1998 the commission set up to make recommendations on this issue reported. The figures adopted by the government were £3.60 for people over 21 and £3 for younger workers (later uprated). This has some marginal impact upon the numbers needing to apply for in-work benefits.

More controversial has been the extent to which measures for single parents seem to be evolving which treat work as an achievable goal for this group too. There is a network of experimental schemes – so far without compulsion – designed to help lone parents into work. They are moving towards an expectation that all single parents without very young children should be active labour market participants, as is the case in many comparable countries. An expectation implies compulsion. Will this follow? As mentioned earlier, one of the earliest policy decisions by the government involved the carrying forward of cuts to benefits to lone parents originally proposed by the Conservatives.

A related measure, affecting a small group, has been the introduction of a requirement that the childless partners of applicants for Job Seekers Allowance should also be required to register for work, and undergo the assessment procedures linked to that.

However, the March 1998 budget did enhance the benefits available for the support of children in general. The child benefit for the first child in all families was increased by £2.50 over the normal indexation increase. A similar increase was made to the 'family premium' used in the calculation of income support and other means-tested benefits and to the rates of payment for children in the lowest income band for those benefits. These measures seem to be having some impact upon the extent of family poverty (Piachaud, 1999).

The Chancellor floated the possibility that child benefit would in future be taxed for those paying higher-rate income tax. This seems in many respects a hollow threat; without a reversion to the joint taxation of couples it could surely only be applied to high-earning women.

One important development in relation to the treatment of single parents was signalled by a Green Paper published early in July 1998 (Department of Social Security, 1998b). There the government set out ideas for the reform of the Child Support Acts. Those Acts continue to sustain a very inefficient system for the collection of money from absent parents, provoking opposition from those required to pay and receiving little support from parents with care responsibilities. A new system is suggested that will use a simpler formula and will bring some benefits to lone-parents. This seems to offer a way to end an unhappy chapter in public policy, implementation failure stemming from an unworkable piece of legislation making impossible demands on an under-funded Child Support Agency. But there may be other problems ahead; simplification will be likely to generate new kinds of 'rough justice' (a *Guardian* report on this news was headlined 'CSA reform "hits low paid"': 7 July 1998).

Disabled People and the Labour Market

The emphasis on work also occurs in government comments on benefits for disabled people. Chapter 6 of the Green Paper contains remarks which, if read in the context of the Conservatives' claim that the shift they made from 'invalidity benefit' to 'incapacity benefit' involved the use of an objective test to ensure that benefits only went to those really unable to do any kind of work, seem either to be nonsense or otherwise very threatening to severely disabled people:

> A key problem with IB is the All Work Test. It writes off as unfit for work people who might, with some assistance, be able to return to work, perhaps in a new occupation. It is an all or nothing test, in the sense that it assesses people as either fit for work or unfit for any work. Thus many people who would be capable of some work with the right help and rehabilitation are instead spending their working lives on benefit. (Department of Social Security, 1998a, p. 54)

Can we really say, so soon after the introduction of Incapacity Benefit, that that last sentence is true? In any case there is already nothing to prevent rehabilitation services being offered to people getting IB.

Again, as with single parents, what seems to be emerging is complicated. The Chancellor sees the introduction of tax credits for disabled workers as the key measure, offering incentives to work. There has been talk of a ' guaranteed minimum income' for disabled people, which (as suggested earlier) means improved means-tested benefits. But the money for this is being realised by restrictions in access to incapacity benefit by those with significant private income sources such as pensions. This involves another attack upon the insurance principle and has attracted the unsuccessful opposition of a substantial number of Labour backbench MPs. Additionally, incapacity benefit claimants are being required to undergo interviews exploring their availability for work and eligibility for training, comparable to those for applicants for job seekers allowance.

Pensions

But what about the really big element in social security spending – pensions? Reference was made above to the exploration of new approaches to public/private partnerships. One pragmatic objection to these is that they do not deal with the issues about current social security policy. New pension schemes do not offer anything for current pensioners. That leaves either a need for more general taxation to cope with that problem or a situation in which social insurance payment obligations are unchanged but new contributions are required from employees towards private pensions. In other words the government has to embark on the politically dangerous course of requiring the young to pay twice – for current pensioners and for themselves. Governments not surprisingly back away from schemes that impose extra costs on today's electorate in order to solve future problems! Of course, it may be objected that – as has been pointed out above – many people already pay both social insurance contributions and private pension contributions. This is merely extending that. The problem is, however, that the latter are voluntary. It is of the essence of a thoroughgoing privatised scheme providing protection to all that its contributions would have to be compulsory.

The Green Paper *Partnership in Pensions* (DSS, 1998c) sought to cope with these problems with a mixed deal:

- Maintenance of the basic flat-rate contributory pension
- Voluntary stakeholder pension schemes designed to offer an alternative to entirely private pensions for those on middle incomes (between roughly £9000 and £18,500 a year) (para. 27) which will be low-cost, flexible and secure, apparently involving private investment under statutory surveillance
- A state second pension for those unable to get into private or stakeholder schemes, essentially low earners and those in caring roles, which they claim will offer a better deal than SERPS. The Green Paper speaks of credited contributions for carers. The extent of expectation of contributions from low earners is not clear

- A minimum income guarantee for current pensioners (which means simply some possibility of higher income-support levels for those over pension age).

Has the government found an ideal middle path?

- more now for the poorest pensioners
- more but not compulsory privatisation but under stronger state protection
- and a deal for low-income workers (including part-time workers and those with periods out of the labour market as carers) which will be better than SERPS.

There are various problems about this. Any advantages of the two new schemes will take a very long while to be realised. In the chapter of the Green Paper giving examples, the year 2050 is mentioned! Furthermore, like all early outlines of complex and costly schemes, it is largely a 'menu without prices' – it is far from clear how much employees will have to pay for the state second pension. However, maybe a realistic welfare reform agenda has to be a very long-term one.

It is also the case that the deal offered to those with lower incomes implies a long period of contributions to pensions which at the end will turn out to be little better than the minimum income guarantee for those unable to contribute at all (see Agulnik *et al.*, 1999).

Conclusion

When first commissioned to write this chapter on the new government's social security policy in summer 1997, I thought there would be very little to say, other than to explain why the government was moving slowly on social security policy. Then in the later part of 1997 social security stories became almost daily events in the newspapers, encouraging a view that the government was moving fast. In early 1998 the debate about the future of social security shifted off the media agenda for a while. Then in March 1998 the Green Paper encouraged more efforts to identify the crucial issues for the future. Later, after a quieter period the Cabinet changes and particularly the resignation of Frank Field, started the whole debate up again. *The Daily Telegraph* cheerfully proclaimed that 'welfare reform' had run into the sand. A commentator more committed to progress on this issue had the following to say about the new Secretary of State:

> Alistair Darling... doubtless thought he meant what he said when declaring that the time had come to stop talking and start acting on welfare reform. But he will quickly find himself mired in the same stasis as Harman and Field. There is no solid Prime Ministerial backing for modernising the system around social insurance and universal benefits; Blair does not believe in it philosophically and, even if he did, Gordon Brown and the Treasury will not pay the costs from (*sic*) moving from one system to another. (Will Hutton in the *The Observer*, 2 August 1998).

The policy direction which has emerged places the solution to the big issues about pensions far in an unknown future (assumed to be one in which employment patterns and economic life are much as they are now). With regard to short-term benefits, it places a dangerously strong emphasis upon increasing attachment to the labour market. It also involves evolution towards negative income tax. The latter seems to be the Chancellor's welfare reform agenda. Where that may run into the mire is that it needs very substantial expenditure increases to lower the rates at which benefits taper off if the poverty-trap problem is to be avoided. I am reliably informed that an intense internal debate is developing around that issue.

What is evident, however, is that while most of the changes are inevitably incremental, the drift of policy continues to be in the direction established by the Conservatives of cutting away at the social insurance system, replacing it by a combination of the further encouragement of private provision and simplified means-tests (including particularly tax credits). The impact of this upon the growth of public expenditure suggested that the Labour government is having more success in curbing social security expenditure than the Conservatives. In a report published early in 2000 it claimed:

> During the previous Parliament benefit spending increased by an average of 4 per cent a year. During the current Parliament, the increase in spending is forecast to be considerably lower, at an average of 0.2 per cent a year, or 1.1 per cent a year if the ...[new tax credits] are included to ensure a consistent time series. Spending has been brought back under control. (Department of Social Security, 2000, ch. 3)

That report goes on to acknowledge the impact of the current state of the economy for this control success, something for which the government obviously claims credit. The underlying question that readers must answer for themselves is whether successful control over social security expenditure growth, in a nation that is a low spender in northern European terms, is necessarily something that the Blair government should boast about?

Acknowledgements

I am very grateful to Geoff Fimister for his help with the preparation of this chapter – collecting press cuttings while I was abroad, letting me see his briefing notes on policy developments and commenting on drafts. I also thank the editors for their helpful reactions to earlier drafts.

13

British Policy in Northern Ireland

Arthur Aughey

Introduction

The Belfast Agreement of 10 April 1998 was acknowledged as the great policy success of the New Labour government. Party conference and public opinion both acknowledged that the plaudits were well deserved. (Hall, 1998, p. 14). In no small measure this had been a personal triumph for the Prime Minister. It may have been the former Secretary of State for Northern Ireland, Marjorie (Mo) Mowlam, who emerged as the darling of party members. However, few would deny that it was the Prime Minister, not Mo Mowlam, who engineered the Agreement in the fateful last week of negotiations. Few seriously doubt that it was also the Prime Minister who encouraged a sufficient number within the unionist electorate to vote for the Agreement in the referendum in May (Mitchell, 1999, p. 169). Subsequently, the Agreement has appeared at its most precarious when, for whatever reason, the Prime Minister has been least involved.

Against the expectations of most seasoned commentators on Northern Ireland, compromises had been arrived at which sustained a precarious settlement. The continuity of policy between the Labour and Conservative governments was openly acknowledged in the referendum campaign. Tony Blair and the former Conservative Prime Minister, John Major, together visited Belfast and made a joint appeal to the electorate. It would be difficult to imagine a clearer expression of political solidarity. And it confirmed the willingness, common to both Labour and Conservative administrations in recent years, to keep Northern Ireland high on the policy agenda. How might this be explained given the different sympathies traditionally held by Labour and Conservative activists?

Northern Ireland is a good example of what Andrew Gamble once called the different perspectives of the politics of support and the politics of power (Gamble, 1974). Conservative supporters might be instinctively sympathetic to the unionist case and Labour supporters instinctively sympathetic to the nationalist case. However, if one were seeking a term which would apply to the policies of successive British governments, Conservative and Labour, it would not be unionism, nor would it be nationalism. The most appropriate term would be *stabilism*, i.e. that the overriding objective is to achieve political stability and that all else (to adapt the famous phrase of Peter Pulzer) is embellishment and detail. The remarks of government officials and the memoirs of ministers lead one to the conclusion that, albeit with differing emphases and prejudices, responsibilities and requirements, both have understood the Northern Ireland problem in Hobbesian terms. The problem British governments have sought to solve can be summed up thus: how can local politicians devise a rational and just compact amongst themselves and their communities in order to get out of a nasty and brutish state of nature and thus to secure the conditions of peace, putting behind them the fanaticism of historic disputes?

At times there has been despair, at times optimism, that such a compact is possible. Different approaches have been suggested but British policy has been defined by a dogged consistency, whatever the immediate setbacks, to return to the task of fashioning a local arrangement between the parties in Northern Ireland. The New Labour government's approach revealed that continuity. Stabilism (the politics of power) is a vital modifier of the traditional unionism associated with the Conservative Party (the politics of support). It goes a very long way to explain the rational thread in what Brendan O'Leary called the 'sound-bottomed contradictions' of Conservative policy in Northern Ireland between 1979 and 1997 (O'Leary, 1997). It is also a vital modifier of the traditional nationalist bias in Labour Party attitudes and it goes a very long way as well to explain Labour's equally sound-bottomed contradictions in the same period, contradictions perfectly abridged in its policy of 'unity by consent'. Indeed, one could argue that as Labour and Conservative both came to embrace the principle of 'neutrality' on Northern Ireland's constitutional position in the 1990s, stabilism was the common denominator which marginalised their residual nationalism and unionism. And that is the key to understanding the common approach by Major and Blair to the Northern Ireland problem.

New Labour's Inheritance: Conservative Policy in the 1990s

The precursor to the events and developments of the 1990s within Northern Ireland was the Anglo-Irish Agreement of 1985. This gave the Irish government a systematic and institutionalised influence on British policy in Northern Ireland. Though opposed by all Unionist parties and later repudiated by Margaret Thatcher herself, Anglo-Irish cooperation has been the foundation principle of all subsequent initiatives. It was against this backcloth that in the summer of 1993 the Conservative government of John Major embarked upon a complex strategy which went under the felicitous name of the peace process. The objective was to find a form of words which would enable the IRA to stop its campaign and which would enable Sinn Fein to abandon its support for 'armed struggle', thereby taking its place in 'normal' politics. The Irish government was enthusiastic about this project for it was very much its own idea. The British government was more cautious and sceptical (even though it too had been conducting secret talks with the IRA about ending the conflict). It feared provoking a complete destabilisation of unionist opinion (Seldon, 1997). After intense negotiations between London and Dublin the principles of this new strategy were set out in the Downing Street Declaration of 15 December 1993.

In the Declaration the British government, supported by the Labour Opposition, restated that it would uphold the 'democratic wish of a greater number of the people of Northern Ireland on the issue of whether they prefer to support the Union or a sovereign united Ireland'. Furthermore, it agreed that 'it is for the people of the island of Ireland alone, by agreement between the two parts respectively, to exercise their right of self-determination on the basis of consent, freely and concurrently given, North and South, to bring about a united Ireland, if that is their wish'. That formulation, confirming the fact of partition but using some of the language of Irish nationalism, was another way of stating the British government's neutrality on the constitutional issue. The Declaration re-expressed that neutrality by stating that the British government has 'no selfish strategic or economic interest in Northern Ireland'.

As a *quid pro quo*, the Conservative government received Irish acceptance that 'the democratic right of self-determination by the people of Ireland as a whole must be exercised with, and subject to the agreement and consent of a majority of the people of Northern Ireland'. This was the principle of consent and the democratic legitimacy of Northern Ireland's place within the United Kingdom. To underline this, the Irish government agreed that 'in the event of an overall settlement' it would 'put forward and support proposals for change in the Irish Constitution which would fully reflect the principle of consent in Northern Ireland'. In other words, it would amend Articles 2 and 3 of its own constitution (which made a territorial claim on Northern Ireland). The Declaration held out the possibility of inclusive talks on the future of Northern Ireland. It stated that if those groups supporting violence were to renounce it, they would be free 'to join in dialogue in due course between the governments and the political parties on the way ahead' after they had shown that they intended to 'abide by the democratic process'. The Declaration was embraced enthusiastically by New Labour.

By the autumn of 1994 the IRA and the main Loyalist paramilitary groupings, after much equivocation, had declared ceasefires. The British and Irish governments' vision of possible new relationships was set out in the Frameworks Document of February 1995. It tried to establish the broad parameters within which all-party talks about the future of Northern Ireland would take place. The Conservative government repeated its undertaking to submit any outcome from such talks to a referendum in Northern Ireland, confirming the so-called 'triple lock'. This formula meant that any agreement would require the consent of the parties and people in Northern Ireland as well as parliament. This was to reassure unionists that nothing would be imposed on them. Again, this formula was agreed by the Labour Opposition.

This political development was overshadowed by argument about decommissioning terrorist weapons. The British and Irish governments established in December 1995 an international commission to review the problem. Its chairman was the former American senator George Mitchell, President Clinton's special adviser on Northern Ireland, who was later appointed chairman of the multi-party talks. The Mitchell Report of 22 January 1996 outlined six principles on non-violence and democratic procedure to which all parties should subscribe. It required the parties to reject the use of violence or the threat of violence to achieve political objectives and to condemn paramilitary behaviour, such as punishment beatings and shootings. Although Sinn Fein and the Loyalist Parties did sign up to Mitchell, this obligated neither the IRA nor the Loyalist paramilitaries and public uncertainty about paramilitary, intentions remained.

The Mitchell Report argued that it was unrealistic to expect decommissioning *before* all-party talks but that some decommissioning should take place *during* the talks. On 9 February 1996, the IRA responded violently, ending its ceasefire by exploding a massive bomb in London's Docklands. Talks on the future of Northern Ireland thus began on 10 June 1996 in unpropitious circumstances. New Labour inherited a peace process without peace and a talks process without Sinn Fein. The prospects for a successful outcome to this initiative looked slim.

Old Labour: Unity by Consent

John Lloyd, a journalist close to Tony Blair, observed that there are two competing views on Northern Ireland within New Labour's governing circles. The first is that Irish nationalism has history on its side and is the coming force. The task is to channel violent nationalism along a democratic path and to persuade it 'to wait until either demographic change or unionist apathy allows a referendum on the future of the province to be won in favour of unity'. This view, argued Lloyd, is probably the most popular view in the party as a whole. The second view holds that Northern Ireland will continue to remain part of the UK for an indefinite period and 'that the main business of both the British and Irish governments and the province's parties is to ensure that political and social life is open to all, and that remaining discrimination is stripped away'. Lloyd (1999, p. 8) believes that this is Blair's own view. From Northern Ireland things looked less ambiguous.

An expectation had developed amongst republicans that a Labour government with a large majority would be able to deliver more to them than a Conservative government uncertain of its majority at Westminster. In the run-up to the general election of June 1997 the IRA bombing campaign had shifted to England in the hope that opinion there wanted peace at any price and that a New Labour government would be in tune with that desire. Unionists also feared that this might be true. The calculation within republican circles – and the equally widespread concern within unionist circles – was based on folk memories of Labour's unelectable turn in the early 1980s. And those inattentive to Tony Blair's approach believed that, in the bonfire of the old Labour vanities which his leadership announced, only Northern Ireland policy would remain unchanged. These popular assumptions were based on Labour's long-standing policy of 'unity by consent'.

How one interpreted the formula of unity by consent depended upon which of its two principles took priority. If one accepted that the principle of consent governed the principle of unity, then, to all intents and purposes, Northern Ireland's place within the UK would be secure. The principle of consent would mean that unity could only arise on the foundations of trust and democratic agreement within Northern Ireland. In the meantime politics should shift to other practical matters.

If, on the other hand, the principle of unity governed the principle of consent then a very different set of expectations emerged. In this case, the balance would be towards those structures designed to facilitate Northern Ireland's transition from its present UK status towards some form of all-Ireland arrangement. It would be a policy which required acquiescence in political arrangements which promoted that end. In other words, a Labour government would have to 'persuade' unionists, meaning, in effect, that it would have to push unionists out of the UK.

Throughout the 1980s, Labour's policy of unity by consent was biased towards the latter of these alternatives. From the 1990s, and explicitly under Tony Blair's leadership, it has been biased towards the former. In other words, the partisan and nationalist bias of old Labour policy has been transformed into the neutral and stabilist bias of New Labour policy. For some, not least Tony Blair himself, this was simply a case of bringing Labour's approach back to reality. It was about being honest, modifying what the party said (the politics of support) in terms of what the leadership believed the party could, and should, do in government (the politics of power). How had this transformation come about?

The old policy can be traced back to the statement by the National Executive Committee at the party's annual conference in 1981. It was a declaration in favour of unity 'by agreement and consent between the two parts of Ireland'. Consent was to be actively campaigned for by Labour and its objective was the peaceful unification of the island. The difficulty lay in encouraging unionist consent in a manner which did not constitute coercion. In other words, Labour policy ran the risk of being either irrelevant (there was no possibility of majority consent in the foreseeable future) or contradictory (consent really meant 'coercion'). One way of trying to resolve the problem was to envisage incremental harmonisation of public policy between Northern Ireland and the Irish Republic. Indeed, it was suggested at one time by Clive Soley MP, Labour spokesman on Northern Ireland, that British welfare benefits to citizens in the North could be re-routed via Dublin in order to encourage a sense of all-Ireland solidarity. Such schemes were generally treated with derision. As one observer put it, amongst other things 'many Irish people did not like being told by the British Labour party that they had better shape up if they wanted unification – too reminiscent of old-fashioned British paternalism, not to say imperialism' (Gibbons, 1995, p. 13).

Another way was to redefine what was meant by the term 'consent' so that it did not unduly hinder the objective of unity. Bew and Dixon have traced the verbal gymnastics which exercised the ingenuity of the Labour Northern Ireland team on this issue. Writing in early 1993 their conclusion was that 'the Labour party has become increasingly ambiguous about what it means by its policy of Irish unity by consent. "Consent" has be redefined, or not defined at all, to imply that a Labour government would unite Ireland without the explicit consent of the majority of people living in Northern Ireland' (Bew and Dixon, 1994, p. 158). Indeed, Kevin McNamara, Labour's spokesman on Northern Ireland from 1987 to 1994, tried to evade precision altogether. In March 1989 he said of consent for Irish unity that it was rather like a rhinoceros: 'I do not know how to define it, but if I see one I'll recognise it. The explicit agreement to transfer sovereignty occupies a similar status' (ibid, p. 160). This was convenient obscurantism for an opposition party but hardly a serious basis for a Labour administration wishing to bring stability to Northern Ireland. An indication of the sort of thinking which had developed under McNamara was the confidential paper, *Options for a Labour Government*, prepared in advance of the 1992 general election. It considered moving towards British–Irish joint sovereignty in Northern Ireland. However, even joint sovereignty was not meant to be permanent. It was envisaged only for 'a period not less than twenty years' (Labour Party, 1991, p. 54). *Options* was to be the high-water-mark of traditional nationalist influence on Labour thinking. John Smith, who replaced Neil Kinnock as Labour leader in 1992, had little opportunity to impress his authority on Irish policy. It was left to Tony Blair to re-position the party.

New Labour, New Realism

In his first engagement as Prime Minister outside London, Tony Blair visited Northern Ireland. Speaking at the Royal Ulster Agricultural Show (RUAS) in Belfast on 16 May 1997, he stated: 'My message is simple. I am committed to Northern Ireland. I am committed to the principle of consent. My agenda is not a united Ireland – and I wonder just how many see it as a realistic possibility in the foreseeable future. Northern Ireland will remain part of the United Kingdom as long as the majority here wish' (*Irish Times*, 17 May 1997). For the biographers of

Gerry Adams, this meant that Blair was at last burying 'old Labour's policy of a United Ireland by consent' (Sharrock and Devenport, 1997, p. 429). This change, though, had happened at least three years earlier.

On becoming leader of the party on 21 July 1994, Blair signalled a break with the old identity by removing McNamara as shadow Northern Ireland secretary and replacing him with Mo Mowlam. Mowlam had been a front-bench spokeswoman on Northern Ireland during 1988–90. A Blairite moderniser, she was not so obviously identified with Irish nationalism as her predecessor. Nevertheless, her views on Ireland disposed her towards the first view identified by Lloyd. For Blair, the Downing Street Declaration had become the new centre of political gravity for Irish policy. Now that the Conservatives had become openly neutral on the Union it was anomalous for Labour to remain biased towards a traditional (and unworkable) nationalist agenda. Following the IRA ceasefire of 31 August 1994, Blair argued that the historic positions of all the political parties had been overtaken by events. There was no longer any requirement on the part of Labour itself to advocate Irish unification. If there was to be persuasion for unity that should be the task of Irish nationalists. It should not be the objective of British policy. Agreement amongst the parties in Northern Ireland was the end to be promoted.

For a period, Mowlam could still propose that 'our policy embraces the aspiration for a united Ireland by consent. That is one of the options available through the joint declaration, which is why Labour can fully support it' (Mowlam, 1995, p. 12). However, consent now had priority. Blair had already made it clear before the party conference in October 1994 that a future Labour government would not be persuaders for Irish unity. As a senior Irish republican source put it at the time: 'Blair's position is a disappointment.' It certainly was. In the 1980s Sinn Fein had put a lot of effort into influencing Labour opinion. This now seemed spent. The sympathy it had once received from prominent figures on the left like Tony Benn and Ken Livingstone was no recommendation to the new leadership (Wilson, 1996, p. 9).

Equally, in his RUAS speech Blair seemed to have a comprehensive vision of the Union which was to prove valuable in helping to sell the Belfast Agreement to the Ulster Unionist Party in April and to the unionist electorate in the May 1998 referendum. The promise of devolution to Scotland and Wales introduced a degree of consistency on the constitution and brought Northern Ireland back towards the mainstream. For instance, Blair told his audience at the RUAS: 'The Union binds the four parts of the United Kingdom together. I believe in the

United Kingdom. I value the Union. I want to see a Union which reflects and accommodates diversity. I am against a rigid, centralised approach. That is the surest way to weaken the Union. The proposals this government are making for Scotland and Wales and for the English regions…will renew and strengthen the Union.' And he went on to link this with the Northern Ireland situation. 'I support this approach for Northern Ireland too, with some form of devolution and cross-border arrangements which acknowledge the importance of relationships in the island of Ireland. This is what the negotiations are about.' There remained a big question-mark over whether the negotiations between the parties then under way could deliver the sort of outcome Blair desired.

The Belfast Agreement

Labour's hope that success was possible involved two interlocking assumptions. These assumptions were, first, that local politicians were capable of recognising the distinction between symbol and substance; and second, that a deal could be done on the basis of politicians accepting the value of substantial advantages even if they had to swallow a certain amount of distasteful symbolism. In short, unionists would have to swallow the symbolism of cross-border cooperation with Dublin in order to secure the substance of Northern Ireland's place within the UK; and nationalists would have to swallow the symbolism of Northern Ireland's place within the UK in order to secure, as the leader of the Social Democratic and Labour Party, John Hume, put it, 'a new beginning in relationships' between the two parts of Ireland. Furthermore, officials believed that there was sufficient evidence to show that the main players, including Sinn Fein, desired to do a deal. Blair, inheriting both the principles and the procedures of the previous Conservative administration, showed the necessary determination to bring this enterprise to a positive conclusion.

The government moved quickly to get Sinn Fein into the talks. Blair had balanced his RUAS speech with the offer of a place in negotiations for Sinn Fein in return for a renewed – and 'unequivocal' – IRA cease-fire. Subsequently, the government conceded the Sinn Fein demand for a time frame for the talks (they were to end by May 1998). It also removed the requirement that the IRA should decommission some arms before Sinn Fein's entry to talks. At noon on 20 July, the IRA brought into effect an 'unequivocal restoration of the cease fire of August 1994'.

The government, having secured this objective, faced the risk of a unionist walkout and the collapse of the process. When the talks did resume in September with Sinn Fein attendance, Ian Paisley's Democratic Unionists and Robert McCartney's UK Unionists left in protest. But the Ulster Unionist Party led by David Trimble and the Loyalist parties remained, and together they constituted a slim majority of the unionist electorate. The continued (and crucial) presence of Trimble was a result of the trust which had developed between him and Blair (Mowlam's relationship with Trimble was poor and often hostile). The understanding and goodwill between the two men was one of the key factors ensuring ultimate agreement on 10 April 1998. Indeed, Trimble's line of communication to the government by-passed Mowlam and went directly through 10 Downing Street. This drew the Prime Minister into the intimate details of the negotiations because he had to show even-handedness with the other parties.

Therefore, the Belfast Agreement owed much to the personal and diplomatic skills of the Prime Minister himself. Indeed, his esteem was such that personal assurances from Blair were sufficient for Trimble finally to overrule dissent within his own negotiating team. It was not the details of the institutional arrangements that threatened Ulster Unionist support. It was the provisions for reform of policing and early release of prisoners. These matters took on a particular significance because there was no explicit connection between the hand-over of IRA arms and Sinn Fein's place in a new Northern Ireland Executive. Here again it was the Prime Minister's reassurance in the final week of the referendum campaign which helped to secure a marginal yes vote amongst unionist electors. In his words: 'Those who have used the twin tactics of ballot box and gun must make a choice. There can be no fudge between democracy and terror' (*Irish Times*, 20 May 1998). A significant proportion of unionists still did not believe the Prime Minister. Indeed, the majority of Trimble's party colleagues at Westminster did not believe him and opposed the Agreement. The referendum result in Northern Ireland was 71.12 per cent for the Agreement and 28.88 per cent against. The percentage of Unionists voting yes was only slightly over 50 per cent. In the Republic of Ireland the figures were 94.39 per cent for and 5.61 per cent against. This can be compared with the results of the elections to the Northern Ireland Assembly in June 1998 which were: UUP 28 seats, SDLP 24, DUP 20, Sinn Fein 18, Alliance Party 6, UKUP 5, Progressive Unionist Party 2, Northern Ireland Women's Coalition 2, Independents (now United Unionist Assembly Party) 3.

The Agreement endorsed in the referendum provided for a 108-member Assembly covering matters devolved to it by Westminster. The Assembly can only take decisions on a cross-community, consensual basis to ensure fairness and equity. An Executive of that Assembly, chaired by a First Minister and Deputy First Minister (in effect balancing the two communities), is responsible for policy on devolved matters such as economic development, education and agriculture. Parties with sufficient seats in the Assembly are automatically eligible for ministerial office allocated according to the d'Hondt procedure. Westminster retains control of matters relating, for instance, to foreign policy, taxation and the European Union. A North/South Ministerial Council was established to consult on cross-border policy cooperation. The Council is accountable to the Northern Ireland Assembly and to the Irish parliament. A British–Irish Council, comprising representatives of the British and Irish governments and members of the newly devolved institutions in Northern Ireland, Scotland and Wales, is to consult on matters of mutual interest. Cooperation between London and Dublin was to continue in a new British–Irish Intergovernmental Conference although there is now provision for members of the Northern Ireland Executive to participate in its deliberations. The Irish government also agreed to amend its constitution to acknowledge Northern Ireland's status as a part of the United Kingdom on the basis of consent.

The outline of the Agreement pre-dates, as we have noted, the New Labour government. However, the spirit of the Agreement fits well with the Blair project of social inclusiveness and political modernisation. It was also sufficiently ambiguous to satisfy both views on Northern Ireland within the party. It might lead ultimately to Irish unity but then again it might secure a reformed and agreed Northern Ireland within the Union. This ambiguity was also apparent in the response of the Northern Ireland parties. The hope contained in the Belfast Agreement is that the old pattern of mutual denial will weaken and that a new pattern of mutual recognition will emerge. Nationalist politics retains the aspiration to Irish unity. Unionism remains committed to the Union. But the possibility presented itself for nationalists to realise the benefits, where possible, of an island community. Unionists too can acknowledge that there may be positive benefits by working constructively at this level. Even some unionist opponents of the Agreement have come to accept this. These all-Ireland communities of interest, if cooperation is to function sensibly, must be defined by unionist as well as nationalist priorities.

Furthermore, unionists might accept that their interests are best served within a framework which acknowledges the cultural diversity of Northern Ireland. There remains deep communal bitterness on both sides. The object of the Agreement is to attenuate that bitterness. If nationalists and republicans participate constructively in a Northern Ireland within the UK which accords them equality of status, then stability is possible. In sum, respect for the principle of consent severely qualifies the aspirational drive to Irish unity. But the changes required in Northern Ireland demand much of unionism.

It has been a measure of the ambition of the Agreement that the major parties of unionism and nationalism are required, almost overnight, to transform themselves from instruments of rhetoric, opposition and mutual frustration (and violence) to instruments of policy and government. The parties needed to have some common point of reference and a common sense of popular responsibility. If the expectations of the Agreement were to be fulfilled then a workable political relationship needed to establish itself. Moreover, this relationship implied a common identification with the central principle of the Agreement, that of mutual respect. In the months following the signing of the Agreement this appeared a naive hope given the historic intensity of old animosities. Those old animosities were bound up with the continuing crisis over decommissioning which has absorbed an enormous amount of time and energy on the part of the Prime Minister and his Northern Ireland Secretaries.

The Decommissioning Blockage

From the perspective of the Labour government, a stable settlement means taking republicanism one step further than it had gone already. In the 1970s the IRA tried to achieve its objective of Irish unity by the use of violence outside democratic politics. In the 1980s it tried to use violence alongside Sinn Fein electioneering. In the 1990s the approach became one of retaining the capacity to use violence inside democratic politics. One purpose of the Downing Street Declaration, the Mitchell Principles and the Belfast Agreement had been to encourage republicanism to make the final transition from the culture of violence to exclusively democratic politics. That meant decommissioning. For the IRA it was not the first step but the last step which seemed to count. Its refusal was always likely to be the factor which might destroy the delicate compromises of the Agreement, compromises which demand trust. Without decommissioning this trust cannot be sustained because unionists are not convinced of republican bona fides. The IRA's rhetoric about the surrender of an 'undefeated army' is irrelevant except in the sense of surrender to the principles of the Belfast Agreement, principles endorsed overwhelmingly by the people of Ireland and from which republicans seek electoral advantage. In short, the ambiguity in the republican position necessary to make the Agreement could no longer be sustained if the Agreement was to function properly. That, in short, was the point made emphatically by Blair during the referendum campaign. He tried to achieve that end in the spring and summer of 1999 in exhaustive efforts to solve the conundrum 'no guns, no government' (the unionist position) and 'no government, no guns' (the Sinn Fein position). He failed.

Moreover, Blair, Mowlam and her successor Peter Mandelson, went to very great lengths to remove every justification for republicans refusing to move to exclusively democratic means. This was done despite sustained Unionist criticism. Early release of prisoners continued. Troop levels were reduced, despite the evidence of continued paramilitary activity involving shootings, punishment beatings and intimidation. For example, in the summer of 1999 members of the IRA were arrested in the United States for the attempted smuggling of 32 handguns into the Irish Republic. Mowlam decided that this did not constitute a breach of the IRA ceasefire. A long-standing republican demand for an inquiry into the events of Bloody Sunday was granted in January 1998. The central recommendations of the Patten Report on policing reform were accepted, much to the dismay of Trimble. Despite the opposition of the Speaker, Sinn Fein MPs were also to be allowed access to the facilities of the House of Commons without having to take the oath of allegiance to the Crown. Crucially, in November 1999 Mandelson achieved what Mowlam had failed to do. After another review of the Agreement conducted by George Mitchell in the autumn of that year, Trimble was persuaded to recommend that his party share power with Sinn Fein. The ruling Unionist Council accepted his recommendation by 58 per cent to 42 per cent. This was based on an understanding that the IRA would cooperate with the International Commission on Decommissioning under General de Chastelain and that there would be some gesture on arms to satisfy Unionist sceptics. Neither happened. Devolved government went 'live' in November 1999. All of these concessions and gestures made no difference. The IRA still refused to move. On 11 February 2000 Mandelson had to choose between losing First Minister

Trimble and with him the last vestiges of unionist support for the Agreement or suspending the devolved institutions. He chose the latter. Direct rule was reimposed.

Conclusion

However, the realities of Northern Ireland politics continued to push towards a compromise. The British government still needed to channel Irish republicanism towards a constructive purpose. That meant re-establishing the institutions of the Belfast Agreement and implementing as quickly as possible those aspects of the Agreement which republicans favour. Sinn Fein also needed the institutions to secure its potential as the major party of Northern nationalism. Moreover, it needed the stability of the Agreement to enhance its electoral prospects in the Irish Republic. The SDLP needed the Agreement to enhance its profile and perhaps to stop the flow of support to Sinn Fein. The Ulster Unionist Party, while severely divided over the merits of the Agreement, has tended to regard any alternative to it as even worse. The compromise hammered out by the British and Irish governments at Hillsborough in early May 2000 envisaged the restoration of devolved government by the end of May; a timetable for achieving the remaining provisions of the Agreement; and the full implementation of the Agreement by June 2001. In effect, the decommissioning deadline was postponed for another year. In return, London and Dublin demanded that the paramilitaries 'state clearly that they will put their arms completely and verifiably beyond use'. The IRA responded on 6 May by stating that it would secure its arms dumps and provide for inspection of some of these dumps 'by agreed third parties' who would report to General de Chastelain. It also claimed that its ceasefire would hold. On 27 May, David Trimble, by the barest of majorities (53 per cent to 47 per cent), secured the support of his party to go back into government with Sinn Fein on the basis of the Hillsborough deal and the explicit commitment by the IRA. Devolution was then restored to Northern Ireland at the beginning of June 2000. On 25 June, the two arms inspectors Martti Ahtisaari and Cyril Ramaphosa, reported that they had carried out their first examination of IRA weaponry.

The view that it is impossible for the Agreement to deliver a lasting settlement is a widely held one. Perhaps the contradictions are too great. Nevertheless, there may be some historically-based optimism. Writing of the partition arrangements of 1923, J.C. Beckett observed that everyone expected them to disintegrate soon. Though the settlement left a legacy of bitterness and sporadic violent disturbances, 'it inaugurated for Ireland a longer period of tranquillity that she had known since the last half of the eighteenth century' (Beckett, 1966). For very different reasons, even if the Belfast Agreement itself falls, that may well be the historian's judgement of the fate of New Labour's policy in Northern Ireland.

14

Foreign and Defence Policy

FERGUS CARR

Introduction

The aims of this chapter are to examine Britain's current role in international affairs and the impact of Tony Blair's Labour government upon foreign and defence policy. Contemporary policy will be contextualised by reference to: the pattern of policies and commitments inherited by the Labour government, the resources available to the government, and the changing nature of the international political system.

The Conservative Legacy and the Changing International Order: 1979–97

The Thatcher era spanned revolutionary changes in international politics. By the time Margaret Thatcher resigned as Prime Minister in November 1990 many of the fundamental features of the Cold War, which had dominated international order for over forty years, were either ending or in the process of change. Revolutions had ended Communist rule in Eastern Europe, Germany had been reunified and the November 1990 Conventional Forces in Europe Treaty (CFE) had substantially reduced the conventional threat to European security. In July 1991 the Warsaw Pact was disbanded and the Strategic Arms Reduction Treaty (START), cutting strategic nuclear forces by a third, was signed. In December 1991 Gorbachev resigned and the Soviet Union ceased to exist. The European order upon which British foreign policy had been predicated for so long had changed irrevocably. Security was being transformed from its Cold War emphasis upon military criteria to wider understandings including economic, political, and societal elements. At question now was the way British interests were structured into a policy which traditionally conditioned participation in Europe with concern for Atlanticism, sovereignty and a wider role.

Although Atlanticism had been a dominant trait of British foreign policy since the Second World War, Margaret Thatcher clearly relished the 'special relationship'. She endorsed Washington's view of the Soviet Union as the 'evil empire', supported American military action in the international system and was a staunch ally in NATO. The Gulf crisis of 1990 gave Thatcher further opportunity to demonstrate the solidity of the Anglo-American alliance and project a British role in the global system. Nuclear deterrence and NATO formed the centrepiece of defence policy in the Thatcher years. NATO defence roles accounted for 95 per cent of the British defence budget. Defence was made the 'first charge on our national resources' in 1979 and by 1985–6 the defence budget had grown one-fifth larger in real terms. The spiralling costs of modern weapon systems however placed increasing strain on the defence budget and a 'funding gap' between resources and commitments resulted. John Nott, Secretary of State for Defence, was charged with conducting a review of policy in 1981 but it was not until 1990 that the 'Options for Change' programme began to implement cuts in force deployments complemented by CFE.

British policy toward the European Community under Margaret Thatcher was uncompromising and often negative in tone. The cost of membership and sovereignty were not new issues in Britain's European relationship but the open and strident tone of Thatcher's approach to her European partners was. She vehemently opposed new levels of 'Euro-Governance'. She did support the adoption of the Single European Act (SEA) agreed at the Luxembourg Summit in 1985 as it set the deadline of 1992 for completion of the single market. Britain also endorsed the formalisation of intergovernmental coordination procedures for foreign policy amongst member states, known as European Political Cooperation (EPC). The SEA, however, created an impetus for further integration to regulate the single market and its development with regard to monetary union. Thatcher dubbed the consequent Social Chapter a 'socialist charter', and resisted moves toward a single currency. When Britain finally entered the ERM on 5 October 1990 she still dissented from the European Council consensus for the following intergovernmental conference on EMU. She declared 'what is the point of trying to get elected to Parliament only to hand over your sterling, and the powers of this House to Europe?' (*Hansard*, 30 October 1990, Col. 873).

John Major did declare that Britain should be at the 'very heart of Europe' but like his predecessor sought to limit integrationist agendas in the EC. The Treaty on European (EU), negotiated at Maastricht in 1991, was presented as a victory for the new Prime Minister. 'Opt-outs' were secured for Britain from key stages of EMU and the Social Chapter. The Treaty did not declare a federal goal and an intergovernmental basis of decision-making was retained for the successor to EPC, the Common Foreign and Security Policy (CFSP). The Treaty declared that CFSP 'shall include all questions related to the security of the European Union, including the framing of a common defence policy, which might in time lead to a common defence' (Article J.4.1). The EU looked to the Western European Union (WEU), whose origins lay in the European alliance which had preceded NATO, to 'elaborate and implement discussions and actions of the Union which have defence implications' (Article J.4.2). Britain, though, firmly opposed any measure which would weaken NATO, and successfully resisted the integration of the WEU into the EU. The WEU was left instead as both the defence arm of the EU and a means to strengthen the European pillar of NATO.

The remaining challenge for John Major was ratification of the Maastricht Treaty. Margaret Thatcher's leadership had enhanced 'Euroscepticism' in the Conservative Party and left deep divisions (see Baker *et al.*, 1995). With an overall majority of just 21 following the 1992 general election, rebel Tory opposition to Maastricht became highly significant. A combination of rebel and Labour votes ensured a parliamentary war of attrition which culminated in the defeat of the government's motion on the Social Chapter on 22 July 1993 and forced John Major to call a vote of confidence. Ratification did not however end the Conservatives' European divisions which soon turned to the single currency issue.

John Major maintained Britain's committment to NATO as 'the bedrock of our defence' (Statement on the Defence Estimates, 1995, Cm 2800, p. 7) and supported the transformation of Alliance Strategy to accord to post-Cold War conditions. NATO's new Strategic Concept of November 1991 provided a new rationale for the Alliance and directly influenced the shape of British defence policy in the 1990s. It acknowledged that the predominant threat faced by the Alliance in the past had given way to risks that were 'multi-faceted in nature and multi-directional'. In the new era, security and stability were seen to have political, economic, social, environmental as well as military elements. In this regard NATO welcomed the emergent new European security architecture including the EC, WEU and Conference on Security and Cooperation in Europe (CSCE). The new Strategic Concept stressed three roles for the Alliance: dialogue, cooperation and collective defence. The first two roles emphasised the new opportunities for political resolution of security issues in Europe. The last role was more traditional but was no longer seen to need a 'comprehensive in-place linear defensive posture in the central region' (North Atlantic Council, 1991). Conventional force levels were to be cut and forces to have enhanced flexibility and mobility to respond to the needs of crisis management. Nuclear forces were to be maintained but at a minimum level with significant reductions in sub-strategic forces.

The implementation of the Strategic Concept required: NATO accommodation and partnership with other European security institutions; a new Alliance relationship with Eastern Europe and Russia; and development of crisis management and peacekeeping strategies.

NATO's relationship with the WEU was consolidated at the January 1994 Alliance Summit which decided to make the collective assets of NATO available:

> on the basis of consultations in the North Atlantic Council, for WEU operations undertaken by the European Allies in pursuit of their Common Foreign and Security Policy. We support the development of separable but not separate capabilities which could respond to European requirements and contribute to Alliance security. (North Atlantic Council, 1994)

This 'pooling' of resources enabled the new European Security and Defence Identity (ESDI) to remain compatible with the Alliance and in accord with British interests. France, though, with other EU member states, still sought the incorporation of the WEU into the EU. Britain rejected incorporation and instead adopted a task-based approach in which the WEU would not have an exclusive role:

> there is no simple criterion that would determine whether the WEU, or NATO, should carry out a particular mission. That would depend on a number of factors, including not only the willingness of the

United States and Canada to participate, but also spread of operations already being undertaken by NATO and the WEU, the complexity of the mission and the risk of escalation. (Cm 2800, p. 16)

NATO's new relationship with Eastern Europe and Russia was essentially to try to balance the promotion of stability in the new Europe with the security interests of the states concerned. The East Europeans, led by the Visegrad countries, sought membership of NATO while Russia opposed its former Warsaw Pact allies joining the Western Alliance and proposed measures to strengthen CSCE instead. NATO's interests in sustaining Russia's commitment to a liberal order, reform and partnership in arms control left the Alliance with a policy dilemma – how not to alienate Moscow while drawing closer to the East Europeans. NATO initially offered dialogue through its North Atlantic Cooperation Council (NACC) in 1991, and then closer association, but not membership, through the Partnership for Peace (PfP) in 1994. As East European demands for membership and Moscow's opposition grew, the British Foreign Secretary Douglas Hurd urged caution. The United States, however, was keen to enlarge NATO and President Clinton drove the agenda forward. In 1995 NATO published its Study on Enlargement which maintained a commitment to open the Alliance to new members while developing a new relationship, in parallel with Russia. This 'balancing act' became Alliance policy for the future.

NATO's commitment to conflict prevention and crisis management led to the Alliance in 1992 to announce its readiness to support on a case-by-case basis peacekeeping activities under the auspices of CSCE and United Nations (UN). NATO supplemented the UN mission to the former Republic of Yugoslavia enforcing the sanctions regime and 'no fly zone' over Bosnia. NATO member countries, including Britain, provided troops for the UN force on the ground, UNPROFOR. As UNPROFOR's role and UN resolutions concerning Muslim 'safe areas' in Bosnia were violated, NATO provided protective air power. This use of NATO airforces proved the most contentious as enforcement strategies were seen to compromise the role of 'peacekeepers' in the delivery of humanitarian aid. In the complex pattern of events which followed the apparent ineffectiveness of international action to protect the Bosnian Muslims, demands grew in the United States to lift sanctions and use air power more freely. Without troops on the ground London and Paris clearly felt Washington's response was irresponsible . The Alliance did however hold and the Europeans sustained their commitment to UNPROFOR and to the post-Dayton Implementation Force. British contributions were some 3,500 personnel to UNPROFOR, rising to 8,000 in 1995 and 10,500 were committed to IFOR in 1996 (Statement on the Defence Estimates, 1996, Cm 3223, ch. 2, p. 1).

Bosnia revealed the complexities of ethnic conflict, the challenges of crisis management and the difficulties of sustaining allied cohesion. For Britain the crisis also revealed that so-called 'low intensity' conflicts still required sophisticated equipment, training and appropriate planning. The government accordingly adjusted its force requirements and defence policy. The 1993 Statement on the Defence Estimates *Defending our Future* (Cm 2270) was termed a 'landmark analysis' by Malcolm Rifkind, Secretary of State for Defence. Three roles were identified which set the framework for defence policy. The first role was to 'ensure the protection and security of the UK (and its dependent territories) even when there is no major external threat' (Cm 2270, p. 7). Nuclear forces were seen, as in the past, to 'provide the ultimate guarantee of the United Kingdom's security'. The second role was to 'insure against a major external threat to the United Kingdom and our allies' (ibid, p. 7). This role was to be discharged through membership of NATO. The final role was to 'contribute to promoting the United Kingdom's wider security interests through the maintenance of international peace and stability' (ibid, p. 7). This role included support directly, or via NATO and the WEU, for UN and CSCE operations. Resources to support these roles were set against a changed strategic environment. The 1990 Defence Review 'Options for Change' was seen as 'inherently cautious' and would be supplemented by a number of selective reductions in force levels beyond those planned. Cuts were signalled for the Navy and Airforce, while to meet the new needs of 'flexibility and mobility', a new helicopter carrier was to be constructed for the Navy and the planned size of the army to be increased from 116,000 to 119,000 (Cm 2270, p. 11). The overall effect though was that the defence programme could be met from a reduced level of expenditure. The adoption of efficiency measures, new management systems and cost studies such as *Frontline First* (see Statement on the Defence Estimates, 1994, Cm 2550) were further designed to secure savings. In 1995 the government reported defence spending was expected to decline by around 14.5 per cent in real terms between 1992–3 and 1997–8, and from 4.2 per cent of GDP in 1991–2 to 2.8 per cent in 1997–8. Expenditure still, however, remained above the current average of aggregate GDP spent on defence by other European NATO countries (Cm 2800, p. 79). It would be Europe, however, not defence expenditure, that would undermine the Conservatives in the general election of 1997.

Manifesto and General Election Pledges in 1997

The Labour Party entered the 1997 general election with a clear lead in the polls. In contrast the Conservatives were considered divided and not a credible party of government (see Harrop, 1997). The central issue of division was Europe and, despite the British opt-out, the focal point of discord was the single currency. John Major adopted a more Euro-sceptical tone, attacked the Social Chapter and hardened his position on the single currency. The Conservatives further depicted Tony Blair as weak and inexperienced on the eve of the EU Amsterdam Summit. Labour's response was to stress its defence of British interests and caution on the single currency. Blair declared that 'if the issue of Britain joining a single currency in the next Parliament arises – and I stress the "if", just as our Manifesto will stress the "if" – then the final say will be with you, the British people in a referendum' (*The Guardian*, 2 April 1997). In fact both Conservative and Labour manifestos pledged a referendum on the single currency but cautioned the need to stay in the relevant negotiations to influence the outcome. Both parties sought to protect British fishing from 'quota hopping', maintain national border controls and ensure NATO's primacy. With the exception of Labour's endorsement of the Social Chapter, the differences between the two with regard to Europe were more of attitude and image than policy. Labour stressed a 'fresh start in Europe, with the credibility to achieve reform'. The Conservatives billed the forthcoming Amsterdam Summit as a 'moment of truth'. Labour pledged to work for reform of CAP, support enlargement of the EU, extend qualified majority voting in some areas but retain the veto in strategic areas such as the budget, immigration, asylum and defence (see Labour Party, 1997, pp. 36–7).

Labour's manifesto promised a retention of Trident and a strong defence against new security challenges. At the Labour Party Conference in October 1997 George Robertson underlined the significance of these pledges, declaring that 'if there is one lesson that we have learned from the General Election and eighteen long years of opposition, it is that the British people will only elect a government which they trust with the defence of our country' (Robertson, 1997c, p. 3). Labour also pledged a strategic defence review and pursuit of multilateral arms control. The manifesto announced a ban on the 'import, export, transfer and manufacture of all forms of anti-personnel landmines'. Labour also warned it would not permit arms sales to regimes that might use arms for internal repression or international aggression. A new priority was also sought for combating global poverty, and for the promotion of human rights and protection of the international environment.

Labour in Office: Continuity and Change in Policy

When New Labour entered office a new foreign policy and a new approach to the world was stressed. Baroness Symons, Parliamentary Under-Secretary of State, Foreign and Commonwealth Office, in a speech entitled 'New Government, New Foreign Policy' explained:

> while British interests may stay the same, British foreign policy has changed. The new government in Britain has a clear plan about how it intends to shape British foreign policy and indeed to shape the world in which Britain lives. (Symons, 1997, p. 1)

At the same time the Labour government quickly signalled strong elements of continuity with the past. The 'special relationship' was strongly underlined with the invitation to President Clinton to address the Cabinet. Tony Blair welcomed the President and did not believe that Britain had to choose between

> its strong relationship in Europe and its strong trans-Atlantic relationship with the United States of America, strong in Europe and strong with the United States. One strength deepens the other. A Britain that is leading in Europe is a Britain capable of ever closer relations also with the United States of America. (Blair, 1997b, p. 1)

The Prime Minister took the theme further in a major speech at the Guildhall in November 1997 on 'The Principles of a Modern British Foreign Policy' (Blair, 1997f). He declared, 'we are the bridge between the US and Europe', and implored, 'let us use it' (ibid, p. 3). In the same speech he made clear Britain's continuing global interests which would be sustained through membership of the UN Security Council, NATO, the G8, Europe, the Commonwealth and 'close alliance with America'. He argued 'we must not reduce our capability to exercise a role on the international stage', and stressed a 'sound defence is a sound foreign policy'. On Europe, Blair did want change – 'we must end the isolation of the last 20 years and be a leading partner' – and warned there was no place for 'misguided little Englander sentiment'. At the same time he stated, 'of course, if Europe embarks on a path that is wrong or repugnant to British interests, we would have to stay apart' (ibid, p2). The Prime Minister saw Britain as taking the lead in the reform of CAP, promoting enlargement, completing the single market and making the single currency work. Finally he stressed the importance of values in foreign policy. He declared that 'we use power and influence for a purpose: for the values and aims we believe in' (Blair, 1997f, p. 3). Robin Cook, the Foreign Secretary, stressed this new sense of purpose in the Mission Statement of the Foreign and Commonwealth Office (FCO):

> Our foreign policy must have an ethical dimension and must support the demands of other peoples for the democratic rights on which we insist for ourselves. The Labour Government will put human rights at the heart of our foreign policy and will publish an annual report on our work in promoting human rights abroad. (Cook, 1997b, p. 2)

The Foreign Secretary believed 'the right to enjoy our freedoms comes with the obligation to support the human rights of others' (Cook, 1997d, p. 1). He argued that governments should observe the basic standards of human rights codified by UN covenants. He saw the business of the Foreign Office as promoting the national interest but also believed that 'promoting our values, taking pride in our principles is in the national interest' (Cook, 1998d, p. 2). Robin Cook announced that the Labour government would encourage other states to reform, sustain critique when they ailed and express solidarity when appropriate. He did not expect a 'perfect world' but believed 'our contribution can make a difference'. Human rights were also linked by the Foreign Secretary to development, arguing that 'without freedom from want and from disease' they were of little value. The Labour government accordingly was to reverse cuts in aid and establish a new Department for International Development. Robin Cook listed a number of policy steps to implement the commitment to human rights, including sanctions, embargos on arms exports, diplomacy and the establishment of a permanent International Criminal Court (Cook, 1997d, pp. 3–5.)

Labour's policy agenda exhibited continuity with the past whilst seeking change, not least in the adoption of an ethical dimension. The capacity of the new government to implement these objectives must be assessed, however, in relation to the specific policy context; the pattern of domestic and international constraints; and the resources available to the administration.

Europe

With Britain's opt-in to the Social Chapter, Robin Cook announced a 'fresh start in Europe for Britain, working with Member States as a partner, not an opponent' (Cook, 1997a, p. 1). Tony Blair warned, though, that 'British national interests must be properly safeguarded and Europe itself has got to re-focus its horizons so that it focuses on the things that really matter to the people' (Blair, 1997a, p. 1). The Prime Minister informed the House of Commons that both objectives had been met at the Amsterdam Summit in June 1997. He reported that Britain had retained national control over immigration, asylum and visas; the veto in foreign policy, defence, treaty change, community finance and tax; and limited the extension of Qualified Majority Voting (QMV). The government had successfully prevented the integration of the WEU into the EU which had been favoured by the majority of member states. Instead the Amsterdam Treaty looked for 'closer institutional relations' (Article J.7). The Treaty further respected the 'obligations of certain member states, which see their common defence realised in the North Atlantic Treaty Organisation…' (Article J.7). The move to enhance the CFSP by greater use of QMV was also checked by the retention of a requirement for unanimity should members' national interests so require (see Article J.113).

The Prime Minister looked to the Treaty chapter on employment and greater cooperation on crime, drugs and the environment as making the EU more relevant to the peoples of Europe (Blair, 1997c, p. 2). The theme became the British government's agenda for its Presidency of the European Union in 1998. Tony Blair saw the Presidency as a test, 'for Britain to show that we can and do offer strong leadership in Europe' and 'for Europe to show that it can embrace the need for change and reform' (Blair, 1997g, p. 1). The problem for British leadership was that in opting out of EMU it stood apart from a key role concerning the majority of member states. Gordon Brown, the Chancellor, rejected opposition to the single currency on constitutional grounds but maintained the economic case for entry had to be 'clear and unambiguous'. The Chancellor set five tests for entry, and concluded, 'British membership of a single currency in 1999 could not meet the tests and therefore is not in the country's economic interests' (*The Times*, 28 October

1997). The eleven member states that did decide to adopt the single currency formed their own economic group, the so-called 'EuroX Group'. While Britain sought to limit this new forum at the Luxemburg summit in December 1997 it could not arrest the need for coordination amongst EMU participating countries. The British government instead sought to seize the initiative on EU enlargement. Robin Cook believed Britain had 'a strategic opportunity especially during our presidency, to emerge as a sponsor and a patron of membership to the European Union for those countires seeking to apply' (*Hansard*, 4 December 1997, Col. 514). In this manner, enlargement and reform of the EU provided the material for British leadership which was denied by 'semi-detachment' over EMU.

NATO and Defence Policy

The Labour government, like its Conservative predecessor, based Britain's security and defence on the North Atlantic Alliance. Tony Blair declared that 'NATO remains the bedrock of our security' (Blair, 1998b, p. 2). The EU was not seen as a potential defence organisation. Robin Cook believed 'such a development would undermine the North Atlantic Alliance and would also create great complications for the different memberships of NATO and the European Union' (Cook, 1997c, p. 1). Labour also sought to maintain the intergovernmental character of defence cooperation and the principle of consensus for decision-making. It was willing to endorse the WEU role in crisis management but as 'a pivot between NATO and the European Union drawing on the skills and assets owned by NATO', and looked 'forward to closer cooperation with NATO and the EU, whilst preserving the essential intergovernmentalism of the existing decision-making process' (Robertson, 1997a, pp. 2–3).

The Labour government endorsed the NATO Madrid Summit decision of July 1997 to enlarge the Alliance. Tony Blair welcomed NATO's membership invitation to Poland, the Czech Republic and Hungary. He told the Commons that the 'priority was a manageable and limited enlargement, involving credible candidates with reliable democratic credentials and a real ability to contribute to collective security' (Blair, 1997e, col.938). In this, Britain supported the United States and rejected a wider enlargement favoured by other states including France. The sensitivity of enlargement to NATO relations with Russia was also of concern to the Labour government. The NATO Russia Founding Act of May 1997 was seen as a 'beginning not an end' (Robertson, 1997d, p. 6). The Founding Act providing for a NATO–Russian Permanent Joint Council and programme of cooperation was strongly supported by Britain. The Act does not, though, necessarily resolve differences between NATO and Russia. The Act will have to withstand differences in policy and domestic politics not least with regard to any future NATO enlargement.

The Labour government's policy on defence commenced with the launch of a Strategic Defence Review. The Review was charged with assessing 'how recent changes in the international arena, and likely developments in the next 15 to 20 years, determine that we should modernise our force structures and capabilities' (Robertson, 1997b, p. 3). The first stage of the Review was to reassess foreign policy objectives, and involved the Ministry of Defence, the Foreign and Commonwealth Office, non-governmental organisations and other specialists. The Defence Secretary believed planning had to address 'likely new challenges from weapons proliferation, the drugs trade, terrorism, ethnic and population pressures, and the break-up of some existing states' (Robertson, 1997b, p. 4). With 17,000 troops deployed in Northern Ireland the Review had also to anticipate the challenge of terrorism.

The government saw the need for forces sufficiently flexible to undertake a wide variety of roles from high intensity combat to humanitarian missions. This included 'maintaining Trident to provide a minimum, but credible and effective, nuclear deterrent which will continue to underpin our collective security' (Robertson, 1997b, p. 7). The problem for conventional forces was maintaining the breadth of tasks envisaged whilst reductions in force levels had followed the end of the Cold War. The Defence Secretary spoke of 'severe overstretch' and 'unprecedented short gaps between operational tours' which affects 'morale, recruitment and retention' (Robertson, 1997b, p. 2). Taken together with the need to enhance rapid deployment, logistic and technical support, the Strategic Defence Review faced a major challenge in reconciling resources with the multi-issue security agenda of the new international order.

The Labour government also made arms control an important focus of defence policy. Labour moved to ban the import, export, transfer and manufacture of all forms of anti-personnel landmines. The government also sought to secure an international ban through the Ottawa process. Labour also looked to prevent the sale of arms to regimes that would use them for internal repression or international aggression. Tony Lloyd, FCO Minister of State, referred to the importance of the Scott Inquiry and its stress upon the legal basis for export controls and parliamentary accountability when describing the development of Labour's new arms exports policy. The government pledged to 'increase the transparency and accountability of decisions on export licences for arms' and ensure the arms trade is properly regulated (Lloyd, 1997, pp. 2–3). In July 1997 Robin Cook announced new criteria for arms exports. Exports would cease of equipment 'which has obvious application for internal repression…(or) for torture' (Cook, 1997e, p. 1). The criteria would take into account respect for human rights and fundamental freedoms in the recipient country. The Foreign Secretary did, however, exempt licences approved by the past Conservative government. This caused controversy amongst those committed to the government's ethical foreign policy when arms sales to Indonesia were permitted as they predated the new criteria (see *The Guardian*, 29 July 1997). When the government did ban further arms sales to Indonesia it faced criticism from the Defence Manufacturers' Association. With British industry accounting for a quarter of the world arms market the challenge for Labour would be to ensure 'success and responsibility go hand in hand' (Cook, 1997e, p. 1). In 1998, allegations of Foreign Office complicity in arms shipments to Sierra Leone by a British company in breach of a United Nations embargo embarrassed the Labour government. While the enquiry into the affair, conducted by Sir Thomas Legg and Sir Robin Ibbs, exonerated Ministers and Officials, it did find 'a number of misjudgements by officials largely due to overload' (Cook, 1998b, p. 2). The Legg Report also found management deficiencies in the Foreign Office. The Report found that there was not a sufficiently high priority for the enforcement of sanctions, that defence intelligence reports were not handled properly and more explicit guidance was needed for dealing with private military companies (Cook, ibid, p. 3). The Foreign Secretary duly announced a series of measures to improve the management of the Foreign Office and open its 'closed culture' (Cook, 1998c, p. 2). As part of that process the number of exchanges of staff with the private sector, the academic world and non-governmental organisations was to increase.

Environmental Policy, Development and Aid

Britain signed the 1992 UN Convention on Climate Change and was committed to returning greenhouse gas emissions to 1990 levels by the year 2000. At the Kyoto Conference in 1997 Britain supported the EU position that developed countries should reduce their greenhouse gas emissions to 15 per cent below 1990 levels by the year 2010 and by at least 7.5 per cent by 2005. While other industrial countries sought lesser targets Britain was prepared to go further to a 20 per cent target. The actual figure agreed at Kyoto was a 6 per cent reduction below 1990 levels to be achieved between 2008 and 2012. John Prescott, Deputy Prime Minister, who played a key role in the negotiations still welcomed the outcome as 'for the first time it commits developed countries to make legally binding cuts in their emissions' (Prescott, 1997, p. 1).

Tony Blair saw the need for 'common action to save our common environment' and the importance of developed countries in assisting the developing world. He explained to the United Nations Special Session on the Environment that is 'why my Government supports the UN aid target; and why we are committed to improving further the quality of our assistance, reversing the decline in Britain's development assistance, and refocusing our efforts on combatting poverty' (Blair, 1997d, p. 1). The Department for International Development was charged with taking forward the agenda for sustainable development. The Department's White Paper looked to support policies 'which create sustainable livelihoods for poor people, promote human development and conserve the environment' (Department for International Development, 1997, p. 3). At the G8 Summit in Denver in June 1997 the Prime Minister pledged that Britain would increase by 50 per cent its support for primary education, basic health care and clean water in sub-Saharan Africa. The focus on Africa reflected government concern to give priority to the poorest countries. For poorer Commonwealth countries it was announced in September 1997 that the UK was willing to cancel aid debt provided the funds released benefited the poor. Labour saw the interrelationship of aid, development and the environmental agenda as integral to its ethical approach to foreign policy.

Britain and the Politics of Intervention

Labour's support for the United Nations and the United States has ensured an interventionist role in the Gulf. Saddam Hussein's refusal to cooperate with UN weapon inspectors and denial of access to so-called 'Presidential sites' led to confrontation. Britain supported Washington's demand that trade sanctions be sustained and deployed naval forces to supplement US carrier forces in the Gulf. Britain's readiness to back the United States was evidence of Labour's continuing endorsement of the transatlantic partnership. Britain has also looked to retain a United States presence in Bosnia and not leave the operation to European auspices alone.

The Kososvo crisis provided further evidence of the importance of the transatlantic alliance to Britain. Kososvo had been an autonomous province of the Federal Republic of Yugoslavia. It enjoyed similar rights to the constituent republics; an assembly, local government etc. but not the republican right to secede. In the 1980s the predominantly Albanian population began to press for republican status. At the same time, Kosovo's Serb minority, some 10 per cent of the population of the province, increasingly looked to Serbia for protection. The migration of Serbs from what was regarded as the heart of the Serbian medieval kingdom reignited Serbian nationalism under the leadership of Slobodan Milosevic. In 1989 Milosevic became President of Serbia and moved to end Kosovo's autonomy. Kosovo Albanian demonstrations against Serbian policy led to the declaration of a state of emergency and the deployment of Serbian forces in Kosovo. In 1990 the Kosovo assembly was suspended and direct rule imposed from Belgrade. As separatism took hold in Yugoslavia, Ibrahim Rugova declared Kosovo's independence but rejected violent resistance to Serb rule. In 1995 the Dayton agreement ended the war in Bosnia but failed to provide a wider settlement for Yugoslvia's minorities. In Kosovo the failure of Dayton radicalised Kosvar Albanian politics and legitimised the strategy of the Kosovo Liberation Army (KLA). The KLA mounted a guerrilla war which mounted in intensity from 1997. In the summer of 1998 Serb offensives against the KLA widened into a campaign against their supporters in the civilian population, resulting in over 1,500 deaths and 300,000 forced from their homes. The United Nations Security Council resolution 1199 demanded that the security forces cease all action against the civilian population of Kosovo. NATO warned of air strikes against Serbia if Belgrade failed to comply with the resolution, and dispatched envoys with United States representatives to negotiate with Milosevic. The resulting agreement limited Serbian forces and their role in Kosovo and provided for an unarmed OSCE mission to verify compliance on the ground. Despite the presence of observers, the situation deteriorated in January 1999 with a fresh Serbian offensive. The six-nation Contact Group called the protagonists to talks in Rambouillet and Paris under British and French co-chairmanship. The Kosovar Albanian delegation signed the proposed peace agreement but the Serbian delegation left the talks without agreement. On the ground, the Serbian offensive intensified and was seen as an attempt to ethnically cleanse the whole province. The OSCE mission was withdrawn on 20 March, and following one final failed intervention by Ambassador Holbrooke, NATO commenced airstrikes on 24 March.

Tony Blair strongly supported NATO's military action. The Prime Minister declared, 'this is a just war, based not on any territorial ambitions but on values. We cannot let the evil of ethnic cleansing stand' (Blair, 1999, p. 2). The British case was that there was no practicable alternative to the use of force to defend human rights. However, the action was not put to the Security Council for authorisation. The argument that force was justified on grounds of overwhelming necessity was one thing; fear of a Russian or Chinese veto at the UN was another. NATO's actions were made more contentious by its reliance on airpower. The refusal of Alliance members to commit ground forces belied a reluctance to accept casualties in such a war. If bombing Serbia was the only possible response, for some commentators it was ineffective and seen to exacerbate rather than redress the plight of the Kosovar Albanians (see Mandelbaum, 1999). By the end of the bombing almost one million people left Kosovo and a half a million were internally displaced (see Roberts, 1999, p. 113). While the Serbian withdrawal from Kosovo negotiated in early June 1999 can be deemed a success for NATO, the plight of the Kosovars and their future remained unanswered. The deployment of KFOR with a substantive British troop contribution met just one element of a needed security policy which should embrace wider economic and political measures for the Balkan region.

The Labour government did recognise the implications of Kosovo for its crisis management policy. Drawing on the lessons of Bosnia, Albania and Kosovo, Robin Cook argued, 'crisis management requires a joined-up approach that brings together the economic, financial and humanitarian assets of the European Union and the military assets of the European countries in NATO' (*Hansard*, 1 December 1999, Column 322). The Foreign Secretary's speech to the Commons took forward the Anglo-French declaration at Saint-Malo in December 1998 which effectively ended the British veto on the integration of the WEU into the EU. The declaration looked for a rapid implementation of the Amsterdam provisions on CFSP. The EU, freed from British opposition, consequently adopted a Common European Policy on Security and Defence at its Cologne and Helsinki summits in 1999. The EU agreed to create by 2003 a rapid reaction force, some 60,000 strong, capable of being deployed in those instances where NATO as a whole was not engaged. London stressed that there was no erosion of NATO's position but by granting the EU the capability for autonomous action in crisis management marked the beginning of a new British strategy for European security.

Conclusion

New Labour's foreign and defence policies have exhibited strong elements of continuity with the past, a policy continuity that reflected in part the pattern of commitments Labour inherited and in part the preferences of the new government. As Labour took office, NATO was already committed to enlargement, the EU to the post-Maastricht Treaty review and Britain to specific deployments such as Bosnia. At the same time, though, Labour chose to endorse Atlanticism, nuclear orthodoxy in defence, and remained wary of deepening integration in the EU. A new agenda was also set in parallel with this process which made Labour's policies a mix of new and old themes, issues and agendas.

The Labour government has launched new initiatives, looked for an ethical dimension to policy and sought change in the institutional structures to which Britain is committed. A new style of foreign policy has followed, but, as we have seen, the record of sustaining such a policy stance is challenging and at times contentious in a spectrum of issues from arms sales to development to the protection of human rights. In a speech to the UN General Assembly, Robin Cook called for reform of the UN system. He maintained that Labour's commitment to the UN had been demonstrated by rejoining UNESCO but looked for a UN that was more 'efficient, representative and properly funded'. With respect to the Security Council, Britain looked to Germany and Japan's inclusion in an expanded permanent membership and a balance between developed and developing in the modernised Council (Cook, 1997f, p. 2). For the EU, Tony Blair identified two challenges: 'how we enlarge Europe to take in the aspirant countries wanting to join the Union; and how we build an economically competitive and prosperous Europe for the future' (Blair, 1998a, p. 5). The Prime Minister saw reform of CAP and the Structural and Cohesion Funds as essential to permit enlargement. He also looked to the formation of a new consensus in favour of Europe in Britain. A 'patriotic alliance' of politicians from all parties 'who are in favour of Europe by in favour of a reformed Europe' (Blair, 1998a, p. 3).

The policies the Labour government has embraced, and is likely to pursue, ensure that Britain retains a global interest in foreign affairs. Tony Blair has stressed that Britain cannot be 'a superpower in a military sense' but believes 'we can make the British presence in the world felt' (Blair, 1997f, p. 1). It is Europe, however, that will clearly form the centre of gravity for future policy with respect to the auspices of both the EU and NATO. The European agenda and issues of Euro-governance in particular, obligate responses in a broad range of policy areas. The EU challenges Labour's European engagement with the single currency, which remains an emotive and potentially politically costly step kept firmly on the policy agenda by the Conservative opposition. The challenge for Labour will be also to sustain the balance of its engagement with Europe while maintaining the Atlantic agenda. The tensions between the EU and the transatlantic frameworks however are ongoing and still to be fully worked out. The EU has also now entered the hallowed ground of security and defence, and while Washington and London have stressed that NATO is not compromised the new EU policy is at the beginning of its development, not the end. For Robin Cook, however, as for previous British governments, the relationships are seen to be complementary and not mutually exclusive.

> Our new relationship with Europe does not in any way detract from Britain's strong friendship with the United States. The two are not contradictory, but reinforce each other. It is because we are now playing a stronger role in Europe that we can be a more effective partner for the US. (Cook, 1998a, p. 8)

Guide to Further Reading

Chapter 1   Introduction: New Labour and 'Blairism'

Driver and Martell (1999) provide the best overview of the debates surrounding New Labour, Gould (1998) and Mandelson and Liddle (1996) provide interesting, if rather one-sided, accounts of the reforms inside the Labour Party, while Giddens (1998) offers a useful view of 'Third Way' thinking.

Chapter 2   Policy, Management and Implementation

For the definitive statement by the Blair government regarding its aims for reforming the British Public Sector, see Cabinet Office (1999). An excellent discussion of 'managerialism' can be found in Pollitt (1992), one of the best guides to the ideological dynamics and practicalities involved in public sector reform. Rhodes (1997) provides a substantial advance on previous reviews of theories of the state. Rhodes explores the forces of globalisation and internationalisation, as well as the evolution of policy networks and the impact this has on making and implementing policy.

Chapter 3   The Europeanisation of British Policy-Making

Dinan (1999b) and Nugent (1999) provide the best textbook account of policy-making in the European Union. Bainbridge and Teasdale (1996) have written a very useful 'A-to-Z' guide to the European Union. George (1994) and Young (1998) offer useful historical accounts of relations between the EC/EU and Britain.

Chapter 4   UK Economic Policy: The Conservative Legacy and New Labour's Third Way

Sloman (2000) is one of many introductory economics texts but readable and up to date. The following offer chapters on particular aspects of policy: Curwen (1997) is not 'glossy' in presentation but solid in analysis; Griffiths and Wall (1997) is detailed and comprehensive with good linkage of theory with policy; Heather, (1997) covers selected topics in an introductory way.

Chapter 5   Welfare to Work? New Labour and the Unemployed

The government's analysis and programme for welfare reform is clearly set out in two Green Papers: HMSO (1998a) and (1998b). Both these Green Papers can be obtained from the following website: http://www.dss.gov.uk/hq/pubs/2810intro.htm) The main criticisms of the Labour government's New Deal policies are clearly outlined in Ivan Turok and David Webster's article in *Local Economy* (1998). A good comparative analysis of policies for the unemployed in the UK and the USA can be found in: King (1995).

Chapter 6   UK Environmental Policy under Blair

A good introduction to the range of issues in environmental study is O'Riordan (2000). A comparable account from a political science perspective is Connelly and Smith (1999). The European dimension in environmental policy is well covered by Hanf and Jansen (1998), and by Lowe and Ward (1998a).

Chapter 7   Law and Order under Blair: New Labour or Old Conservatism?

A range of issues relating to criminal justice and policing policy are examined in depth in Maguire, Morgan, and Reiner (1997). An overview of sentencing policy can be found in Dunbar and Langdon (1998). The 'policing/probation' interface and the 'public protection' agenda is examined critically in Nash, (1999a). A comprehensive study of British policing is contained in Leishman, Loveday and Savage (2000). A broad coverage of criminal justice issues is provided in Wasik, Gibbons and Redmayne (1999).

Chapter 8   Health Policy

Ham (1999) is an accessible and reasonably comprehensive account of health care in Britain, which provides a good starting point. Satler (1998) is an incisive exploration of the processes of change in the NHS, and pays due regard to 'professional politics'. Hunter (1999) covers a dynamic and frequently neglected area in health policy. Moon and North (2000) focuses on the increasingly important place of general practice and general practitioners in the NHS.

Chapter 9   Housing Policy

Balchin and Rhoden (1998) is a very sound introductory text, often used as a 'first port of call' by people interested in the economics, finance, politics, land use planning, and management aspects of housing policy. DETR (2000a) (The

Housing Green Paper) is the Blair government's overview of housing policy; essential reading. Marsh and Mullins (1998) is a discussion of housing policy in the context of citizenship, relating housing to broader issues of policy-making. Wilcox (1999) is an essential 'enquire within' book; good commentaries and most of the statistics you are likely to need from one of the 'big names' in housing policy research.

Williams (1997) focuses on the issue of sustainability in housing policy, that is, the formulation of policies which meet needs, can be afforded, and have a reasonable chance of success in the medium and longer term.

Chapter 10   Education Policy

Glennerster (1998) provides a concise but thorough analysis and evaluation of all aspects of education policy from 1974 until 1997. Barber (1997) focuses on the compulsory sector and includes a clear statement of the the New Labour perspective on raising standards. Smithers and Robinson (2000) provides a very recent account of developments in the FE sector. Watson (1998) gives an overview of the impact of the Dearing report on HE.

Chapter 11   The Personal Social Services

A knowledge of the origins of social services departments adds to an understanding of their present operation. The reflections of nine leading Fabians at the very beginnings of the social services departments thirty years ago is provided by Townsend et al. (1970). A good treatment of community care which analyses the major issues (including partnership and user and carer empowerment) is Means, and Smith (1998). A familiarity with Labour's policies in this area is best obtained by reading the White Paper, *Modernising Social Services.*

Chapter 12   Social Security: Welfare Reform or Piecemeal Adjustment?

McKay and Rowlingson (1999) is an excellent up-to-date textbook on social security. The government itself has gone to great lenghts to explain its own policies, and the three key official sources are the Green Paper *A New Contract for Welfare* (DSS, 1998a), Partnership in Pensions (DSS, 1998c) and *The Changing Welfare State: Social Security Spending* (DSS, 2000).

Chapter 13   British Policy in Northern Ireland

Excellent analyses of the constitutional questions relating to Northern Ireland can be found in Hazell and Sinclair (1999) and Hazell, Russell, Seyd and

Sinclair (2000). On the Belfast Agreement, see Doyle, Bruce and Edwards (1998). Taylor (1999) includes a chapter by Mark Hayes on New Labour and Northern Ireland. A survey of the political consequences of the Belfast Agreement is to be found in Ruane and Todd (1999). Cox, Guelke and Stephen (2000) is an impressive and wide-ranging collection of essays on most aspects of New Labour policy in Northern Ireland.

Chapter 14   Foreign and Defence Policy

Wheeler and Dunne (1998) provide a review of the key issues concerning the ethical dimension of Labour's foreign policy including a case study on Indonesia. Roberts (1999) analyses NATO's humanitarian war over Kosovo. Carr (1999) examines the interrelationships of Europe and British party politics. For a useful guide to the changing nature of security in Europe and the consequences for foreign and defence policy, see Sperling and Kirchner (1997).

Bibliography

ACOP (1988) *More Demanding than Prison* (Wakefield: Association of Chief Officers of Probation).

Agulnik, P. *et al.* (1999) *Partnership in Pensions? Responses to the Pensions Green Paper*, Centre for Analysis of Social Exclusion paper 24 (London: London School of Economics).

Andersen, S. S. and Eliassen, K. A. (1993) 'The EC as a New Political System', in S. S. Andersen, and K. A. Eliassen (eds), *Making Policy in Europe: The Europeification of National Policy-Making* (London: Sage).

Anderton, B., Riley, R. and Young, G. (2000) *New Deal for Young People: First Year Analysis of Implications for the Macroeconomy*, ESR 33, Employment Service Research and Development Branch, Sheffield.

Armstrong, H. and Blake, J. (1998) 'Question Time', *Roof*, July/August, pp. 19–21.

Association of Police Authorities (APA) (1998) *Annual Report 1998* (London: APA).

Atkinson, A.B. (1994) *State Pensions for Today and Tomorrow*, Welfare State Programme Discussion Paper 104 (London).

Atkinson, R. and Savage, S. (1994) 'The Conservatives and Public Policy', in S. P. Savage, R. Atkinson, and L. Robins, (eds), *Public Policy in Britain* (London: Macmillan).

Audit Commission (1985) Obtaining Better Value from Further Education (London: HMSO).

Audit Commission/OFSTED (1993) *Unfinished Business: Full-Time Further Education Courses for 16–19 Year Olds* (London: HMSO).

The Audit Commission (1996) *What the Doctor Ordered. A Study of GP Fundholders in England and Wales* (London: HMSO).

The Audit Commission (1997) *Coming of Age. Improving Care Services for Older People* (London: HMSO).

Audit Commission (1998a) *Local Authority Performance Indicators 1996/97: Education Services* (London: HMSO).

Audit Commission (1998b) *Changing Partners* (London: HMSO).

Audit Commission (1999) *Held in Trust: The LEA of the Future* (London: The Stationery Office).

Baggott, R. (1994) *Health and Health Care in Britain* (London: Macmillan).

Bainbridge, T. and Teasdale, A. (1996) *The Penguin Companion to European Union* (London: Penguin).

Baker, D., Fountain, I., Gamble, A. and Ludlam, S. (1995) 'Backbench Conservative Attitudes to European Integration', *Political Quarterly,* 66, pp. 221–33.

Balchin, P. (1996) *Housing Policy* (London: Routledge).

Balchin, P. and Rhoden, M. (1998) (eds), *Housing: The Essential Foundations* (London: Routledge).

Baldock, J. (1998) 'The Personal Social Services and Community Care', in P. Alcock, A. Erskine and M. May (eds), *The Student's Companion to Social Policy*, (Oxford: Blackwell), pp. 306–12.

Balls, E. (1998) 'Open Macroeconomics in an Open Economy', *Scottish Journal of Political Economy*, 45(2), pp. 113–31.

Barber, M. (1997) *The Learning Game* (London: Indigo/Cassell).

Barlow, J. and Duncan, S. (1994) *Success and Failure in Housing Provision* (London: Perganon).

Barratt Brown, M. and Coates, K. (1996) *The Blair Revelation. Deliverance for Whom?* (Nottingham: Spokesman).

Barro, R. J. (1994) 'Personal View: Party Politics of Growth', *Financial Times*, 1 November, p. 20.

Bartlett, W. (1991) 'Quasi-Markets and Contracts: A Markets and Hierarchies Perspective on NHS Reforms' *Public Money and Management*, 11(3), pp. 53–60.

Beatson, M. (1995) 'Progress Towards a Flexible Labour Market', *Employment Gazette*, 103(2), pp. 55–65.

Beckett, J. C. (1966) *The Making of Modern Ireland, 1603–1923* (London: Faber & Faber).

Beecham, L. (2000) 'UK GPs Will have to Show They Are Fit to Practice', *British Medical Journal,* 317, p. 98.

Begg, D., Fischer, S. and Dornbusch, R. (1994) *Economics*, 4th edn (Maidenhead: McGraw-Hill).

Berwick, D.M., Enthoven, A. and Bunker, J.P. (1992) 'Quality Management in the NHS: The Doctor's Role', *British Medical Journal*, 304, pp. 235–9.

Bew, P. and Dixon, P. (1994) 'Labour Party Policy and Northern Ireland', in B. Barton, and P. J. Roche (eds), *The Northern Ireland Question: Perspectives and Policies* (London:Avebury).

Bingham, Lord (1997) 'The Sentence of the Court', Police Foundation Lecture, 10 July 1997, Lord Chancellor's Press Office.

Bingham, Lord (1998) 'The Mandatory Life Sentence for Murder', Newsam Memorial Lecture, given at the Police Staff College, 13 March.

Blair, T. (1996) *New Britain. My Vision of a Young Country* (London: Macmillan).

Blair, T. (1997) Speech given at the Aylesbury Estate, Southwark, London (June).

Blair, T. (1997a) Press Conference Noordwijk (23 May 1997), http://www.fco.gov.uk/texts/1997/may/23/Nordwijk.txt

Blair, T. (1997b) Transcript of Remarks by the Prime Minister and President Clinton, No 10 Downing Street, London (29 May 1997), http://www.fco.gov.uk/t1997/may/29/clinton.txt

Blair, T. (1997c) *Press Conference Amsterdam Summit* (18 June 1997), http:www.fco. gov.uk.texts/1997/jun/18/amst.txt

Blair, T. (1997d) 'Common Action to Save our Common Environment', United Nations Special Session on the Environment (23 June 1997), http:www.fco.gov.uk.texts/1997/jun23/ungass.txt

Blair, T. (1997e) 'NATO Summit in Madrid', Statement in House of Commons, 9 July 1997, *Hansard* 1997, July, Col 938.

Blair T. (1997f) 'The Principles of Modern British Foreign Policy', Guildhall Speech, London (10 November, 1997), http://193.114.50.5/texts/1997/nov/10/guildhal

Blair, T. (1997g) 'Europe Working for People', Speech at the EU Presidency Launch, Waterloo, London (5 December 1997), http:www.fco.gov.uk/texts/1997/dec/05/launch.txt

Blair, T. (1998a) 'A Modern Britain in a Modern Europe', The Hague (20 January, 1998), http://193.114.50/5 texts/1998/jan20/hague.txt

Blair, T. (1998b) 'NATO's Role in the Modern World', http://www.fco.gov.uk/news/speechtext.asp?170

Blair, T. (1998c) *The Third Way: New Politics for a New Century* (London: Fabian Society).

Blair, T. (1999a) 'Facing the Modern Challenge: The Third Way in Britain and South Africa', Speech given in the Parliament Building, Cape Town, South Africa, 8 January 1999.

Blair, T. (1999b) Speech to Labour Party Conference, Bournemouth, 28 September 1999.

Blair, T. (1999c) 'The Fight Against Poverty – "The One Nation Coalition of Haves and Have Nots', Centrepoint, London, 16 December 1999.

Blair, T. (1999d) New Year Message, Sedgefield, 29 December 1999.

Blair, T. (1999e) Speech by the Prime Minister to the Economic Club of Chicago, http://www.fco.gov.uk/speechtext

Blair, T. (2000) Centenary Anniversary Speech to the Labour Party, 27 February 2000.

Blair, T. and Schroeder, G. (No date) 'Europe: The Third Way/Die Neue Mittee' [Online]. Available from: http://www.labour.org.uk/views/items/00000053.html [Accessed: 10 June 1999].

Bland, P. (1999) 'Trade Union Membership and Recognition 1997–98: An Analysis of Data from the Certification Officer and the Labour Force Survey', *Labour Market Trends*, 107(7), pp. 343–53.

Blowers, A (1987) 'Transition or Transformation? Environmental Policy under Thatcher', *Public Administration,* 65, pp. 277–94.

Blyton, P. and Turnbull, P. (1998) *The Dynamics of Employee Relations*, 2nd edn (Basingstoke: Macmillan).

Bosanquet, N. and Zarzecka, A. (1995) 'Attitudes to Health Services 1983 to 1993', *Health Care UK 1994/5* (London: King's Policy Institute).

Bradbeer, J. B. (1990) 'Environmental Policy', in S. P. Savage and L. Robins (eds), *Public Policy under Thatcher* (London: Macmillan).

Bradbeer, J. B. (1994) 'Environmental Policy: Past and Future Agendas', in S. P. Savage, R. Atkinson and L. Robins (eds), *Public Policy in Britain* (London: Macmillan).

Bradbury, J. and Mawson, J. (eds) (1997) *British Regionalism and Devolution* (London: Jessica Kingsley).

Bramley, G. (1998) 'Why Does Need Add Up', *Roof*, Nov/Dec, pp. 23–5.

Bratton, W. (1998) 'Crime is Down in New York City: Blame the Police', in N. Dennis (ed.), *Zero Tolerance: Policing a Free Society* (London: Institute of Economic Affairs).

Brindle, D. (1997) 'NHS managers' jobs targeted to provide cash for patient care', *The Guardian*, 23 May, p. 5.

Brittan, S. (1993) 'Economic Viewpoint: Endogenous Growth – Treat with Care', *Financial Times*, 4 March, p. 18.

Britton, A. J. C. (1991) *Macroeconomic Policy in Britain 1974–87* (Cambridge: Cambridge University Press).

Brown, G. (1999) 'Modernising the British Economy – The New Mission for the Treasury', Speech at the Institute of Fiscal Studies 30th Anniversary Lecture, 27 May 1999.

Brown, W., Deakin, S. and Ryan, P. (1997) 'The Effects of British Industrial Relations Legislation 1979–97' *National Institute Economic Review*, 161 (July), pp. 69–83.

Brownlee, I. (1998) *Community Punishment: A Critical Introduction* (Harlow: Longman).

Bulmer, S. and Burch, M. (1998) 'Organizing for Europe: Whitehall, the British State and European Union', *Public Administration*, 76(4).

Burrows, R. and Joseph, D. (1997) *The Changing Population in Social Housing in England* (York: Joseph Rowntree Foundation).

Burrows, R. Pleace, N. and Quilgars, D. (1997) *Homelessness and Social Policy* (London: Routledge).

Butler, P. (1994) 'Managers and Fundholders Clash on GP Fundholding', *Health Service Journal*, 104 (5395), p. 7.

Cabinet Office (1988) *Improving Management in Government: The Next Steps* (London: HMSO).

Cabinet Office (1994) *The Civil Service: Continuity and Change*, Cm 2627 (London: HMSO).

Cabinet Office (1995) *The Civil Service: Taking Forward Continuity and Change* (London: HMSO).

Cabinet Office (1997) *Opening up Quangos* (London, HMSO).

Cabinet Office (1998a) *Finding Your Way Around Whitehall and Beyond* (London: HMSO).

Cabinet Office (1998b) *Public Bodies 1997* (London: HMSO).

Cabinet Office (1998c) *The 1997 Next Steps Report*, Cm 3889 (London: HMSO).

Cabinet Office (1999) *Modernising Government*, Cm 4310 (London: HMSO).

Campbell, C. and Wilson, G. (1995) *The End of Whitehall: Death of a Paradigm* (Oxford: Blackwell).

Carers National Association (1997) *Still Battling? The Carers Act One Year On* (London: Carers National Association).

Carr, F. (1999) 'Europe and Foreign Affairs', in R. Kelly (ed.), *Changing Party Policy in Britain* (Oxford: Blackwell).

Carr, F. and Cope, S. (1994a) 'Britain and Europe: From Community to Union', in S. P. Savage, R. Atkinson, and L. Robins, (eds), *Public Policy in Britain* (Basingstoke: Macmillan).

Carr, F. and Cope, S. (1994b) 'Implementing Maastricht: The Limits of European Union', *Talking Politics*, 6(3).

Carter, N and Lowe, P. (1998) 'Britain: Coming to Terms with Sustainable Development?, pp. 17–39 in K. Hanf and A.-I. Jansen, (eds), *Governance and Environment in Western Europe* (Harlow: Longman).

Castle, B and Townsend, P. (no date) *We CAN Afford the Welfare State* (London).

Chambers, R. and Belcher, J. (1993) 'Work Patterns of General Practitioners Before And after the Introduction of the 1990 Contract', *British Journal of General Practice,* 43, pp. 410–12.

Charman, S. and Savage, S. (1999) 'New Labour, New Politics of Law and Order', in M. Powell, (ed.), *New Labour, New Welfare State* (London: Polity Press).

Chryssochoou, D. (1999) 'Eurogovernance: Theories and Approaches to the EU', in F. Carr, and A. Massey, (eds), *Public Policy in the New Europe* (Cheltenham: Edward Elgar).

Cini, M. (1996) *The European Commission: Leadership, Organisation and Culture in the EU Administration* (Manchester: Manchester University Press).

CML/DETR (1999) *Housing Finance,* no. 44 (November), p. 18, Table 3.

Coakley, J. and Harris, L. (1992) 'Financial Globalisation and Deregulation' in J. Michie (ed.), *The Economic Legacy 1979–1992* (London: Academic Press) pp. 37–57.

Coker, J. B. and Martin, J. P. (1985) *Licensed to Live* (Oxford: Blackwell).

Coman, J. (1998) 'Crossroads on the Third Way', *The European,* 21 September, p. 7.

Congdon, T. (1999) 'Fashion and Continuity in British Fiscal Policy', *Economic Affairs,* 19(1), pp. 18–23.

Connelly, J. and Smith, G. (1999) *Politics and the Environment: From Theory to Practice* (Harlow: Longman).

Considine, M. and Painter, M. (eds) (1997) *Managerialism: The Great Debate* (Melbourne: Melbourne University Press).

Cook, R. (1997a) 'Britain Opts in to the Social Chapter', FCO Press Release, London (4 May 1997), http:www.fco.gov.uk/texts/1997/may04/socialch.txt

Cook, R. (1997b) 'British Foreign Policy: FCO Mission Statement', London (12 May 1997) http://www.fco.uk/texts/1997/may/12/mspc.txt

Cook, R. (1997c) 'European Security', WEU, Ministerial Meeting, Paris (13 May 1997), http://www.fco.gov.uk/news/newstext

Cook, R. (1997d) 'Human Rights into a New Century', FCO, London (17 July 1997), http://www.fco.uk/texts/1997/July/17/hrspeech.text

Cook, R. (1997e) 'New Criteria to ensure Responsible Arms Trade', FCO Daily Bulletin (28 July 1997), http://www.fco.gov.uk/texts/1997/jul/28/bulletin.txt

Cook, R. (1997f) 'A United Nations for the Twenty-First Century', Speech to the United Nations General Assembly, New York (23 September, 1997), http://www.coi.gov.uk/coi/depts/gte/coi574 5d .ok

Cook, R. (1998a) 'Europe and America: The Decisive Partnership', European Institute, Washington (15 January 1998), http://www.fco.gov.uk/news/speech text.asp?34

Cook, R. (1998b) Statement by the Foreign Secretary, House of Commons, 27 July 1998, http://www.fco.gov.uk/news/newstext.asp?1354

Cook, R. (1998c) Edited Transcript of an Interview by the Foreign Secretary, BBC Radio, London, 28 July 1998, http://www.fco.gov.uk.news/ newstext.asp?1357

Cook, R. (1998d) Speech to the Amnesty International Human Rights Festival, 16 October 1998, http://www.fco.gov.uk/news/speechtext.asp?161

Cope, S., Leishman, F. and Starie, P. (1996) 'Reinventing and Restructuring', in F. Leishman, B. Loveday and S. Savage, (eds), *Core Issues in Policing* (London: Longman).

Cox, M., Guelke, A. and Stephen, F. (eds) (2000) *A Farewell to Arms? From 'Long War' to Long Peace in Northern Ireland* (Manchester: Manchester University Press).

Crail, M. (1997) 'Cash on Delivery', *Health Service Journal*, 107 (5578), p. 9. 9.

Curtice, J. (1997) 'Anatomy of a Non-Landslide', *Politics Review*, 7(1), pp. 2–8.

Curwen, P. (1997a) 'Taxation', in P. Curwen (ed.), *Understanding the UK Economy* (London: Macmillan), pp. 166–85.

Curwen, P. (1997b) 'The European Union', in P. Curwen (ed.), *Understanding the UK Economy* (London: Macmillan) pp. 265–97.

Curwen, P. (1997c) 'Employment and Unemployment' in P. Curwen (ed.), *Understanding the UK Economy* (London: Macmillan) pp. 325–65.

Curwen, P. (1997d) 'Macroeconomic Policy' in P. Curwen (ed.), *Understanding the UK Economy* (London: Macmillan) pp. 522–44.

Curwen, P. and Hartley, K. (1997) 'Industry and Policy II: Privatisation', in P. Curwen (ed.), *Understanding the UK Economy* (London: Macmillan) pp. 477–502.

Day, P. and Klein, R. (1991) 'Britain's Health Care Experiment', *Health Affairs*, Fall, pp. 39–59.

Denham, A. (1996), *Think Tanks of the New Right* (Aldershot: Dartmouth).

Dennis, N. and Halsey, A.H. (1988) *English Ethical Socialism* (Oxford: Clarendon Press).

Department for Education and Employment (DfEE) (1997) *Excellence in Schools* (London: HMSO).

Department for Education and Employment (DfEE) (1998a) *The Learning Age: A Renaissance for a New Britain*, Cm.3790 (London: The Stationery Office).

Department for Education and Employment (DfEE) (1998b) *Higher Education for The 21st Century: A Response To The Dearing Report* (London: DfEE).

Department for Education and Employment (DfEE) (1998c) *Departmental Report, The Government's Expenditure Plans,* Department for Education and Employment (London: HMSO).

Department for Education and Employment (DfEE) (1999) *Learning to Succeed: A New Framework for Post-16 Learning*, Cm.4392 (London: The Stationery Office).

Department for Education and Employment (DfEE) (2000a) *New Deal for Young People and Long-Term Unemployed People aged 25+, Statistical First Release*, SFR 05/00, 24 February, (London: DfEE).

Department for Education and Employment (DfEE) (2000b) *New Deal for Lone Parents, Statistical First Release*, SFR 06/00, 2 March (London: DfEE).

Department of Education and Science (DES) (1972) *Education: A Framework for Expansion* (London: HMSO).

Department of Education and Science (DES) (1991) *Higher Education: A New Framework*, Cm.1541 (London: HMSO).

Department of Education and Science (DES) (1992) *Choice and Diversity: A New Framework for Schools* (London: HMSO).

Department of Employment (1990) *Motivation, Unemployment and Employment Department Programmes*, Research Paper 80 (London: Department of Employment).

Department of the Environment (DoE) (1977) *Housing Policy: A Consultation Document*, Cmnd 6851 (London: HMSO).

Department of the Environment (DoE) (1987) *Housing: The Government's Proposals*, Cmnd 214 (London: HMSO).

Department of the Environment (DoE) (1995a) *Our Future Homes*, Cmnd 2901 (London: HMSO).

Department of the Environment (DoE) (1995b) *Projections of Households in England to 2016* (London: HMSO).

Department of the Environment (DoE) (1996a) *English Housing Condition Survey* (London: HMSO).

Department of the Environment (DoE) (1996b) *Housing Need* (London: HMSO).

Department of the Environment, Transport and the Regions (DETR) (1997a) *An Economic Model of the Demand and Need for Social Housing* (London: HMSO).

Department of the Environment, Transport and the Regions/Welsh Office (DETR) (1997b) *Replacing CCT with a Duty of Best Value; Next Steps* (unnumbered circular) (London: HMSO).

Department of the Environment, Transport and the Regions (DETR) (1998a) *Modernising Local Government: Improving Local Services Through Best Value* (London: DETR).

Department of the Environment, Transport and the Regions (DETR) (1998b) *Regional Development Agencies' Regional Strategies* (London: DETR).

Department of the Environment, Transport and the Regions (DETR) (1999a) *1989/9 Survey of English Housing* (London: DETR).

Department of the Environment, Transport and the Regions (DETR) (1999b) *DETR Annual Report* (London: DETR).

Department of the Environment, Transport and the Regions (DETR) (1999c) *Housing in the South East: The Inter-relationship between Supply, Demand and Land Use Policy*, available at: http://www.planning.detr.gov.uk/ sehou/index.htm [Accessed: 8 April 2000].

Department of the Environment, Transport and the Regions (DETR) (2000a) *The Housing Green Paper: 'Quality and Choice'* (London: HMSO).

Department of the Environment, Transport and the Regions (DETR) (2000b) *Best Value*, documents available at: http://www.housing.detr.gov.uk/ information/bvhf/index.htm [Accessed: 15 April 2000].

Department of the Environment, Transport and the Regions (DETR) (2000c) *DETR Annual Report* (London: DETR).

Department of Health (DoH) (1989) Caring for People: Community Care in the Next Decade and Beyond, Cm 849 (London: HMSO).

Department of Health (DoH) (1998a) *Statistical Bulletin: Community Care Statistics 1998. Residential Personal Social Services for Adults* (London: HMSO).

Department of Health (DoH) (1998b) *Modernising Social Services: Promoting Independence, Improving Protection, Raising Standards* (London: HMSO).

Department of Health (DoH) (1998c) *The Government's Objectives for Children's Social Services* (London: HMSO).

Department of Health (DoH) (1999a) *Statistical Bulletin: Community Care Statistics 1998. Day and Domiciliary Personal Social Services for Adults (England)* (London: HMSO).

Department of Health (DoH) (1999b) *Me, Survive, Out There? New Arrangements for Young People Living in and Leaving Care* (London: HMSO).

Department of Health (DoH) (1999c) *National Standards for Residential and Nursing Homes for the Elderly: Consultation Document* (London: HMSO).

Department of Health (DoH) (2000a) *No Secrets: Guidance on Developing and Implementing Multi-Agency Policies and Procedures to Protect Vulnerable Adults from Abuse* (London: HMSO).

Department of Health (DoH) (2000b) *Better Care, Higher Standards: A Charter for Long Term Care* (London: HMSO).

Department of Health (DoH) (2000c) *The NHS Plan: A Plan for Investment, A Plan for Reform*, Cm 4848-1 (London: HMSO).

Department of Health and Social Security (DHSS) (1983) *NHS Management Inquiry* (the Griffiths Report) (London: DHSS).

Department for International Development (1997) *Eliminating World Poverty: A Challenge for the 21st century* (White Paper), http://www.oneworld.org/dfid/whitepaper/preview.htm.

Department of Social Security (DSS) (1997) *Social Security Statistics (1997)* (London: HMSO).

Department of Social Security (DSS) (1998a) *A New Contract for Welfare*, Cm 3805 (London: HMSO).

Department of Social Security (DSS) (1998b) *Children First: A New Approach to Child Support* (London: Department of Social Security).

Department of Social Security (DSS) (1998c) *Partnership in Pensions* (London: HMSO).

Department of Social Security (DSS) (2000) *The Changing Welfare State: Social Security Spending* (London: Department of Health).

Dinan, D. (1999a) 'Treaty Change in the European Union: The Amsterdam Experience', in L. Cram, D. Dinan, and N. Nugent, (eds), *Developments in the European Union* (Basingstoke: Macmillan).

Dinan, D. (1999b) *Ever Closer Union: An Introduction to European Integration* (Basingstoke: Macmillan).

Dixon, G. and Glennerster, H. (1995) 'What Do We Know About Fundholding in General Practice?', *British Medical Journal*, 311, pp. 727–30.

DoH (1988) *Public Health in England. Report of the Acheson Committee of Inquiry into the Future Development of the Public Health Function*, Cm 289 (London: HMSO).

Dolton, P. and O'Neill, D. (1996) 'Unemployment Duration and the Restart Effect: Some Experimental Evidence', *Economic Journal*, no. 106 (March), pp. 387–400.

Downes, D. and Morgan, R. (1997) 'Dumping the "Hostages to Fortune"'? The Politics of Law and Order in Post-War Britain', in R. Reiner, R. Morgan, and M. Maguire, (eds), *Oxford Handbook of Criminology* (Oxford: Oxford University Press).

Downs, A. (1972) 'Up and Down with Ecology', *Public Interest*, 28, pp. 38–50.

Doyle, J. Bruce, S. and Edwards, O. D. (1998) *Scottish Affairs*, 25 (autumn).

Driver, S. and Martell, L. (1997) 'New Labour's Communitarianisms', *Critical Social Policy*, 17(3), pp. 27–44.

Driver, S. and Martell, L. (1999) *New Labour. Politics after Thatcherism* (Cambridge: Polity Press).

Dunbar, I. and Langdon, A. (1998) *Tough Justice: Sentencing and Penal Policies in the 1990s* (London: Blackstone Press Ltd).

Dunleavy, P. (2000) 'Slippery polls', *The Guardian*, 31 January, p. 18.

Dyson, K. (1994) *Elusive Union: The Process of Economic and Monetary Union in Europe* (Harlow: Longman).

Elcock, H. (1991), *Change and Decay? Public Administration in the 1990s* (Harlow: Longman).

Engel, M. (1998) 'Hague and Co Offer Music Hall Portrayal of Disintegration that Fails to Bring House Down', *The Guardian*, 10 October.

Etzioni, A. (1995) *The Spirit of Community* (London: Fontana Press).

Eurostat (1997) *News Release: Government Spending in the EU,* 19 December, Luxembourg: Eurostat.

Farnham, D. and Pimlott, J. (1995) *Understanding Industrial Relations*, 5th edn (London: Cassell).

Faulkner, D. (1997) 'A Prison Service for the 21st Century', *Prison Service Journal*, Iss 109.

Featherstone, K. (1999) 'The Political Dynamics of Economic and Monetary Union', L. in Cram, D. Dinan, and N. Nugent, (eds), *Developments in the European Union* (Basingstoke: Macmillan).

FEFC (1997) Fundamental Review of the Funding Methodology, Circular 97/31 (Coventry: FEFC).

Field, F. (1996) *Stakeholder Welfare* (London: Institute of Economic Affairs).

Field, F. (1997a) 'Re-inventing Welfare: A Response to Lawrence Mead', in L. Mead, *From Welfare to Work: Lessons from America* (London: Institute for Economic Affairs, Health and Welfare Unit).

Field, F. (1997b) *Reforming Welfare* (London: Social Market Foundation).

Field, F. (1998) Keith Joseph Memorial Lecture.

Finn, D. (1986) *Training Without Jobs: New Deals and Broken Promises*, (Basingstoke: Macmillan).

Finn, D. and Taylor, D. (1990) *The Future of Jobcentres: Labour Market Policy and the Employment Service*, Employment Paper No. 1 (London: Institute for Public Policy Research).

Foster, C. and Plowden, F. (1996), *The State Under Stress* (Milton Keynes: Open University Press).

Friedman, M. (1997) 'Why Europe Can't Afford the Euro', *The Times*, 19 November, p. 22.

Gamble, A. (1974) *The Conservative Nation* (London: Routledge & Kegan Paul).

Gamble, A. and Kelly, G. (2000) 'The British Labour Party and Monetary Union', *West European Politics*, 23(1).

Gamble, A. and Payne, A. (eds) (1996) *Regionalism and World Order* (Basingstoke: Macmillan).

Gay, O. (1998) *The Scotland Bill: Devolution and Scotland's Parliament*, London, House of Commons Research Paper, 98/1, House of Commons.

General Medical Council (1999) Consultation on Fitness to Practice, www.gmc-uk.org/n_hance/fitness/consultation/ftpconsultation.htm

George, S. (1991) *Politics and Policy in the European Community* (Oxford: Oxford University Press).

George, S. (1994) *An Awkward Partner: Britain in the European Community* (Oxford: Oxford University Press).

George, S. (1996) 'The European Union, 1992 and the Fear of "Fortress Europe" ', in A. Gamble, and A. Payne, (eds), *Regionalism and World Order* (Basingstoke: Macmillan).

Gibbons, I. (1995) 'Realism Essential', *Fortnight*, February.

Giddens, A. (1998) *The Third Way. The Renewal of Social Democracy*, (Cambridge: Polity Press).

Giddens, A. (1999) *Runaway World: How Globalisation Is Reshaping Our Lives* (London: Profile Books).

Gilroy, R. and Woods, R. (1994) *Housing Women* (London: Routledge).

Glennerster, H, (1998) 'Education' in H. Glennerster and J. Hills (eds*), The State of Welfare: The Economics of Social Spending* (Oxford: Oxford University Press).

Glennerster, H., Matsanganis, M. and Owens, P. with Hancock, S. (1994) *Implementing GP Fundholding. Wild Card or Winning Hand?* (Buckingham: Open University Press).

Goddard, J. (1997) 'New Labour: The Party of Law and Order?', Unpublished paper presented to Political Studies Association Conference, April 1997.

Goodman, A., Johnson, P. and Webb, S. (1997) *Inequality in the UK* (Oxford: Oxford University Press).

Gould, P. (1998) *The Unfinished Revolution. How the Modernisers Saved the Labour Party* (London: Little, Brown and Company).

Gravatt, J. and Silver, R (2000) 'Partnerships with The Community', in Smithers and Robinson (eds) (2000).

Gray, T. S. (ed.) (1995) *UK Environmental Policy in the 1990s* (Basingstoke: Macmillan).

Greer, P. (1994) *Transforming Central Government: The Next Steps Initiative* (Milton Keynes: Open University Press).

Griffiths, A. and Wall, S. (eds) (1997) *Applied Economics: An Introductory Course*, 7th edn (Harlow: Addison Wesley Longman).

Griffiths, Sir Roy (1988) *Community Care: Agenda for Action* (London: HMSO).

Haas, E. B. (1964) 'Technocracy, Pluralism and the New Europe', in S. R. Graubard (ed.), *A New Europe?* (Boston: Houghton Mifflin).

Hall, S. (1998) 'The Great Moving Nowhere Show', *Marxism Today*, Nov/Dec.

Ham, C. (1992) *Health Policy in Britain. The Politics and Organisation of the National Health Service,* 3rd edn (Basingstoke: Macmillan).

Ham, C. (1999) *Health Policy in Britain*, 4th edn (Basingstoke: Macmillan).

Harman, H. (1998) 'Welfare Reform: Theory into Practice', *Fabian Review*, 110 (1), pp. 2–3.

Harrison, S. and Choudhry, N. (1996) 'General Practice Fundholding in the UK National Health Service: Evidence to Date', *Journal of Public Health Policy*, 17 (3), pp. 331–46.

Harrison, S., Hunter, D.J., Marnoch, G. and Pollitt, C.J. (1992) *Just Managing: Power and Culture in the National Health Service* (London: Macmillan).

Harrop, M. (1997) 'The Pendulum Swings: The British Election of 1997', *Government and Opposition*, 32 (3), pp. 305–19.

Hattersley, R. (2000) 'Put down your gun, Gerry', *The Guardian*, 6 March.

Hay, C. (1997) 'Blaijorism: Towards a One-Vision Polity?', *Political Quarterly*, 68, pp. 372–8.

Hayes-Renshaw, F. and Wallace, H. (1997) *The Council of Ministers* (Basingstoke: Macmillan).

Hazell, R. and Sinclair, D. (1999) 'The British Constitution in 1997–98: Labour's Constitutional Revolution', *Parliamentary Affairs*, 52 (2) (April), pp. 161–79.

Hazell, R., Russell, M., Seyd, B. and Sinclair, D. (2000) 'The British Consitution in 1998–99: The Continuing Revolution', *Parliamentary Affairs*, 53 (2) (April), pp. 242–62.

Heather, K. (1997) *Understanding Economics* (Hemel Hempstead: Harvester Wheatsheaf).

Hennessy, P. (1989), *Whitehall* (London: Fontana).

Hennessy, P. (1999) 'Tony Blair, the Caesar of our times', *Daily Telegraph*, 13 July, p. 20.

Hensher, M. and Edwards, N. (1996) 'Driving Range,' *Health Service Journal*, 106 (5518) pp. 18–19.

Hirst, P. and Thompson, G. (1996) *Globalization in Question* (Cambridge: Polity Press).

Hix, S. (2000) 'Britain, the EU and the Euro', in P. Dunleavy, A. Gamble, I. Holliday, and G. Peele (eds), *Developments in British Politics 6* (Basingstoke: Macmillan).

HMSO (1990) *Crime, Justice and Protecting the Public*, Cm 965 (London: HMSO).

HMSO (1994) *Jobseeker's Allowance*, Cm 2687 (London: HMSO).

HMSO (1998a) *New Ambitions for Our Country: A New Contract for Welfare*, Cm 3805 (London: HMSO).

HMSO (1998b) *A New Contract for Welfare: The Gateway to Work*, Cm 4102 (London: HMSO).

HM Treasury (No date) *Government's Economic Strategy* [Online]. Available from: http://www.hm-treasury.gov.uk/pub/html/e_info/overview/1_goes.html [Accessed: 11 June 1999].

HM Treasury (1998a) *UK Membership of the Single Currency: An Assessment of the Five Economic Tests* [Online]. Available from: http://www.hm-treasury.gov.uk/pub/html/docs/emumem/main.html [Accessed: 9 November 1998].

HM Treasury (1998b) *The Public Sector Balance Sheet* (London: HM Treasury).

HM Treasury (1998c) White Paper, *Modern Public Services for Britain: Investing in Reform: Comprehensive Spending Review: Spending Plans 1999–2002*, Cm.4011 (London: The Stationery Office).

HM Treasury (1999) *Public Expenditure Statistical Analyses 1999–2000* (London: The Stationery Office).

HM Treasury (2000) *Budget 2000* (London: The Stationery Office. House of Commons No. 346).

Holloway, D. (1999) The Audit Commission, Managerialism and The Further Education Sector, *Journal of Vocational Education and Training*, 51 (2) pp. 229–43.

Holmes, M. (ed.) (1996) *The Eurosceptical Reader* (Basingstoke: Macmillan).

Home Office (1997a) No *More Excuses – A New Approach To Tackling Youth Crime: A Consultation Paper* (London: Home Office).

Home Office (1997b) *Review of Delay in the Criminal Justice System* (The Narey Report) (London: HMSO).

Home Office (1998a) *Reducing Offending*, Home Office Research Study 187 (London: HMSO).

Home Office (1998b) *Prisons Probation: Joining Forces to Protect the Public* (London: HMSO).

Home Office (1998c) Supporting Families: A Consultation Document (London: HMSO).

Home Office (1998d) *Compact: Getting it Right Together*, Cm 4100 (London: HMSO).

Hough, M. and Roberts, J. (1998) *Attitudes to Punishment: Findings from the British Crime Survey*, Home Office Research Study 179 (London: Home Office).

Holmans, A. (1991) 'The 1997 Housing Policy Review in Retrospect', *Housing Studies*, vol. 6, pp. 206–19.

Holmans, A. (1995) *Housing Demand and Need in England 1991–2011* (York: Joseph Rowntree Foundation).

Holmans, A., Morrison, N. and Whitehead, C. (1998) *How Many Homes will we Need?* (London: Shelter).

Horton, S. and Farnham, D. (eds) (1996), *Managing the New Public Services*, 2nd edn, (Basingstoke: Macmillan).

Horton, S. and Farnham, D. (eds) (1999), *Public Management in Britain*, (Basingstoke: Macmillan).

Hudson, B. (1987) *Justice Through Punishment* (London: Macmillan).

Hughes, O. (1998), *Public Management and Administration*, 2nd edn, (Basingstoke: Macmillan).

Hunter, D. J. (1999) *Managing for Health. Implementing the New Health Agenda* (London: Institute for Public Policy).

Hurd, Lord (1998) 'Jack Straw's Battle on Tiptoe', *Prison Service Journal*, Iss 117.

Hutton, W. (1995) *The State We're In* (London: Jonathan Cape).

Incomes Data Services (2000) *The Impact of the Minimum Wage in 1999/2000*, IDS Report 802 (February).

Independent Commission on Policing in Northern Ireland (1999) *A New Beginning: Policing in Northern Ireland* (London: Independent Commission on Policing in Northern Ireland).

Institute of Fiscal Studies (2000) *Fiscal Reforms since May 1997: Distributional Consequences of the Last Four Budgets* [Online]. Available: http://www1.ifs.org.uk/budgets/

Jordan, A. (1998) 'The Impact on UK Environmental Administration', pp. 173–94 in Lowe and S. Ward (eds), *British Environmental Policy and Europe: Politics and Policy in Transition*, (London: Routledge).

Jordan, A. (2000) 'Environmental Policy', in P. Dunleavy, A. Gamble, I. Holliday, and G. Peele (eds), *Developments in British Politics 6* (Basingstoke: Macmillan).

Joseph Rowntree Foundation (1994) *Inquiry into Planning for Housing* (York: Joseph Rowntree Foundation).

Kaiser, W. (1996) *Using Europe, Abusing the Europeans: Britain and European Integration, 1945–63* (Basingstoke: Macmillan).

Karn, V. (1993) 'Remodelling a HAT: The Implementation of the Housing Action Trust Legislation 1987–92' in P. Malpass and R. Means (eds) *Implementing Housing Policy* (Buckingham: Open University Press).

Kemp, P. (1998) *Housing Benefit: Time for Reform* (York: Joseph Rowntree Foundation).

Kennedy, M. C. (1996) 'Macroeconomic Policy', in M.J. Artis (ed.), *The UK Economy: A Manual of Applied Economics* (Oxford: Oxford University Press), pp. 123–54.

Kenny, M. and Smith, M. J. (1997) '(Mis)understanding Blair', *Political Quarterly*, 68, pp. 220–30.

Keohane, R. O. and Hoffmann, S. (1991) 'Institutional Change in Europe in the 1980s', in Keohane, and Hoffmann, (eds), *The New European Community: Decisionmaking and Institutional Change* (Boulder: Westview Press).

King, D. (1995) *Actively Seeking Work? The Politics of Unemployment and Welfare Policy in the United States and Great Britain* (University of Chicago Press).

King, M. (1994) 'The Transmission Mechanism of Monetary Policy', *Bank of England Quarterly Bulletin*, 34(3), pp. 261–7.

Kirchner, E. J. (1992) *Decision Making in the European Community: The Council Presidency and European Integration* (Manchester: Manchester University Press).

Klein, R. (1995) *The New Politics of the NHS* (London: Longman).

Kleinmann, M. *et al.* (1999) *No Excuse Not to Build* (London: Shelter).

Krieger, J. (1999) *British Politics in the Global Age: Can Social Democracy Survive?* (Cambridge: Polity Press).

Labour Party (1983) *The New Hope for Britain: Labour's Manifesto 1983* (London: Labour Party).

Labour Party (1989) *Meeting the Challenge, Make the Change: A New Agenda for Britain. Final Report of Labour's Policy Review for the 1990s* (London: Labour Party).

Labour Party (1991) *Options for a Labour Government* (London: Labour Party).

Labour Party (1993) *Selling Our Security* (London: The Labour Party).

Labour Party (1996) 'Renewing the National Health Service: Labour's Agenda for a Healthier Britain,' *International Journal of Health Services,* 26 (2), pp. 269–308.

Labour Party (1997a) New Labour because Britain deserves better (London: John Smith House).

Labour Party (1997b) *Labour Party Manifesto* (London: The Labour Party).

Ladrech, R. (1994) 'Europeanization of Domestic Politics and Institutions: The Case of France', *Journal of Common Market Studies*, 32(1).

Lancet, The (1989) Editorial: ' The New GP Contract; Will Patients Suffer?', *The Lancet*, 29 April, pp. 936–8.Bantam Press.

Lawson, N. (1992) *The View from No. 11: Memoirs of a Tory Radical* (London: Bantam Press).

Layard, R. (1996) *Preventing Long Term Unemployment* (London: Employment Policy Institute).

Lea, J. and Young, J. (1984) *What is to be Done About Law and Order?* (London: Penguin).

Lee, P. and Murie, A. (1997) *Poverty, Housing Tenure and Social Exclusion* (Bristol: Policy Press).

Leese, B. and Bosanquet, N. (1996) 'Changes in General Practice Organization: Survey of General Practitioners' Views on the 1990 Contract and Fundholding', *British Journal of General Practice,* 46, pp. 95–99.

Leishman, F., Loveday, B. and Savage, S. (eds) (1996) *Core Issues in Policing* (London: Longman).

Leng, R., Taylor, R. and Wasik, M. (1999) *Crime and Disorder Act 1998* (London: Blackstone Press).

Lloyd, J. (1999) 'Will Peter Secure Peace in Ireland?', *New Statesman and Society*, 18 October.

Lloyd, T. (1997) *Controlling the Arms Trade: A New Agenda for the 21st Century* (London: Chatham House) (9 June 1997). http://www.fco.gov.uk/texts/1997/jun/09/arms.txt

Local Government Association/Association of Directors of Social Services (1998) *Social Services ADSS/LGA Budget Survey* (London: ADSS/LGA).

Lodge, M. (2000) 'Isomorphism of National Policies? The "Europeanisation" of German Competition and Public Procurement Law', *West European Politics*, 23(1).

Lowe, P. and Ward, S. (eds) (1998a) *British Environmental Policy and Europe* (London: Routledge).

Lowe, P. and Ward, S. (1998b) 'Britain in Europe: Themes and Issues in National Environmental Policy' pp. 3–30 in P. Lowe, and S. Ward, (eds), *British Environmental Policy and Europe: Politics and Policy in Transition* (London: Routledge).

Labour Party (1995a) *A New Economic Future for Britain: Economic and Employment Opportunities for All*, Final report of the Economic Policy Commission (London).

Labour Party (1995b) *Labour's New Deal for the Under-25s* (London).

Ludlow, P. (1991) 'The European Commission', in R. O. Keohane, and S. Hoffmann, (eds), *The New European Community: Decisionmaking and Institutional Change* (Boulder: Westview Press).

Lustgarten, L. (1986) *The Governance of the Police* (London: Sweet & Maxwell).

Lynes, T. (1997a) 'Supplementary Pensions in Britain: Is There Still a Role for the State?', Paper given at European Institute for Social Security seminar in Dublin.

Lynes, T. (1997b) 'The British Case', in M. Rein and E. Wadensjö (eds), *Enterprise and the Welfare State* (Cheltenham: Edward Elgar).

Macaulay, T. B. (1854), *Critical and Historical Essays, Volume 1* (London: Longman, Brown, Green and Longman).

Maguire, M., Morgan, R. and Reiner, R. (eds) (1997) *Oxford Handbook of Criminology* (Oxford:Oxford University Press).

Malpass, P. (1996) 'Policy Review: The Unravelling of Housing Policy in Britain', *Housing Studies*, vol. 11, pp. 459–70.

Malpass, P. and Means, R. (eds) (1993) *Implementing Housing Policy* (Buckingham: Open University Press).

Mandelbaum, M. (1999) 'A Perfect Failure: NATO's War Against Yugoslavia', *Foreign Affairs*, 78 (5), pp. 2–8.

Mandelson, P. and Liddle, R. (1996) *The Blair Revolution* (London: Faber).

Marquand, D. (1998) 'The Blair Paradox', *Prospect*, May, pp. 19–24.

Marr, A. (1998) 'Blair's big secret: he's a Liberal', *The Observer*, 26 July, p. 21.

Marsh, A. and Mullins, D. (1998) (eds), *Housing and Public Policy: Citizenship and Control* (Buckingham: Open University Press).

Martin, J. (1998) *What Works Among Active Labour Market Policies: Evidence from OECD Countries' Experiences*, OECD Occasional Papers (Paris).

Massey, A. (1993), *Managing the Public Sector* (Aldershot: Edward Elgar).

Massey, A. (1995a) *After Next Steps: The Massey Report* (London: Cabinet Office) (OPSS).

Massey, A. (1995b), 'Civil Service Reform and Accountability', *Public Policy and Administration*, 10 (1).

Massey, A. (1999), *The State of Britain: A Guide to the UK Public Sector* (London: Public Management and Policy Association).

Matthews, R. (1989) *Privatising Criminal Justice* (London: Sage).

Mawson, J. and Spencer. K. (1997) 'The Government Offices for the English Regions: Towards Regional Governance?', *Policy and Politics*, 25 (1), pp. 71–84.

Maynard, G. (1991) 'Britain's Economic Recovery', in G. Bird and H. Bird (eds), *Contemporary Issues in Applied Economics* (Aldershot: Edward Elgar) pp. 137–47.

McCormick, J. (1991) *British Politics and the Environment* (London: Earthscan).

McKay, S. and Rowlingson, K. (1999) *Social Security in Britain* (Basingstoke: Macmillan).

McKinsey Global Institute (1998) *Driving Productivity Growth in the UK Economy* (McKinsey & Company).

McVicar, M. (1990) 'Education Policy: Education as a Business?', in S. Savage, and L. Robins, *Public Policy Under Thatcher* (Basingstoke: Macmillan).

McVicar, M. and Robins, L. (1994) 'Education Policy: Market Forces or Market Failure?', in S. Savage, R. Atkinson and L. Robins, (eds), *Public Policy In Britain* (Basingstoke: Macmillan).

McWilliams, W. (1985) 'The Mission Transformed: Professionalisation of Probation between the Wars', *Howard Journal of Criminal Justice*, 24 (4), pp. 257–74.

McWilliams, W. (1986) 'The English Probation System and the Diagnostic Ideal', *Howard Journal of Criminal Justice*, 25 (4), pp. 241–60.

McWilliams, W. (1992) 'The Rise and Development of Management Thought in the English Probation System', in R. Statham and P. Whitehead (eds), *Managing the Probation Service Issues for the 1990s* (Harlow: Longman).

Mead, L. (1997) *From Welfare to Work: Lessons from America* (London: Institute for Economic Affairs).

Meager, N. (1998) 'Evaluating Active Labour Market Measures for the Long-Term Unemployed', *Policies,* InforMISEP No. 62, Journal of European Employment Observatory, Employment Commission DGV, Brussels.

Means, R. and Smith, R. (1998) *Community Care Policy and Practice,* 2nd edn (Basingstoke: Macmillan).

Middlemas, K. (1979) *Politics in Industrial Society* (London: Andre Deutsch).

Middlemas, K. (1995) *Orchestrating Europe: The Informal Politics of European Union 1973–1995* (London: Fontana Press).

Middleton, R. (1996) *Government Versus the Market: The Growth of the Public Sector, Economic Management and British Economic Performance, c. 1890–1979* (Cheltenham: Edward Elgar).

Mikosz, D. (1998) 'The Third Way', *Fabian Review,* 110 (1), p. 13.

Milward, A. S. (1992) *The European Rescue of the Nation-State* (London: Routledge).

Mitchell, G. (1999) *Making Peace* (Belfast: Alfred A. Knopf).

Mohan, J. (1991) 'Privatization in the British Health Service: A Challenge to the NHS', in J. Gabe, M. Calnan and M. Bury (eds), *The Sociology of the Health Service* (London: Routledge).

Mohan, J. (1997) 'Market Testing/Market Failure. Health Service Privatisation in Theory and Practice, 1979–96', in N. North and Y. Bradshaw (eds), *Perspectives in Health Care* (London: Macmillan).

Moon, G. and North, N. (2000) *Policy and Place: General Medical Practice in the UK* (Basingstoke: Macmillan).

Mooney, G.H. and Healey, A. (1991) 'Strategy Full of Good Intentions', *British Medical Journal,* 303 pp. 1119–20.

Moran, M. and Prosser, T. (eds) (1994) *Privatization and Regulatory Change in Europe* (Milton Keynes: Open University Press).

Moravcsik, A. (1999) *The Choice for Europe: Social Purpose and State Power from Messina to Maastricht* (London: UCL Press).

Morgan Report (1997) *Safer Communities: The Local Delivery of Crime Prevention through the Partnership Approach* (London: Home Office).

Mowlam, M. (1995) 'A Rosier Future?', *Fortnight,* February.

Muellbauer, J. (1990) *The Great British Housing Disaster and Economic Policy* (London: Institute for Public Policy Research).

Murray, C. (1990) *The Emerging British Underclass* (London: Institute of Economic Affairs).

Mussa, M. (2000) Comment at a Press Conference on World Economic Outlook, 12 April 2000, Washington DC [Online]. Available: http://www.imf.org/external/np/tr/2000/Trooo412.HTM [Accessed: 14 April 2000].

Naisbitt, B. (1991) 'Monetary Policy in the 1980s', in G. Bird and H. Bird (eds), *Contemporary Issues in Applied Economics* (Aldershot: Edward Elgar) pp. 189–203.

NAO (National Audit Office) (1997a) *The Further Education Funding Council for England* (London: HMSO).

NAO (National Audit Office) (1997b) *The Management of Growth in the English Further Education Sector,* (London: HMSO).

Nash, M. (1994/5) 'Explaining or Excusing Crime – the Michael Howard Solution', *Talking Politics*, 7 (2).

Nash, M. (1999a) *Police, Probation and Protecting the Public* (London: Blackstone Press).

Nash, M. (1999b) 'Enter the Polibation Officer', *International Journal of Police Science and Management*, 4(1) (January).

NATFHE (1998) Evidence to the House of Commons Education and Employment Committee in Education and Employment Committee, 1998, Appendix 53, cited in Smithers and Robinson (eds) (2000).

National Commission on Education (1993) *Learning to Succeed* (London: Heinemann).

National Committee of Inquiry into Higher Education (NCIHE) (1997) *Higher Education in The Learning Society, Summary Report* (London: NCIHE).

NCSR (1999) '*Unknown Destinations in the New Deal*', unpublished report, National Centre for Social Research.

NDTF (1999) *Lasting Value: Recommendations for Increasing Retention within the New Deal,* New Deal Task Force, (London: DfEE).

Newburn, T. (1995) *Crime and Criminal Justice Policy* (Harlow: Longman).

NHS Executive (1994) *Developing NHS Purchasing and GP Fundholding: Towards a Primary Care-Led NHS* (Leeds: NHS Executive).

NHS Executive (1998) *A First Class Service*, HSC 1998/113 (Leeds: NHS Executive).

North, N. (1997) 'Politics and Procedures: The Strategy Process in a Health Commission', *Health and Social Care in the Community*, 6 (5), pp. 375–83.

North, N. (1998) 'Implementing Strategy: The Politics of Health Care Commissioning', *Policy and Politics*, 26 (1), pp. 5–14.

North Atlantic Council (1991) *The Alliance's Strategic Concept* (Brussels: NATO Office of Information and Press).

North Atlantic Council (1994) *Declaration of Heads of State and Government* (Brussels: NATO Office of Information and Press).

Nugent, N. (1999) *The Government and Politics of the European Union* (Basingstoke: Macmillan).

OECD (Organisation for Economic Cooperation and Development) (1975) *Education Development Strategy in England and Wales* (Paris: OECD).

OECD (1994) *The OECD Jobs Study: Evidence and Explanation* (Paris: Organisation for Economic Cooperation and Development).

OECD (1998a) *Economic Outlook* (Paris: OECD).

OECD (1998b) *The Battle against Exclusion: Social Assistance in Australia, Finland, Sweden and the United Kingdom* (Paris: OECD).

Office of Fair Trading(1999) *What Does the Act Say?* [Online]. London: Crown Copyright. Available: http://www.oft.gov.uk/ht...ntroduction/what_does_the_act_say.html [Accessed: 10 March 2000].

Office of Health Economics (1997) *Compendium of Health Statistics,* 10th edn, (London: OHE).

O'Leary, B. (1997) 'The Conservative Stewardship of Northern Ireland, 1979–97: Sound-Bottomed Contradictions or Slow Learning?', *Political Studies*, 45 (4), pp. 663–77.

O'Leary, J. (1998) 'Town Planning and Housing Development' in P. Balchin and M. Rhoden (eds) *Housing: The Essential Foundations* (London: Routledge).

ONS (1997) *Adult Literacy in Britain* (London: HMSO).

ONS (2000) *Labour Market Statistics March 2000: First Release*, 15 February (London: Office for National Statistics).

O'Riordan, T. (1991) 'Stability and Transformation in Environmental Government', *Political Quarterly*, 62, pp. 167–85.

O'Riordan, T. (ed.) (2000) *Environmental Science for Environmental Management*, 2nd edn (Harlow: Prentice Hall).

O'Toole, B. (1990) 'T. H. Green and the Ethics of Senior Officials in British Central Government', *Public Administration*, 68 (3).

Oulton, N. (1995) 'Supply Side Reform and UK Economic Growth: What Happened to the Miracle?' *National Institute Economic Review*, 154 (November), pp. 53–70.

Parker, H. (1989) *Instead of the Dole* (London: Routledge).

Parkin, M., Powell, M. and Matthews, K. (1998) *Economics*, 4th edn (Harlow: Addison-Wesley).

Payne, J. (1991) *Women, Training and the Skills Shortage: The Case for Public Investment* (London: Policy Studies Institute).

Payne, J., Lissenburgh, S., White, M. and Payne, C. (1996) *Employment Training and Employment Action: An Evaluation by the Matched Comparison Method*, Research Series No.74 (London: DfEE).

Pease, K. (1997) 'Crime Prevention', in R. Reiner, *et al.* (eds), *Oxford Handbook of Criminology* (Oxford: Oxford University Press).

Peck, J. (1998) 'New Labourers: Making a New Deal for the "workless class"', paper presented at the annual conference of the Royal Geographical Society/Institute of British Geographers, Guildford, 5–8 January.

Peters, B. G. (1992) 'Bureaucratic Politics and the Institutions of the European Community', in A. M. Sbragia, (ed.), *Euro-Politics: Institutions and Policymaking in the 'New' European Community* (Washington, DC: The Brookings Institution).

Peterson, J. (1995) 'Decision-making in the European Union: Towards a Framework for Analysis', *Journal of European Public Policy*, 2(1).

Phillips, M. (1998) 'Changing Wildlife Law', *Ecos*, 19(1), pp. 73–8.

Piachaud, D. (1999) 'New Labour and Poverty', paper given at the Social Policy Association Conference, Roehampton.

PM (1997) Speech by the Prime Minister the Rt Hon Tony Blair MP at the Aylesbury Estate, Southwark, on Monday 2 June, London.

Pollitt, C. (1990) *Managerialism and the Public Services: The Anglo American Experience* (Oxford: Basil Blackwell).

Pollitt, C. (1992) *Managerialism and the Public Services: Cuts or Cultural Change?*, 2nd edn (Oxford: Blackwell).

Pollitt, C. (1995) *Management Techniques for the Public Sector: Pulpit and Practice* (Canadian Centre for Management Development).

Pollock, A., Brannigan, M. and Liss, P.E. (1995) 'Rationing Health Care: From Needs to Markets?', *Health Care Analysis*, 3, pp. 299–314.

Powell, M. (1997) *Evaluating the National Health Service* (Buckingham: Open University Press).

Prais, S.J. (1995) *Productivity, Education and Training: An International Perspective* (Cambridge: Cambridge University Press).

Prescott, J. (1997) 'Historic Agreement reached in Kyoto on Climate Change', Department of the Environment, Transport and the Regions (11 December 1997). http://www.coi.gov.uk/ coi/depts/gte/coi5745d.ok

Prescott, J. (2000) *Hansard. House of Commons Debates*, 7 March 2000, Col. 865.

Price, D. (1997) 'Profiting from Closure: The Private Finance Initiative and the NHS', *British Medical Journal*, 315, pp. 179–80.

Prison Service Journal (1998) 'Editorial', *Prison Service Journal*, May.

Radical Statistics Health Group (1995) 'NHS "Indicators of Success": What Do They Tell Us?', *British Medical Journal*, 310 pp. 1045–50.

Ranade, W. (1997) *A Future for the NHS?*, (2nd edn) (London: Longman).

Rea, D.M. (1995) 'Unhealthy Competition: The Making of a Market for Mental Health', *Policy and Politics*, 23(2), pp. 141–55.

Reiner, R. (1992) *Politics of the Police* (Brighton: Harvester Wheatsheaf).

Report of the Royal Commission on Long Term Care (1999) *With Respect to Old Age*, Cm 4192 (London: Stationery Office).

Rhodes, R. A. W. (1997) *Beyond Westminster and Whitehall* (London: Unwin Hyman).

Roberts, A. (1999) 'NATO's Humanitarian War over Kosovo', *Survival*, 41 (3), pp. 102–23.

Robertson, G. (1997a) 'European Security', WEU Ministerial Meeting, Pairs (13 May 1997), http://www.fco.gov.uk/news/newstext

Robertson, G. (1997b) Speech on the Strategic Defence Review, Royal United Services Institute, London (18 September 1997), http:www.mod.uk/ speeches/sofs18–9htm

Robertson, G. (1997c) Labour Party Conference 1997, http://www.Labour.org.uk/ cgi-labour/conference

Robertson, G. (1997d) 'Building European Security and the role of Defence Policy' (4 September1997), http://www. mod.uk.speeches/sofs 4–9.html

Roddan, D. (1998) 'Prison Policy under Labour a year after the Election', *The Howard League Magazine*, Iss 1.

Roof (1998) 'Fast Facts', *Roof*, July/August, p. 40.

Roof (2000) *Roof Briefing*, April (London: Shelter).

Rose, C (1990) *The Dirty Man of Europe: The Great British Pollution Scandal* (London: Simon & Schuster).

Ross, G. (1998) 'European Integration and Globalization', in R. Axtmann, (ed.) *Globalization and Europe: Theoretical and Empirical Investigations* (London: Pinter).

Routledge, P. (1998) *Gordon Brown. The Biography*, (London: Simon & Schuster).

Ruane, Joseph and Todd, Jennifer (eds) (1999) *After the Belfast Agreement: Analysing Political Change in Northern Ireland* (Dublin: UCD Press).

Rutherford, A. (1998) 'One Year On', *The Howard League Magazine*, Iss 1.

Ryan, M. and Ward, T. (1989) *Privatisation and the Penal System* (Milton Keynes: Open University Press).

Sainsbury, R. (1996) 'Rooting out Fraud – Innocent until Proved Fraudulent.' *Poverty*, 93, pp. 17–20.

Samuels, M. (1998) *Towards Best Practice: An Evaluation of the First Two Years of the Public Sector Benchmarking Project 1996–98* (London: Cabinet Office).

Satler, B. (1998) *The Politics of Change in the Health Service* (Basingstoke: Macmillan).

Savage, S.P. (1990) 'A War on Crime? Law and Order Policies in the 1980s', in S.P. Savage, and L. Robins, (eds), *Public Policy Under Thatcher* (London: Macmillan).

Savage, S.P. and Nash, M. (1994) 'Yet Another Agenda for Law and Order', *International Criminal Justice Review*, 4.

Savage, S.P. and Charman, S. (1996) 'In Favour of Compliance', *Policing Today*, 2 (1).

Savage, S.P., Charman, S. and Cope, S. (1997) 'ACPO: A Force to be Reckoned With?', *Criminal Lawyer*, April.

Savage, S.P. (1998a) 'The Politics of Criminal Justice Policy', in I. McKenzie, (ed.), *Law, Power and Justice in England and Wales* (New York: Praeger).

Savage, S. P. (1998b) 'The Changing Geography of Police Governance', *Criminal Justice Matters*, June.

Savage, S., Charman, S. and Cope, S. (2000) 'The Policy Context', in F. Leishman, B. Loveday, and S. Savage (eds), *Core Issues in Policing* (London: Pearson Education).

School Exclusion Unit (1997) *Truancy and School Exclusion*, Cm 3957 (London: HMSO).

Scichor, D. and. Sechrest, D. K. (eds) (1996) *Three Strikes and You're Out; Vengeance as Public Policy* (California: Sage).

Scott, P. (1996) *The Meanings of Mass Higher Education* (Buckingham: SRHE/Open University Press).

Secretary of State for Health (1989) *Working for Patients*, Cm 555 (London: HMSO).

Secretary of State for Health (1992) *The Health of the Nation: A Strategy for Health in England*, Cm 1896 (London: HMSO).

Secretary of State for Health (1997) *The New NHS. Modern, Dependable*, Cm 3807 (London: Stationery Office).

Secretary of State for Scotland (1997) *Designed to Care. Renewing the National Health Service in Scotland*, Cm 3811 (Edinburgh: The Scottish Office).

Secretary of State for Wales (1998) *NHS Wales; Putting Patients First* (London: Stationery Office).

Selbourne, D. (1997) *The Principle of Duty*, 2nd edn (London: Abacus Rowntree Foundation).

Seldon, A. (1997) *Major: A Political Life* (London: Weidenfeld and Nicholson) pp. 415–24.

Shapiro, R. J. (1994) Letters to the Editor: 'Government Must Play Part to Achieve Endogenous Growth' *Financial Times*, 7 November, p. 18.

Sharrock, D. and Devenport, M. (1997) *Man of War, Man of Peace?: The Unauthorized Biography of Gerry Adams* (London: Macmillan).

Shaw, R. (1996) 'Supervising the Dangerous in the Community', in N. Walker (ed.), *Dangerous People* (London: Blackstone Press Ltd).

Shaw, S. (1992) 'A Short History of Prison Privatisation', *Prison Service Journal*, Iss 87.

Shaw, S. (1998) 'Interview with Stephen Shaw', *Prison Service Journal*, Iss 117.

Sloman, J. (2000) *Economics*, 4th edn (Hemel Hempstead: Prentice Hall Europe).

Sloman, J. and Sutcliffe, M. (1998) *Economics for Business* (Hemel Hempstead: Prentice Hall Europe).

Smith, M. (1999) *The Core Executive in Britain* (Basingstoke: Macmillan).

Smith, R. (1998) 'All Changed, Changed Utterly', *British Medical Journal*, 316, pp. 1917–18.

Smith, T. A. (1979) *The Politics of the Corporate Economy* (London: Martin Robertson).

Smithers, A. and Robinson, P. (eds) (2000) *Further Education Reformed* (London: Falmer Press).

Sperling, J. and Kirchner, E. (1997) *Recasting the European Order* (Manchester: Manchester University Press).

Starie, P. (1999) 'Globalisation, the State and European Economic Integration', *Journal of European Area Studies*, 7(1).

Statement on the Defence Estimates (1993) *Defending our Future*, Cm 2270 (London: HMSO)

Statement on the Defence Estimates (1994) *Frontline First*, Cm 2550 (London: HMSO).

Statement on the Defence Estimates (1995) *Stable Forces in a Strong Britain*, Cm 2800 (London: HMSO).

Statement on the Defence Estimates (1996) Cm 3223, http://www.official.docoments.co.uk/ document/mod/defence/deffc.htm

Stephens, P. (1996) *Politics and the Pound: The Conservatives' Struggle with Sterling* (London: Macmillan).

Straw, J. (1995) 'Straw and Order', *New Statesman and Society*, 15 September.

Straw, J. (1998) 'Foreword', in *Joining Forces to Protect the Public – Prisons-Probation Review* (London: HMSO).

Sutherland, Sir Stewart (1999) *With Respect to Old Age: Long Term Care Rights and Responsibilities*, Report by the Royal Commission on Long Term Care, Cm 4192–1 (London: HMSO).

Sweeney, K. and McMahon, D. (1998) 'The Effect of Jobseeker's Allowance on the Claimant Count', *Labour Market Trends*, 106 (4) (HMSO), pp. 195–203.

Symons, Baroness (1997) 'New Government, New Foreign Policy', http://www.fco.gov. uk/news/speechtext

Taylor, Gerald R. (1999) *The Impact of New Labour* (London: Macmillan).

Taylor, P. (1996) *The European Union in the 1990s* (Oxford: Oxford University Press).

Therborn, G. (1995) *European Modernity and Beyond* (London: Sage).

Thomas, D. A. (1997) 'The Crime (Sentences)Act 1999', *Criminal Law Review*, pp. 83–92.

Thompson, N. (1996) 'Supply Side Socialism: The Political Economy of New Labour', *New Left Review*, no. 216, pp. 37–54.

Timmins, N. (1995) *The Five Giants: A Biography of the Welfare State* (London: HarperCollins).

Townsend, P. *et al.* (1970) *The Fifth Social Service: A Critical Analysis of the Seebohm Proposals* (London: Fabian Society).

Toynbee, P. (1999) 'Labour's plan to eradicate poverty is underway. Really', *The Guardian*, 21 July, p. 18.

Treasure, T. (1998) 'Lessons from the Bristol Case', *British Medical Journal*, 316, pp. 1885–6.

Tsoukalis, L. (1996) 'Economic and Monetary Union: The primacy of High Politics', in H. Wallace and W. Wallace (eds), *Policy-making in the European Union* (Oxford: Oxford University Press).

TUC (1999) *Labour Market Briefing*, February, (London: Trades Union Congress).

Turock, I. and Webster, D. (1998) 'The New Deal: Jeopardised by the Geography of Unemployment?', *Local Economy*, 12(4).

Vane, H. R. and Thompson, J. L. (1992) *Current Controversies in Macroeconomics: An Intermediate Text* (Aldershot: Edward Elgar).

Wallace, W. (1983) 'Less than a Federation, More than a Regime: The Community as a Political System', in H. Wallace, W. Wallace and C. Webb (eds), *Policy-making in the European Community* (Chichester: John Wiley).

Wasik, M., Gibbons, T. and Redmayne, M. (1999) *Criminal Justice: Texts and Materials* (Harlow: Addison Wesley Longman).

Watson, D. (1998) *Lifelong Learning and the University – a Post-Dearing Agenda* (Falmer Press).

Wheeler, N. and Dunne, T. (1998) 'Good International Citizenship: A Third Way for British Foreign Policy', *International Affairs*, 74 (4), pp. 847–70.

White, M. and Lakey, J. (1992) *The Restart Effect* (London: Policy Studies Institute).

White, M., Lissenburgh, S. and Bryson, A. (1997) *The Impact of Public Job Placing Programmes* (London: Policy Studies Institute).

White, R. and Haines, F. (1996) *Crime and Criminology* (Oxford: Oxford University Press).

Whitehead, C. (1997) 'Changing Needs, Changing Incentives: Trends in the UK Housing System', in P. Williams (ed.) *Directions in Housing Policy: Towards Sustainable Housing Policies for the UK* (London: Paul Chapman).

Whitehead, M. (1993) 'Is it Fair? Evaluating the Equity Implications of the NHS Reforms', in R. Robinson and J. Le Grand (eds), *Evaluating the NHS Reforms* (London: King's Fund Institute).

Wilcox, S. (1999) *Housing Finance Review 1999/2000* (York: Joseph Rowntree Foundation).

Wilcox, S. *et al.* (1993) *Local Housing Companies* (York: Joseph Rowntree Foundation).

Williams, P. (ed.) *Directions in Housing Policy: Towards Sustainable Housing Policies for the UK* (London: Paul Chapman).

Wilson, D. and Ashton, J. (1998) *What Everyone Should Know about Crime and Punishment* (London: Blackstone Press Ltd).

Wilson, J. Q. and Kelling, G. (1982) 'Broken Windows', *The Atlantic Monthly*, March.

Wilson, R. (1996) 'No Great Expectations, Just a Little Hope for a Fresh Approach', *New Statesman and Society*, 10 May.

264 *Bibliography*

Working Group on Post-School Basic Skills (1999) *A Fresh Start: Basic Skills for Adults* (London: DfEE).

Worrall, A. (1997) *Punishment in the Community: The Future of Criminal Justice* (London: Longman).

Young, H. (1998) *This Blessed Plot: Britain and Europe from Churchill to Blair* (London: Macmillan).

Young, J. (1997) 'Left Realist Criminology: Radical in its Analysis, Realist in its Policy', in M. Maguire, R. Morgan, and R. Reiner (eds), *Oxford Handbook of Criminology*, (Oxford: Oxford University Press).

Young, J. W. (1997) 'Foreign, Defence and European Affairs', in B. Brivati and T. Bale (eds), *New Labour in Power: Precedents and Prospects* (London: Routledge).

Index